Armstrong's Handbook of Performance Management

Also available by Michael Armstrong

Armstrong's Handbook of Management and Leadership

Armstrong's Handbook of Human Resource Management Practice

Armstrong's Essential Human Resource Management Practice

Armstrong's Handbook of Strategic Human Resource Management

Armstrong's Handbook of Reward Management Practice

How to Manage People

How to be an Even Better Manager

Human Capital Management (with Angela Baron)

The Reward Management Toolkit (with Ann Cummins)

Evidence-based Reward Management (with Duncan Brown and Peter Reilly)

www.koganpage.com

FIFTH EDITION

Armstrong's Handbook of Performance Management

An evidence-based guide to delivering high performance

Michael Armstrong

LONDON PHILADELPHIA NEW DELHI

First published in Great Britain and the United States in 1994 by Kogan Page Limited as *Performance Management*
Second edition 2000
Third edition 2006
Fourth edition 2009 published as *Armstrong's Handbook of Performance Management*
Fifth edition published in 2015
Reprinted 2015 (three times)

2nd Floor, 45 Gee Street	1518 Walnut Street, Suite 1100	4737/23 Ansari Road
London EC1V 3RS	Philadelphia PA 19102	Daryaganj
United Kingdom	USA	New Delhi 110002
www.koganpage.com		India

© Michael Armstrong, 1994, 2000, 2006, 2009, 2015

The right of Michael Armstrong to be identified as the author of this work has been asserted by him in accordance with the Copyright, Designs and Patents Act 1988.

ISBN   978 0 7494 7029 6
E-ISBN 978 0 7494 7030 2

British Library Cataloguing-in-Publication Data

A CIP record for this book is available from the British Library.

Library of Congress Cataloging-in-Publication Data

Armstrong, Michael, 1928-
    Armstrong's handbook of performance management : an evidence-based guide to delivering high performance / Michael Armstrong. – Fifth edition.
        pages cm
    ISBN 978-0-7494-7029-6 – ISBN 978-0-7494-7030-2 (ebk)   1. Employees–Rating of.   2. Performance standards.   3. Performance.   I. Title.   II. Title: Handbook of performance management.
    HF5549.5.R3A758 2015
    658.3'125–dc23
                                                                                    2014027013

Typeset by Graphicraft Limited, Hong Kong
Print production managed by Jellyfish
Printed and bound by CPI Group (UK) Ltd, Croydon, CR0 4YY

CONTENTS

To David Turner, 1945–2009:
a good friend and colleague
with whom I worked happily
and productively for many years.

Introduction

Performance management is a systematic and continuous process for improving organizational performance by developing the performance of individuals and teams. This book deals with performance management as a system consisting of interlocking elements designed to achieve a purpose, that of improving individual, team and organizational performance. These elements consist of the processes of planning for performance improvement and personal development, goal setting, monitoring performance, providing feedback, analysing and assessing performance and reviewing performance. Performance management makes a vital contribution not only to improving individual and team performance but also to support the key human resource management activities of human capital management, enhancing levels of engagement, talent management, learning and development and reward.

The impact of performance management

The Work Foundation research into performance management conducted by Armstrong and Ward (2005) reached the following conclusion about the impact of performance management:

> Performance management has the potential to improve the performance of organizations and act as a lever to achieve cultural change. A focus on performance can bring real rewards for organizations. Performance management can be the key space or mechanism for dialogue in an organization. An organization's choice of where to focus its attention in relation to performance management may in part determine its future and can certainly guide its culture.

Features of performance management

A survey of performance management practices in 156 organizations conducted by e-reward in 2014 revealed the following percentages of respondents using different performance management features (the chapter in this book in which these features are described is shown in brackets):

- Performance review – 91 per cent (8)
- Goal setting – 90 per cent (5)
- Personal development plans – 79 per cent (16)
- Overall rating linked to contribution or performance pay – 59 per cent (9)
- Performance improvement plans – 51 per cent (1)
- Overall rating *not* linked to contribution or performance pay – 20 per cent (9)
- 360-degree feedback – 19 per cent (6)
- Use of balanced scorecard – 17 per cent (5)

Performance management systems

The various features of performance management are combined together into a performance management system – a set of inter-related activities and processes which are treated as an integrated and key component of an organization's approach to managing performance through people and developing the skills and capabilities of its human capital. Performance management systems are described in Chapter 1.

The problem with performance management

There can be no doubt that the management of performance is the most important thing an organization has to do and an effective performance management system is the best way to do it. But it is not easy. Performance management can promise much more than it achieves.

Pulakos (2009) quoted a Watson Wyatt survey which established that only 30 per cent of workers felt their company's performance management system helped them improve their performance. He asked the question 'What makes performance management so hard?' His answer was as follows:

> Managers avoid performance management activities, especially providing developmental feedback to employees because they don't want to risk damaging relationships with the very individuals they count on to get work done.

Employees avoid performance management activities, especially discussing their development needs with managers because they don't want to jeopardize their pay or advancement.

The issues affecting the performance of performance management are discussed in Chapter 4.

Themes

This book describes how performance management works. But it also addresses the issues which determine and influence its effectiveness. In so doing, a number of recurrent themes have emerged, namely:

- Performance management is strategic in the sense that it enables the goals of individuals and teams to be aligned to the strategic goals of the organization.
- It is a continuous process not an annual ritual.
- Keep it simple! The performance management system should not be over-elaborate or bureaucratic.
- It should be owned and driven by line management. It is not the property of the HR department.
- Performance management won't work without enthusiastic support from top management.
- Neither will it work without the willing and effective contribution of line managers. And this will not be forthcoming if the procedures are too complicated or if, when introducing the scheme, comprehensive consultation, communication and training has not taken place.
- Performance management is about developing people in order to improve their performance. It is not just about generating ratings to inform performance pay decisions and it is certainly not about weeding out undesirables.
- Performance management involves a continuing dialogue between managers and the people they manage. The dialogue is based on goal achievement, performance analysis and constructive feedback, and leads to performance improvement and personal development plans. It is not a mechanism for coercion or control.

Plan of the book

Part One of the book deals with the fundamental aspects of performance management. Chapter 1 describes the elements of a performance management system but also notes the limitations of this model and examines the reality of performance management – the problems of making it work and the requirements for success. This is followed by a history of performance management in Chapter 2 – much current practice is based on past experience in such areas as management by objectives and performance appraisal. To understand performance management it is necessary to take account of its strong conceptual base consisting of various aspects of organizational behaviour and motivation theory and these are covered in Chapter 2.

Part Two expands the description of the performance management system in Chapter 1 by describing the processes and skills used in setting goals, providing feedback, conducting performance reviews, assessing performance, coaching and dealing with under-performers.

Part Three is concerned with the applications of performance management. It examines how it can be applied to manage organizational and team performance and how it supports a number of key HR activities, namely: employee engagement, talent management, reward management and learning and development. It also covers how performance management functions in international firms.

Part Four describes performance management in action. Consideration is given to the extent to which it impacts on performance, the current state of performance management is revealed by research and how a number of organizations have modelled their performance management systems.

Part Five deals with how performance management should be developed and managed and examines the role of line managers upon whom the effectiveness of performance management largely depends. It also covers performance management training and, importantly, the evaluation of performance management.

Appendix A contains a comprehensive toolkit which provides practical guidance on analysing current performance arrangements and developing, implementing, operating and evaluating performance management systems.

Appendix B contains a number of case studies specially commissioned from e-reward.

References

Armstrong, K and Ward, A (2005) *What Makes for Effective Performance Management?* London, The Work Foundation

e-reward (2014) *Survey of Performance Management*, Stockport, e-reward

Pulakos, E D (2009) *Performance Management: A new approach for driving business results*, Malden MA, Wiley-Blackwell

PART ONE
Performance management fundamentals

PART ONE
Performance
management
fundamentals

The essence of performance management

The purpose of this chapter is to define performance management and provide an overall description of the aims, principles and operation of a performance management system taking into account the reality of performance management and the factors that contribute to its effectiveness. To understand fully the essence of performance management Chapter 2 explains how the features of today's version evolved from its origins in merit rating, performance appraisal and management by objectives.

This chapter and the succeeding chapters in Parts One and Two of this book concentrate on performance management for individuals. But most if not all of the approaches described can and should be applied to performance management for teams as covered in Chapter 13.

Performance management defined

Performance management is the continuous process of improving performance by setting individual and team goals which are aligned to the strategic goals of the organization, planning performance to achieve the goals, reviewing and assessing progress, and developing the knowledge, skills and abilities of people.

Here are some other definitions:

- 'Performance management is a continuous process of identifying, measuring and developing the performance of individuals and teams

and aligning performance with the strategic goals of the organization.'
(Aguinis, 2005)

- 'Performance management is the system through which organizations
  set work goals, determine performance standards, assign and
  evaluate work, provide performance feedback, determine training
  and development needs and distribute rewards.' (Briscoe and Claus,
  2008)

- 'Performance management is a broad set of activities aimed at
  improving employee performance.' (DeNisi, and Pritchard, 2006)

- 'Performance management is the key process through which work
  gets done. It's how organizations communicate expectations and
  drive behaviour to achieve important goals; it's also about how
  organizations identify ineffective performers for development
  programmes or other personnel actions.' (Pulakos, 2009)

- 'Performance management is regarded as a continuous,
  future-orientated and participative system; as an ongoing
  cycle of criteria setting, monitoring, informal feedback from
  supervisors and peers, formal multi-source assessment, diagnosis
  and review, action-planning and developmental resourcing.'
  (Shields, 2007)

Performance management is managing the business. Line managers are there
to manage performance and performance management helps them to do
this – it is a natural process of management. It is not an HR-directed annual
ritual. And it is not simply a process of appraising people once a year.
Performance management is a continuous process whilst traditional performance appraisal tended to be just an annual event.

Performance management is a powerful means of ensuring that the organization's strategic goals are achieved. It contributes to the achievement of
culture change and it is integrated with other key HR activities, especially
human capital management, talent management, learning and development
and reward management. Thus performance management helps to achieve
horizontal integration and the 'bundling' of HR practices so that they are
inter-related and therefore complement and reinforce each other. Performance management can also play an important part in increasing levels of
employee engagement.

Aims of performance management

The overall objective of performance management is to develop and improve the performance of individuals and teams and therefore organizations. As the Lloyds Banking Group states: 'When done well, it ensures that we are all clear about what success looks like and the part we each play in delivering this success'. A strategic approach (strategic performance management) means that performance management processes such as setting goals are explicitly designed to align individual objectives with the organization's strategic objectives.

As noted by Verweire and Van Den Berghe (2004) performance management involves creating motivation and commitment to achieve objectives. Shields (2007) pointed out that 'it provides performance direction and recognition without which employees will be at a loss as to the nature and level of work effort required'. Performance management aims to develop the capacity of people to meet and exceed expectations and to achieve their full potential to the benefit of themselves and the organization. It is about ensuring that the support and guidance people need to develop and improve is readily available.

A definition of what performance management systems are there to do was provided by Lee (2005):

> The real goals of any performance management system are threefold – to correct poor performance, to sustain good performance and to improve performance... All performance management systems should be designed to generate information and data exchange so that the individuals involved can properly dissect performance, discuss it, understand it, and agree on its character and quality.

As explained by Shields (2007) effective performance management has two other important purposes. First, it can communicate to employees the strategic goals of the enterprise and specify what the organization expects from them in terms of behaviour and results in order to achieve those goals. This means defining what doing a good job entails. Second, it can help with relationship building between employees and their managers. Involving both managers and their staff in performance planning and review can widen the dialogue between them and enhance inter-personal trust.

A summary of what management and individuals can gain from performance management is given in Table 1.1.

TABLE 1.1   What management and individuals can gain from performance management

What management can gain	What individuals can gain
The opportunity to: • integrate individual, team and corporate objectives; • guide individual and team effort to meeting overall business needs; • motivate and engage employees; • recognize individual contribution; • plan individual careers (talent management); • introduce relevant and effective learning and development programmes to meet identified needs.	They will: • know what is expected of them; • know how they stand; • know what they need to do to reach their goals; • be able to discuss with their manager their present job, their development and training needs and their future.

Respondents to the e-reward 2014 survey of performance management reported that their most important performance management objective was:

- to improve organizational performance – 33 per cent;
- to align individual and organizational objectives – 22 per cent;
- to develop a performance culture – 17 per cent;
- to improve individual performance – 14 per cent;
- to align individual behaviour to organizational values – 6 per cent;
- to provide the basis for personal development – 3 per cent;
- to inform performance pay decisions – 3 per cent.

Note the low priority given to informing performance pay decisions.

Here is a typical statement of objectives from one respondent to the e-reward 2005 survey:

To support culture change by creating a performance culture and reinforcing the values of the organization with an emphasis on the importance of these in getting a balance between 'what' is delivered and 'how' it is delivered.

A financial sector organization produced the following definition of the purpose of its performance management system.

> The aim is to improve performance. Rather than just saying that somebody's been very effective and ticking a box, the process is actually to sit down and have a discussion around the requirements of the role, dealing with what aspects are being done well and what aspects are not so good. Overall the purpose is to make it clear to people how their performance links in with the performance of the business.
>
> Managing performance is about coaching, guiding, appraising, motivating and rewarding colleagues to help unleash potential and improve organizational performance. Where it works well it is built on excellent leadership and high quality coaching relationships between managers and teams. Through all this our colleagues should be able to answer three straightforward questions:
>
> 1 What is expected of me? How will I be clear about what is expected of me in terms of both results and behaviour?
>
> 2 How am I doing? What ongoing coaching and feedback will I receive to tell me how I am doing and how I can improve?
>
> 3 What does it mean for me? How will my individual contribution, potential and aspirations be recognized and rewarded?

The following description of the purpose of performance management was produced by Hitachi Europe:

The process is as much about building relationships with employees in order to agree what is reasonably attainable in the year as it is about setting objectives. It is effective because it focuses people's intentions and produces new thinking on the way they work rather than simply continuing to perform at the same level day-in-day-out.

A definition of the aims of performance management produced by CEMEX UK is given in Appendix B.

Overall principles of performance management

The overarching principles governing effective performance management were defined by Egan (1995):

> Most employees want direction, freedom to get their work done, and encouragement not control. The performance management system should be a control system only by exception. The solution is to make it a collaborative development system, in two ways. First, the entire performance management process – coaching, counselling, feedback, tracking, recognition, and so forth – should encourage development. Ideally, team members grow and develop through these interactions. Second, when managers and team members ask what they need to be able to do to do bigger and better things, they move to strategic development.

Strebler *et al* (2001) suggested that the following principles were required for performance management to work effectively:

- Have clear aims and measurable success criteria.
- Be designed and implemented with appropriate employee involvement.
- Be simple to understand and operate.
- Make its use fundamental to achieving all management goals.
- Allow employees a clear 'line of sight' between their performance goals and those of the organization.
- Focus on role clarity and performance improvement.
- Be closely allied to a clear and adequately resourced training and development infrastructure.
- Make crystal clear the purpose of any direct link to reward and build in proper equity and transparency safeguards.
- Be regularly and openly reviewed against its success criteria.

The views of practitioners on the principles of performance management as identified in the research conducted by Armstrong and Baron (1998, 2004) were as follows:

- 'Performance management is what managers do: a natural process of management.'
- 'A management tool which helps managers to manage.'
- 'It's about how we manage people – it's not a system.'
- 'Driven by corporate purpose and values.'
- 'To obtain solutions that work.'
- 'Only interested in things you can do something about and get a visible improvement.'
- 'Focus on changing behaviour rather than paperwork.'
- 'Based on accepted principles but operates flexibly.'
- 'Focus on development not pay.'
- 'Success depends on what the organization is and needs to be in its performance culture'.

Two further important principles were suggested by Sparrow and Hiltrop (1994): first, that top management must support and be committed to the system, and second, that line managers should own and drive it. The latter will only take performance management seriously if it is clear to them that top managers believe in it and act accordingly. And performance management will only work if line managers want it to work and are capable of doing so. Both these principles emphasize that the bad old days of performance appraisal as the property of the personnel or HR department are over. The role of line managers is explored in Chapter 24.

Ethical principles

Performance management should also operate in accordance with agreed and understood ethical principles. These have been defined by Winstanley and Stuart-Smith (1996) as follows:

1 *Respect for the individual* – people should be treated as 'ends in themselves' and not merely as 'means to other ends'.

2 *Mutual respect* – the parties involved in performance management should respect each other's needs and preoccupations.

3 *Procedural fairness* – the procedures incorporated in performance management should be operated fairly in accordance with the principles of procedural justice.

4 *Transparency* – people affected by decisions emerging from performance management processes should be given the opportunity to scrutinize the basis upon which decisions were made.

Procedural justice requires that performance management decisions are made in accordance with principles which safeguard fairness, accuracy, consistency, transparency and freedom from bias, and properly consider the views and needs of employees. Folger *et al* (1992) set out the benefits of procedurally just performance management based on the components of due process. They labelled such systems 'due process performance management' and argued that they do not bring about gross reallocations of power between managers and employees, but rather require only that managers be open to employees' input and responsive to justifiable questions and concerns about performance standards and judgements.

Organizational researchers such as Taylor *et al* (1995) have gathered a strong body of evidence showing that employees care a great deal about the justice of performance management practices and staffing. This work generally has found that the more just or fair employees consider such systems to be, the more satisfied and accepting they are of the resultant outcomes, even when those outcomes are less than desirable. They found that procedurally just performance systems may also increase managers' own positive outcomes. The strength of these findings has led some researchers such as Folger and Cropanzano (1998) to propose that the provision of fair procedures is a more powerful foundation for the management of employees than is the provision of financial rewards.

Performance management systems

A performance management system as described in this section and modelled in Figure 1.1 is a set of inter-related activities and processes. These are treated

FIGURE 1.1   The performance management cycle

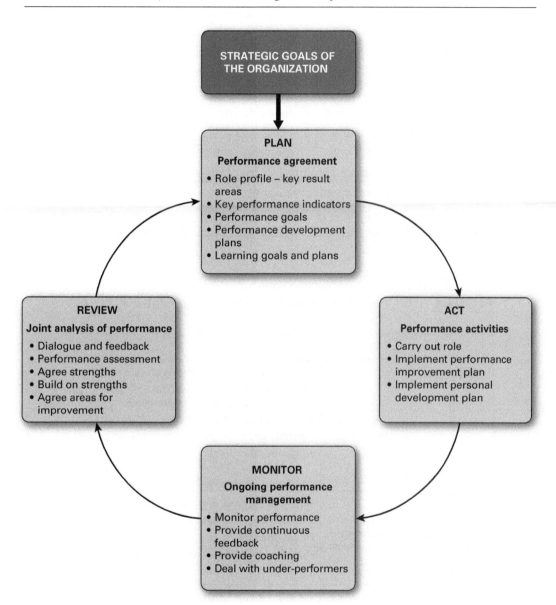

as integrated and key components of an organization's approach to managing performance through people and developing the skills and capabilities of its human capital. The system flows from the organization's goals and then operates as a continuous and self-renewing cycle. There are other ways of modelling the system which are illustrated in Chapter 21. Some represent it as a cycle and others as a flow chart but they all contain the basic elements of the model used here and all illustrate the ways in which these elements form a continuous process.

The cycle shown in Figure 1.1 resembles the cycle for continuous improvement defined by William Deming (1986). This is not a coincidence. This is what performance management is about.

Figure 1.2 shows how performance management activities take place over the year and then performance management activities are described in more detail.

FIGURE 1.2   Summary of performance management activities over the year

Start of year	Performance agreement	• Define role profiles, updating as necessary. • Ensure that role profiles set out updated key result areas and competency requirements. • Define goals and standards of performance. • Identify and define key performance indicators. • Draw up development plans.
Continuing dialogue	Ongoing performance management	• Monitor progress and review evidence of achievement. • Provide informal feedback as required. • Provide coaching as required. • Update role profiles and objectives as necessary.
End of year	Performance review	• Prepare for performance review by analysing achievements (work and learning) against objectives. • Identify specific strengths and weaknesses on the basis of evidence. • Assess overall performance. • Provide feedback. • Use conclusions of performance review as the basis for next year's performance and development agreement.

Performance agreement

A performance agreement is the outcome of the decisions made jointly by the manager and the individual during the planning part of the performance management sequence. It provides a foundation for managing performance throughout the year and for guiding improvement and development activities. It is used as a reference point when planning and reviewing performance and is therefore a key component of a performance management system. It contains agreements on expectations in the form of the results, competencies and actions required, defined as performance and learning goals, and on action plans to develop performance and abilities. The basis for these agreements is a role profile which is jointly developed by the two parties.

Role profiles

An important part of performance planning is the agreement or updating of a role profile for the role holder. A full role profile defines:

- *Overall purpose* – what the role exists to achieve.
- *Key result areas* – elements of a role for which clear outputs and standards exist, each of which makes a significant contribution to achieving its overall purpose. It is best to restrict KRAs to no more than five or six.
- *Knowledge and skill requirements* – what the role holder should know and be able to do.
- *Behavioural competency requirements* – the types of behaviour required for the successful performance of a role.

However, the process may be made less complex for line managers by grouping together knowledge and skill and behavioural competency requirements under the heading of 'critical success factors' or 'role requirements' meaning those aspects of a role that must go well to ensure success. This not only simplifies the profile but also provides a more positive and forward-looking basis for development planning. An example of a role profile is given in Figure 1.3.

The prior information needed to prepare or update a role profile is a list of the corporate key result areas and strategic goals and the organization's competency framework. If there is no framework it is highly desirable that

FIGURE 1.3   Example of a role profile

Role title: Database administrator

Overall purpose of role: Responsible for the development and support of databases and their underlying environment.

Key result areas

- Identify database requirements for all projects that require data management in order to meet the needs of internal customers.
- Develop project plans collaboratively with colleagues to deliver against their database needs.
- Implement project plans in accordance with defined criteria, within the predefined budget and within the agreed time scale.
- Support underlying database infrastructure to ensure that the level of service delivery required is achieved.
- Ensure security of the database infrastructure through adherence to established protocols and develop additional security protocols where needed.

Role requirements

Need to know:

- Oracle database administration.
- Operation of oracle forms SQL/PLSQL, Unix administration, shell programming.

Able to:

- Analyse and choose between options where the solution is not always obvious.
- Develop project plans and organize own workload on a time scale of 1–2 months.
- Adapt to rapidly changing needs and priorities without losing sight of overall plans and priorities.
- Interpret budgets in order to manage resources effectively within them.
- Negotiate with suppliers.
- Keep abreast of technical developments and trends, bring these into day-to-day work when feasible and build them into new project developments.

Competencies:

- Aim to get things done well and set and meet challenging goals, create own measures of excellence and constantly seek ways of improving performance.
- Analyse information from range of sources and develop effective solutions/recommendations.
- Communicate clearly and persuasively, orally or in writing, dealing with technical issues in a manner which can be readily understood by internal clients.
- Work participatively on projects with technical and non-technical colleagues.
- Develop positive relationships with colleagues as the supplier of an internal service.
- Fully aware of business needs in developing and operating the database.
- Use high levels of analytical thinking to deal with complex issues and the use of an effective logical approach to address work-related issues and problems.

one should be created as it will provide the basis for the role profile, the definition of behavioural expectations and the important behavioural aspects of the performance review. Role profiles may include the general competency framework headings or specific competencies may be defined for a particular role as illustrated in Figure 1.3.

An example of a competency framework for managers is given in Appendix A (Table A4). Guidance on preparing competency frameworks (competency modelling) is provided by Armstrong (2014, chapter 51).

To define a role profile it is necessary to refer to this prior information and then obtain answers to the following questions:

1 What is the overall purpose of the role?

2 How does the role contribute to the achievement of the organization's strategic goals?

3 What are the key result areas in the role which define what has to be achieved? (No more than five or six.)

4 What will indicate how well the role holder has performed in each key result area (the key performance indicators)?

5 How are the key result areas aligned to the key result areas of the organization?

6 What is the role holder expected to know to be able to carry out the role?

7 What skills are needed to carry out the role?

8 By reference to the headings in the organizational competency framework, what behavioural competencies are required for successful role performance?

Key performance indicators

Key performance indicators (KPIs) are the metrics or other sources of information which indicate how outcomes can be measured or recognized.

Performance goals

Performance goals define the results individuals are expected to achieve. The expected results will be defined within the framework of the role profile and by reference to the key performance indicators established for key result areas.

Wherever possible, goals are quantified as targets which indicate what has to be achieved over a period of time in terms of quantified results or the completion of a project. But they can be expressed as qualitative performance standards which state that a key aspect of the job will have been well done if something specific happens.

Further guidance on preparing role profiles, establishing key performance indicators and setting goals is provided in Chapter 5 and in the training manual included with the supplementary material to this book.

The process of setting goals is covered more extensively in Chapter 5.

Action planning

Action planning involves achieving agreement between the manager and the individual in three areas:

1 *Achieving goals* – any actions required by the individual *and* the manager to achieve the overall objectives of the job,

2 *Performance development plans* – these will spell out what employees, in conjunction as necessary with their managers, need to do in specified areas of their jobs such as reaching sales or productivity targets, working accurately, providing services to internal customers, cutting costs, reducing waste, meeting deadlines. In any development area, goals are set on what has to be done and by when, and agreement reached on how the expected results will be achieved. If there are any behavioural performance problems such as being uncooperative or lack of effort, plans are agreed on how the problems can be overcome. The plan should be focused; too many goals will only dissipate improvement efforts.

3 *Personal development plans* – learning plans to achieve learning goals for which individuals are responsible with the support of their managers and the organization (see Chapter 16). Again the goals should be limited to make them more attainable. Lloyds Banking Group combines 2 and 3 under the general heading of 'development plan' and stipulate that it should contain no more than three development areas. If a rating system is used plans can be made on how improvement in the rating can be achieved.

Act

Action by individuals means that they manage their own performance with guidance as required from their manager or team leader. They are there to meet the demands of their roles as defined at the planning stage in the form of key result areas, goals, competency requirements and action plans.

Ongoing performance management

Perhaps one of the most important features of performance management is that it is a continuous process which can be described as ongoing performance management or 'managing performance throughout the year'. This means regularly monitoring outcomes against plans and ensuring that corrective action is taken when necessary. It involves individuals monitoring and managing their own performance and managers giving feedback, support and guidance. Feedback and the recognition of good work by the manager (see Chapter 6) is provided as and when appropriate, which means at the time or immediately after an event has occurred rather than being saved up for a later formal performance review session. It also means updating objectives, and continuous learning on the job or through coaching. Another requirement is to deal with underperformers in good time so that improvements can take place.

Review

Although performance management is a continuous process it is still useful to have a formal review once or twice yearly. This provides a focal point for the consideration of key performance and development issues and leads to the completion of the performance management cycle by providing the basis for updating performance agreements. The performance review meeting is an important means of ensuring that the five primary performance management elements of agreement, feedback, assessment, positive reinforcement, and dialogue can be put to good use. The conduct of performance reviews is covered in Chapter 8.

Performance reviews may be carried out by a manager with an individual on a one-to-one basis and the results are usually recorded on a performance management form as described in Chapter 23. 360-degree feedback (multisource assessment) may be used (see Chapter 7).

The reality of performance management

The performance management cycle described above is a model but like all models it has its limitations. It is normative in that it seems to prescribe a norm or standard pattern as best practice by presenting an ideal picture of what a performance management system should look like and how it should work. But how it works will largely depend on the context in which it operates. Fletcher (1993) noted the evolution in many organizations of a number of separate but linked processes applied in different ways according to the needs of local circumstances and staff levels. Some organizations reject the concept of a bureaucratic, centrally controlled and uniform system of performance management which is implied by the model, and instead accept that, within an overall policy framework, different approaches may be appropriate in different parts of the organization and for different people.

One problem with the model as presented here is that it can encourage an over-elaborate approach. Systems designers may be tempted to cover every aspect of the model in detail and turn what should be a natural and straightforward management process into a bureaucratic nightmare with complex procedures and intricate paper- or computer-based forms. Managers don't like this and won't do it properly, if at all. Employees generally regard it as yet another control mechanism imposed from above.

When developing a performance management system the watchwords are 'keep it simple'. Remember that line managers may be even more reluctant to do it well if they have to follow over-elaborate procedures and understand obscure jargon. The important thing to do is to ensure that the basic processes are explained and illustrated in communications about the system and training programmes.

Another problem with the model is the suggestion that there is a smooth transition from the organization's strategic goals to individual goals. But this is much more difficult than it sounds. Strategic goals at organizational level may not always translate easily into individual goals because organizational goals are not defined well enough or are too remote from the work of individual employees. Many commentators have extolled the virtue of alignment; few have made practical suggestions about how it can be achieved.

It can also be argued that strategic goals will inevitably be determined by top management without consulting employees, and that simply 'cascading' goals downwards contradicts the performance management principle that people should be involved in agreeing their own goals. The answer to this objection is that, although at individual level account should be taken of overarching goals, individuals can usefully take part in discussions on how they can further the achievement of those goals.

Thereafter, the model indicates a steady progression through the stages of performance management, each of them linked together. This is both logical and desirable but in reality it may be difficult to achieve. The natural tendency of managers is to compartmentalize these activities, if they carry them out at all. They do not always appreciate how they are connected and what they should do to ensure that the cycle does work smoothly.

Performance management is applied in many different ways according to the context in which it is used. These ways will not necessarily conform to those prescribed by the model. The contextual factors include the type of operation and the organization's structure. Importantly they also include the organization's culture as expressed in its philosophy or norms (explicit or implicit) on how people should be managed and the prevailing management style, for example, the degree to which it is controlling or participative. As Stoskopf (2002) put it: 'A [performance management] system with the most academically correct competencies or performance measures may fail if it does not fit with the company's culture or workforce'. Pulakos *et al* (2008) summed this up as follows:

> Performance management is often referred to as the 'Achilles heel' of HRM. All modern organizations face the challenge of how best to manage performance. That is, they must determine the best ways to set goals, evaluate work and distribute rewards in such a way that performance can be improved over time. While all firms face similar challenges, the way a firm responds to these challenges will depend on where the firm is located and the context within which it is operating. Differences in culture, technology or simply tradition make it difficult to directly apply techniques that have worked in one setting to a different setting.

The employee relations climate is also important. As Haines and St-Onge (2012) noted this particularly applies to the quality of relationships between managers and their subordinates. The beliefs of management on the extent to which HRM interventions such as performance management can make a difference to business outcomes can be significant. The application of performance management will also be affected by the importance attached to talent management, learning and development, and paying for performance.

Many organizations have a performance management system which, at least in its essentials, resembles the one described in the model but which has been adapted to fit the needs of the business and its people. Others, however, if they do anything at all, still use old-style, tick box, top-down performance appraisal systems which provide an easy way out (managers need do little more than fill up the forms or answer the standardized questions in a web-based system) and act as a means of exercising control. The 'rank and yank' procedure is an example of the latter which is a mainly American method of ranking employees according to their performance and then dismissing (yanking) a proportion of those in the lower levels, eg the bottom 10 per cent.

Irrespective of the context, performance management is difficult. Some years ago Keith Grint (1993), referring to performance appraisal, asserted that: 'Rarely in the history of business can such a system promise so much and deliver so little'. More recently, Duncan Brown (2011) observed on the basis of research conducted by the Institute for Employment Studies that: 'The main areas of concern [about performance management] were the skills and attitudes of reviewing managers, the consistency and quality of approach across large organizations, the complexity of the paperwork and the value of outputs... Performance management, it appears, isn't working.

The reality of performance management is that the issues it faces are formidable. They include the design of the system, its implementation, and its operation, especially the role of line managers. These are described in Chapter 3 with suggestions on how they can be dealt with bearing mind the requirements for success set out below.

Requirements for success

Many prescriptions have been offered on the requirements for successful performance management.

Research conducted by Lawler *et al* (2012) led to the overall conclusion that:

> What organizations need to do is to create performance management systems
> that are integrated with the other human resource management systems they
> have and the overall talent management strategy of the organization. Indeed,

they need to go beyond just integrating it with the talent management practices of the organization; they need to make sure it is integrated with the strategy of the organization. There has always been, and our data say there continues to be, a strong correlation between the effectiveness of performance management systems and the degree to which they are driven by the business strategy of the organization.

Haines and St-Onge (2012) established through their research that performance management is most likely to be successful when:

- more performance management training in coaching and giving constructive feedback is provided;
- employee recognition is emphasized;
- the corporate culture values engagement;
- performance management is strategically integrated with human resource management and the business plans of the organization;
- human capital is valued;
- there is a positive employee relations climate.

They also noted that: 'Performance management effectiveness is not only a function of system design or best practices, but also of programme implementation and execution in different organizational contexts'.

Research by Biron *et al* (2011) identified four performance management facilitators: (1) taking a broad view of performance management that includes both strategic and tactical elements; (2) involving senior managers in the process; (3) clearly communicating performance expectations and (4) formally training performance raters.

Mone and London (2010) pointed out that trust provides a necessary foundation for performance management. Managers must endeavour to create a climate of trust by acting as advocates for their employees, showing confidence and interest in them, being open with them, and acting with integrity (doing what they say they will do).

All these approaches will help but what emerged from the research conducted by Armstrong and Baron (1998 and 2004) was that what mattered was not so much the design of the system (which can reproduce the performance management model without too much difficulty) but getting the system implemented and working well on a continuing basis. The three key factors affecting the quality of implementation and operation they identified were:

- The commitment, encouragement and support of senior management – as Lawler and McDermott (2003) commented: 'The behaviour of management is also an indication of how important the performance management system is and as a result is likely to have a strong influence on how the system is actually implemented'.

- The involvement of line managers in developing the scheme and the quality of communications, training, guidance and advice provided to them.

- The rigour with which the organization evaluated the effectiveness of performance management and its determination to put things right, often through training.

Support from top management will be forthcoming if they believe or are persuaded to believe that there is a business case for performance management as a means of delivering increased organizational effectiveness.

Involving line managers in the design of the system and thoroughly communicating to them its purpose, significance and methods of operation will help to gain their commitment. Training is an obvious way to overcome the lack of skill often displayed by line managers. But it is not an easy solution. It demands time and effort. Typically, a new or revised system is launched with a half day or at most a whole day briefing and training session which can only touch the surface. There are strong arguments for providing a suite of one day learning events, one serving as a general introduction to performance management and others dealing separately with each of the main skills managers have to use, namely: goal setting, providing feedback, conducting performance reviews and coaching as described in Chapter 25. These should be supplemented by individual coaching. But organizations are often unwilling to allocate much time to training or coaching. Unless they do, performance management will never live up to its expectations.

Another requirement for success is that the system should fit the situation of the organization. For example, a monolithic system may not be appropriate in a divisionalized or multinational organization. In these circumstances it may be sufficient to set out basic operational principles and leave it to the individual units to decide how best to apply them. Even a centralized system needs to avoid being over-bureaucratic.

The evaluation of how well performance management is working in practice can provide valuable evidence on the need for improvement – generally or in the skills of individual managers. As described in Chapter 26, evaluation requires quite a lot of effort but is easy to do. It can lead to specific improvement programmes as detailed in the eight point plan at the end of Chapter 26.

Examples of approaches to performance management

Performance management stages in AstraZeneca

1 *Business role clarification* – clear statement of agreed role and objectives.

2 *Performance planning* – agreement of targets to achieve the 'plan–do–evaluate' elements of managing performance.

3 *Performance development* – agree skills required and prepare individual development plan.

4 *Performance measurement* – provide ongoing feedback and an annual summary of an employee's performance (no overall ratings).

Civil Service basic design principles

- Stretching objectives agreed at the beginning of the year.
- Individuals know the competencies and behaviours they are expected to demonstrate.
- Regular discussions during year between individuals and their managers to discuss progress.
- Formal meeting at the end of the year to record whether objectives have been achieved and levels of competence demonstrated.

What makes good performance management – Scottish Parliament

- New staff know what is expected of them from the outset.
- Everyone is clear about corporate goals and works towards them.

- Objectives are SMART.
- A system exists to accommodate day-to-day performance feedback.
- Evidence is available to support assessments.
- The personal development plan is used to help self-developmental activities or improve performance.
- The line manager provides and the jobholder undertakes the training needed to support the individual and the organization.

Thames Valley Police performance and development review process

- Key to the performance management strategy.
- Establishes strong employment relationships.
- Provides a route to individual, team and organizational performance planning.
- Secures future training and development.

References

Aguinis, H (2005) *Performance Management*, Upper Saddle River NJ, Pearson Education

Armstrong, M (2014) *A Handbook of Human Resource Management Practice*, 13th edition, London, Kogan Page

Armstrong, M and Baron, A (1998) *Performance Management: The New Realities*, London, CIPD

Armstrong, M and Baron, A (2004) *Managing Performance: Performance Management in Action*, London, CIPD

Biron, M, Farndale, E and Paauwe, J (2011) Performance management effectiveness: lessons from world-leading firms, *International Journal of Human Resource Management*, 22 (6), pp 1294–1311

Briscoe, D B and Claus, L M (2008) Employee performance management: policies and practices in multinational enterprises, in P W Budwah and A DeNisi (eds), *Performance Management Systems: A global perspective*, Abingdon, Routledge

Brown, D (2011) Performance management – can it ever work? *Manager*, Summer, p 16

Deming, W E (1986) *Out of the Crisis*, Cambridge MA, Massachusetts Institute of Technology Centre for Advanced Engineering Studies

DeNisi, A S and Pritchard, R D (2006) Performance appraisal, performance management and improving individual performance: a motivational framework, *Management and Organization Review*, 2 (2), pp 253–77

Egan, G (1995) A clear path to peak performance, *People Management*, 18 May, pp 34–37

e-reward (2005) *Survey of Performance Management Practice*, Stockport, e-reward

e-reward (2014) *Survey of Performance Management*, Stockport, e-reward

Fletcher, C (1993) Appraisal: an idea whose time has gone? *Personnel Management*, September, pp 34–37

Folger, R and Cropanzano, R (1998) *Organizational Justice and Human Resource Management*, Thousand Oaks CA, Sage

Folger, R, Konovsky, M A and Cropanzano, R (1992) A due process metaphor for performance appraisal, in B M Staw and L L Cummings (eds), *Research in Organizational Behavior*, Greenwich CT, JAI Press

Grint, K (1993) What's wrong with performance appraisal? A critique and a suggestion, *Human Resource Management Journal*, Spring, pp 61–77

Haines, V Y and St-Onge, S (2012) Performance management effectiveness: practices or context? *International Journal of Human Resource Management*, 23 (6), pp 1158–75

Lawler, E E and McDermott, M (2003) Current performance management practices: examining the impacts, *WorldatWork Journal*, 12 (2), pp 49–60

Lawler, E E, Benson, G S and McDermott, M (2012) What makes performance appraisals effective? *Compensation & Benefits Review*, 44 (4), pp 191–200

Lee, C D (2005) Rethinking the goals of your performance management system, *Employment Relations Today*, 32 (3), pp 53–60

Mone, E M and London, M (2010) *Employee Engagement Through Performance Management: A practical guide for managers*, New York, Routledge

Pulakos, E D (2009) *Performance Management: A new approach for driving business results*, Malden MA, Wiley-Blackwell

Pulakos, E D, Mueller-Hanson, R A and O'Leary, R S (2008) Performance management in the US, in A Varma, P S Budhwar and A DeNisi (eds), *Performance Management Systems: A global perspective*, Abingdon, Routledge

Shields, J (2007) *Managing Employee Performance and Reward*, Port Melbourne, Cambridge University Press

Sparrow, P and Hiltrop, J M (1994) *European Human Resource Management in Transition*, Harlow, Prentice Hall

Stoskopf, G A (2002) Taking performance management to the next level, *Workspan*, 45 (2), pp 28–30

Strebler, M T, Bevan, S and Robertson, D (2001) *Performance Review: Balancing objectives and content*, Brighton, Institute for Employment Studies

Taylor, M S, Tracy, K B, Renard, M K, Harrison, J K and Carroll, S J (1995) Due process in performance appraisal: A quasi-experiment in procedural justice, *Administrative Science Quarterly*, 40, pp 495–523

Verweire, K and Van Den Berghe, L (2004) Integrated performance management: New hype or new paradigm? in K Verweire and L Van Den Berghe (eds), *Integrated Performance Management*, Thousand Island CA, Sage, pp 1–14

Winstanley, D and Stuart-Smith, K (1996) Policing performance: the ethics of performance management, *Personnel Review*, 25 (6), pp 66–84

The evolution of performance management

02

This chapter presents a survey of the antecedents of performance management and how it evolved as the process described in the last chapter. Its aim is to increase understanding of the different elements of performance management by analysing how they developed over the years.

The beginnings and thereafter

According to Koontz (1971), the first known example of performance appraisal took place during the Wei dynasty (AD 221–65) when the emperor employed an 'imperial rater' whose task it was to evaluate the performance of the official family. In the 16th century Ignatius Loyola established a system for formal rating of the members of the Jesuit Society.

The first formal monitoring systems, however, evolved out of the work of Frederick Taylor and his followers before the First World War. Rating for officers in the US armed services was introduced in the 1920s and this spread to the UK, as did some of the factory-based American systems. Merit rating came to the fore in the United States and the UK in the 1950s and 1960s, when it was sometimes re-christened performance appraisal. Management by objectives then came and largely went in the 1960s and 1970s, and simultaneously, experiments were made with assessment techniques such as behaviourally anchored rating scales. A revised form of results-orientated performance appraisal emerged in the 1970s and still exists today. The term performance management was first used in the 1970s but it did not become a recognized process until the latter half of the 1980s.

Merit rating

Merit rating was the process of assessing how well someone was regarded in terms of personality traits such as judgement or integrity and qualities such as leadership or cooperativeness. The term 'merit' recalled classroom judgements made by teachers. Merit rating often involved the quantification of judgements against each factor, presumably in the belief that the quantification of subjective judgements made them more objective.

W D Scott was the American pioneer who introduced rating of the abilities of workers in industry prior to the First World War. He was very much influenced by F W Taylor (1911) and invented the 'Man to Man Comparison' scale, which was Taylorism in action. Many of the developments that have followed, even to this day, are a form of Taylorism, which is F W Taylor's concept of scientific management, meaning the use of systematic observation and measurement, task specialization and, in effect, the reduction of workers to the level of efficiently functioning machines.

The W D Scott scale was modified and used to rate the efficiency of US army officers. It is said to have supplanted the seniority system of promotion in the army and initiated an era of promotion on the basis of merit. The perceived success of this system led to its adoption by the British army.

The pioneering efforts of Scott were developed in the 1920s and 1930s into what was termed the Graphic Rating Scale, used for reports on workers and for rating managers and supervisors. A typical manager's or supervisor's scale included 'tick box' assessments of various qualities, for example:

Consider his success in winning confidence and respect through his personality:

(a) inspiring   (b) favourable   (c) indifferent   (d) unfavourable   (e) repellent

---

Times have changed.

The justification made for the use of this sort of scale was that ratings were 'educational'. They ensured, it was said, that those making the reports analysed subordinates in terms of the traits essential for success in their work. The educational impact on employees was described as imparting knowledge that they were being judged periodically on vital and important traits.

The original scale was said to have been based on thorough research by W D Scott and colleagues into what were the key criteria for rating people at work. But the principle of the scale and the factors used were seized on with enthusiasm by organizations on both sides of the Atlantic as merit rating or, later, performance appraisal flourished. This was without any research and analysis of the extent to which the factors were relevant (or whether dubbing someone 'repellent' was a good idea). Surveys conducted by the CIPD (Armstrong and Baron, 1998 and 2004) and e-reward (2005) revealed that there are organizations still using lists of competencies that include items that look suspiciously like some of the traits identified 70 years or more ago. They seemed to have been lifted down from some shelf (or extracted from a 'dictionary of competencies') without any research into the extent to which they were appropriate in the context of the organization. Merit rating still exists in some quarters even if it is now called performance management.

Some companies use the total merit score as the basis for ranking employees, and this is translated into a forced distribution for performance pay purposes; for example, the top 10 per cent in the ranking get a 5 per cent increase, the next 20 per cent a 4 per cent increase and so on. To iron out rating inconsistencies one manufacturing company used a diabolical device that they called 'factorising'. This meant producing an average score for the whole company and amending the allocation of points in each department to ensure that their scores corresponded with the company average. It can be imagined that line managers did not take kindly to the implication that there were no differences between departmental performances.

Attacks on merit rating

Attacks on merit rating were often made on the grounds that it was mainly concerned with the assessment of traits. These could refer to the extent to which individuals were conscientious, imaginative, self-sufficient and cooperative, or possessed qualities of judgement, initiative, vigour or original thinking. Traits represent 'pre-dispositions to behave in certain ways in a variety of different situations' (Chell, 1992). Trait theorists typically advance the following definition of personality: 'More or less stable internal factors that makes one person's behaviour consistent from one time to another and different from the behaviour other people would manifest in comparable situations' (Hampson, 1982). But the belief that trait behaviour is independent of situations (the work system) and the people with whom an individual is interacting is questionable. Trait measures cannot predict how a person will respond in a particular situation. And there is the problem of how anyone can be certain that someone has such and such a trait. Assessments of traits are only too likely to be prompted by subjective judgements and prejudices. These attacks led to the notion of performance appraisal as described below.

Performance appraisal

The term 'performance appraisal' as an alternative to merit rating emerged in the 1950s. The differences between the two were often small but the emphasis shifted towards reviewing how people performed their work rather than just trying to assess traits.

As defined by the Advisory, Conciliation and Arbitration Service (ACAS):

> Appraisals regularly record an assessment of an employee's performance, potential and development needs. The appraisal is an opportunity to take an overall view of work content, loads and volume, to look back at what has been achieved during the reporting period and agree objectives for the next.

Appraisal schemes were often over-elaborate and bureaucratic. They usually had ratings of performance factors such as volume of work, quality of work, knowledge of job, dependability, innovation, staff development and communication. They generally included an overall rating which could be expressed as a points score and used to rank employees and provide the basis for forced ranking (dividing the rank order into a hierarchy of performance grades and grading people according to their rank order). Scope might be allowed for self-assessment, and the forms frequently included spaces for training requirements and the assessment of potential. There was often an arrangement for 'countersigning' managers to make comments; this was usually the appraiser's manager – who was originally called the 'grandfather', which later changed to 'grandparent'.

The appraisal was typically an annual event; a meeting convened by a manager in which a top-down opinion was expressed about the performance of a subordinate, followed by a rating.

A view about how performance appraisal functioned was expressed by Long (1986) on the basis of the Institute of Personnel Management's research into performance appraisal:

There is no such thing as the perfect performance review system. None is infallible, although some are more fallible than others. Some systems, despite flaws, will be managed fairly conscientiously, others, despite elegant design, will receive perfunctory attention and ultimately fail. The relative success or failure of performance review, as with any other organizational system, depends very much on the attitudinal response it arouses.

The requirements for success were indeed demanding. These were described by Lazer and Wikstrom (1977): 'A "good" performance appraisal scheme must be job related, reliable, valid for the purposes for which it is being used, standardized in its procedures, practical in its administration and suited to the organization's culture.'

The term performance appraisal is now generally limited to the performance assessment aspect of performance management.

Attacks on performance appraisal

A strong attack on the practice of performance appraisal was mounted by McGregor in his highly influential *Harvard Business Review* article, 'An uneasy look at performance appraisal' (1957). He made the following suggestion:

Douglas McGregor on performance appraisal

The emphasis should be shifted from appraisal to analysis. This implies a more positive approach. No longer is the subordinate being examined by his superior so that his [sic] weaknesses may be determined; rather he is examining himself, in order to define not only his weaknesses but also his strengths and potentials... He becomes an active agent, not a passive 'object'. He is no longer a pawn in a chess game called management development.

McGregor proposed that the focus should be on the future rather than the past in order to establish realistic targets and to seek the most effective ways of reaching them. The accent of the review is therefore on performance, on actions relative to goals.

He went on to write:

There is less a tendency for the personality of the subordinate to become an issue. The superior, instead of adopting the position of a psychologist or a therapist, can become a coach helping subordinates to reach their own decisions on the specific steps that will enable them to reach their targets. In short, the main factor in the management of individual performance should be the analysis of the behaviour required to achieve agreed results, not the assessment of personality. This is partly management by objectives, which is concerned with planning and measuring results in relation to agreed targets and standards, but retains the concept that individual performance is about behaviour as well as results (a notion that management by objectives ignored).

A research project conducted by Rowe (1964) in the UK came to broadly the same conclusion as McGregor – that managers do not like 'playing at being God' in rating the personalities of their subordinates:

Managers admitted they were hesitant [to appraise] because what they wrote might be misunderstood, because they might unduly affect a subordinate's future career, because they could only write what they were prepared to say and so on.

One comment made by a manager to Rowe was that: 'You feel rather like a schoolmaster writing an end-of-term report'. Rowe's conclusions were that:

- Appraisers were reluctant to appraise.
- The follow-up was inadequate.
- No attempt should be made to clarify or categorize performance in terms of grades. The difficulty of achieving common standards and the reluctance of appraisers to use the whole scale made them of little use.

These comments, especially the last one, are as relevant today as they were when they were made some time ago.

Performance appraisal problems

Perhaps the biggest problem with performance appraisal schemes was that appraisal was not regarded as a normal and necessary process of management. It only happened once or at most twice a year. It was generally a top-down affair and managers tended to go through the motions when they reluctantly held their yearly appraisal meeting. As described by Armstrong and Murlis (1994) it too often became 'a dishonest annual ritual'.

Another problem with performance appraisal was that it was too often perceived as the property of the personnel department. This was where the forms were kept and where decisions were made about performance-related pay. Line managers frequently criticized the system as being irrelevant. They felt they had better things to do and at worst ignored it and at best paid lip service to completing the forms, knowing that they had to make ratings to generate performance pay. Indeed, managers have been known to rate first in accordance with what pay increase individuals should have and then write their comments to justify their marks. In other words, human beings behaved as human beings. Individuals were said to be wary of appraisals and as likely to be demotivated by an appraisal meeting as to be motivated.

The concept of 'Appraisal: an idea whose time has gone?' was advanced by Fletcher (1993) as follows:

> What we are seeing is the demise of the traditional, monolithic appraisal system … In its place are evolving a number of separate but linked processes applied in different ways according to the needs of local circumstances and staff levels. The various elements in this may go by different names, and perhaps the term appraisal has in some ways outlived its usefulness.

Management by objectives

The management by objectives (MBO) movement claimed that it overcame the problems of merit rating and traditional appraisal schemes. It was based on the writings of Peter Drucker and Douglas McGregor.

Peter Drucker

The term 'management by objectives' was first coined by Peter Drucker (1955) as follows:

Peter Drucker on management by objectives

What the business enterprise needs is a principle of management that will give full scope to individual strength and responsibility and at the same time give common direction of vision and effort, establish teamwork and harmonize the goals of the individual with the common weal. The only principle that can do this is management by objectives and self-control.

Drucker emphasized that 'an effective management must direct the vision and efforts of all managers towards a common goal'. This would ensure that individual and corporate objectives are integrated and would also make it possible for managers to control their own performance: 'Self-control means stronger motivation: a desire to do the best rather than just enough to get by. It means higher performance goals and broader vision.'

Douglas McGregor

McGregor's (1960) contribution arose from his Theory Y concept. He wrote: 'The central principle that derives from Theory Y is that of integration: the creation of conditions such that the members of the organization can achieve their own goals best by directing their efforts towards the success of the organization'. This is McGregor's principle of 'management by integration and self-control', which he insisted should be regarded as a strategy – a way of managing people:

Douglas McGregor on the principle of integration and self-control

The tactics are worked out in the light of the circumstances. Forms and procedures are of little value... 'selling' management a programme of target setting and providing standardized forms and procedures is the surest way to prevent the development of management by integration and self-control.

This principle may not have entered the vocabulary of performance management but is fully absorbed into current thinking about it. Many writers and management consultants recycle McGregor's philosophy without ever acknowledging its source.

Management by objectives defined

Management by objectives was defined by John Humble (1972), a leading British enthusiast, as: 'A dynamic system that seeks to integrate the company's need to clarify and achieve its profit and growth goals with the manager's need to contribute and develop himself [sic]. It is a demanding and rewarding style of managing a business.' His illustration of the dynamic nature of

FIGURE 2.1   The management by objectives cycle

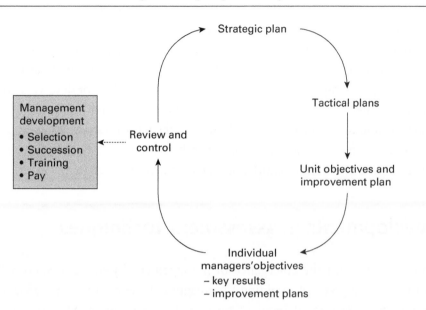

the system is given in Figure 2.1. It shows its cyclical nature of management by objectives and thus anticipated the way in which the performance management cycle was modelled. The derivation of individual objectives from the strategic, tactical and unit plans also anticipates the importance attached in performance management to aligning individual and corporate strategic goals.

Management by objectives discredited

Management by objectives was adopted enthusiastically by many companies in the 1960s and 1970s. But it became discredited by the 1990s – why?

The demise of management by objectives was mainly due to the process becoming over-systematized (often under the influence of package-orientated management consultants). In addition, too much emphasis was placed on the quantification of objectives. The originators of the concept may not have advocated lots of forms and they recognized, as John Humble did, that qualitative performance standards could be included in the system, by which was meant 'a statement of conditions which exist when the result is being satisfactorily achieved'. But these principles were often ignored in practice. In addition, management-by-objectives frequently became a top-down affair with little dialogue, and it tended to focus narrowly on the objectives of individual managers without linking them to corporate or team goals (although this link was supposed to happen, and it was certainly a major part of Drucker's original concept). The system also tended to concentrate on managers, leaving the rest of the staff to be dealt with by an old-fashioned merit-rating scheme, presumably because it was thought that they did not deserve anything better. Furthermore, the elaborate procedures involved were resented by managers and difficult to maintain. However, the basic concept of management-by-objectives had considerable influence first on results-based performance appraisal and then, significantly, on performance management.

Developments in assessment techniques

Concurrently with the emergence of management by objectives, consideration was being given to avoiding the misguided use of traits in performance assessment. The critical incident approach developed by Flanagan (1954) changed the focus to the observation of behaviour. Behavioural anchored rating scales (Smith and Kendall, 1963) and behavioural observation scales (Latham and Wexley, 1977) provided for the quantification of behavioural performance. These approaches are described in Chapter 9.

Much research was carried out later on rating, for example, by Bernardin and Buckley (1981), Sulsky and Balzer (1988) and Murphy and Balzer (1989). Such activity reflected the preoccupation of some American academics with rating techniques. This still persists today, in contrast to the UK approach, which has become more concerned with developing performance than rating it. Further consideration to assessment and rating techniques is given in Chapter 9.

Rating research led to the emergence in the early 1990s of multi-source or 360-degree feedback that provided for upwards and lateral assessments as well as the traditional top-down rating (Hedge *et al*, 2001).

Results-based performance appraisal

In the 1970s a revised approach to performance appraisal was developed under the influence of the management by objectives movement. It was called 'results-based appraisal' because it incorporated the agreement of objectives and an assessment of the results obtained against these objectives. Ratings were usually retained of overall performance and in relation to individual objectives. Trait ratings were also used, but these were later replaced in some schemes by competency ratings. This form of performance appraisal received a boost during the later 1980s because of the increased use of performance-related pay based on performance ratings.

Enter performance management

The concept of performance management incorporates some of the notions and approaches of management by objectives and results-based perform-ance appraisal but it includes a number of significantly different features as described below.

Early days

The earliest reference to performance management in the literature was made by Warren (1972). On the basis of his research in a manufacturing company he defined the features of performance management as follows.

Features of performance management as defined by Warren in 1972

- Expectations – a large group of employees – preferably all – must be told clearly, objectively and in their own language what is specifically expected of them.

- Skill – a large group of employees must have the technical knowledge and skill to carry out the tasks.

- Feedback – workers must be told in clear terms, without threats, how they are doing in terms of expectations.

- Resources – employees must have the time, money and equipment necessary to perform the expected tasks at optimal level.

- Reinforcement – employees must be positively reinforced for desired performance.

These requirements may not be expressed in quite the same language today, but they are just as relevant.

Another early use of the term performance management was made by Beer and Ruh (1976). Their thesis was that: 'performance is best developed through practical challenges and experiences on the job with guidance and feedback from superiors.' They described the performance management system at Corning Glass Works, the aim of which was to help managers give feedback in a helpful and constructive way, and to aid in the creation of a developmental plan. The features of this system that distinguished it from other appraisal schemes were as follows:

- emphasis on both development and evaluation;
- use of a profile defining the individual's strengths and development needs;
- integration of the results achieved with the means by which they have been achieved;
- separation of development review from salary review.

Although this was not necessarily a model performance management process it did contain a number of characteristics that are still regarded as good practice.

The concept of performance management then lay fallow for some years but began to emerge in the United States as a new approach to managing performance in the mid-1980s. However, one of the first books exclusively devoted to performance management was not published until 1988 (Plachy and Plachy). They described what had by then become the accepted approach to performance management as follows.

Performance management as described by Plachy and Plachy in 1988

Performance management is communication: a manager and an employee arrive together at an understanding of what work is to be accomplished, how it will be accomplished, how work is progressing toward desired results, and finally, after effort is expended to accomplish the work, whether the performance has achieved the agreed-upon plan. The process recycles when the manager and employee begin planning what work is to be accomplished for the next performance period. Performance management is an umbrella term that includes performance planning, performance review, and performance appraisal. Major work plans and appraisals are generally made annually. Performance review occurs whenever a manager and an employee confirm, adjust, or correct their understanding of work performance during routine work contacts.

In the UK the first published reference to performance management was made at a meeting of the Compensation Forum in 1987 by Don Beattie, Personnel Director, ICL, who described how it was used as 'an essential contribution to a massive and urgent change programme in the organization' and had become a part of the fabric of the business.

By 1990 performance management had entered the vocabulary of human resource management in the UK as well as in the United States. Fowler (1990) defined what has become the accepted concept of performance management:

> Management has always been about getting things done, and good managers are concerned to get the right things done well. That, in essence, is performance management – the organization of work to achieve the best possible results. From this simple viewpoint, performance management is not a system or technique, it is the totality of the day-to-day activities of all managers.

Performance management established

Full recognition of the existence of performance management was provided by the research project conducted by the Institute of Personnel Management (1992). The following definition of performance management was produced as a result of this research: 'A strategy that relates to every activity of the organization set in the context of its human resources policies, culture, style and communications systems. The nature of the strategy depends on the organizational context and can vary from organization to organization.'

It was suggested that what was described as a 'performance management system' (PMS) complied with the textbook definition when the following characteristics were met by the organization.

Institute of Personnel Management (1992): definition of a performance management system

- It communicates a vision of its objectives to all its employees.

- It sets departmental and individual performance targets that are related to wider objectives.

- It conducts a formal review of progress towards these targets.

- It uses the review process to identify training, development and reward outcomes.

- It evaluates the whole process in order to improve effectiveness.

- It expresses performance targets in terms of measurable outputs, accountabilities and training/learning targets.

- It uses formal appraisal procedures as ways of communicating performance requirements that are set on a regular basis.

- It links performance requirements to pay, especially for senior managers.

With the exception of the link to pay, which applies to many but not all performance management schemes, these characteristics still hold good today.

The IPM 1992 survey revealed that in the organizations with performance management systems, 85 per cent had performance pay and 76 per cent rated performance (this proportion is lower in later surveys). The emphasis was on objective setting and review that, as the authors of the report mentioned, 'leaves something of a void when it comes to identifying development needs on a longer-term basis... there is a danger with results-orientated schemes in focusing excessively on what is to be achieved and ignoring the how'. It was noted that some organizations were moving in the direction of competency analysis but not very systematically.

Two of the IPM researchers (Bevan and Thompson, 1991) commented on the emergence of performance management systems as integrating processes that mesh various human resource management activities with the business objectives of the organization. They identified two broad thrusts towards integration:

1 Reward-driven integration, which emphasizes the role of performance pay in changing organizational behaviour and tends to undervalue the part played by other human resource development activities. This appeared to be the dominant mode of integration.

2 Development-driven integration, which stresses the importance of HRD. Although performance pay may operate in these organizations, it is perceived to be complementary to HRD activities rather than dominating them.

Performance management: the next phase

The 1998 IPD research project (Armstrong and Baron, 1998) revealed that in many instances performance management practices had moved on since 1992. In the organizations covered by the survey the following trends were observed:

- Performance management was regarded as a number of interlinked processes.

- Performance management was seen as a continuous process, not as a once-a-year appraisal, thus echoing Fowler's (1990) comment that: 'In today's fast-moving world, any idea that effective performance management can be tied neatly to a single annual date is patently absurd.'

- The focus was on employee development rather than on performance-related pay.

- A shift had taken place towards getting line managers to accept and own performance management as a natural process of management.

- Some organizations rejected the concept of a bureaucratic, centrally controlled and uniform system of performance management, and instead accepted that, within an overall policy framework, different approaches may be appropriate in different parts of the organization and for different people.

Another important trend in the 1990s was the increased use of competencies for recruitment and people development purposes. This led to more focus on the nature of performance, which was recognized as being not only about what was achieved but also about *how* it was achieved. The result was the 'mixed model' of performance management as described by Hartle (1995), which covers competency levels and the extent to which behaviour was in line with the core values of the organization, as well as objective-setting and review. At the same time the notion emerged of what Sparrow (2008) called value-based performance management: that is, including assessments of the extent to which individuals uphold a defined list of core organizational values in the performance review procedure.

The next development was the recognition that performance management had to focus on organizational as well as individual effectiveness. It was not enough to hope that processes for improving individual performance would necessarily result in improvements in organizational performance. A strategic approach is required which involves fitting the performance management strategy to the firm's business strategy and context, and supporting the business and HR strategies through activities designed to improve organizational capability such as human capital management, talent management and the development of high-performance cultures.

Why performance management?

Performance management arrived in the later 1980s partly as a reaction to the negative aspects of merit rating and management by objectives referred to earlier and partly because of increased emphasis on high performance. Its strength is that it is essentially an integrated approach to managing performance on a continuous basis. The appeal of performance management in its fully realized form is that it is holistic – it pervades every aspect of running the business and helps to give purpose and meaning to those involved in achieving organizational success.

Of course, performance management at first incorporated many of the elements of performance appraisal for example, rating, objective setting and review, performance pay and a tendency towards trait assessment. However, performance management is significantly different from previous approaches in that:

1 It is regarded as a continuous process not a single event.

2 It is treated as a normal and necessary function of management rather than an HR procedure.

3 The emphasis is on dialogue and agreement rather than top-down appraisal.

4 It is owned by line managers rather than HR.

References

Advisory, Conciliation and Arbitration Service (1988) *Employee Appraisal*, London, ACAS

Armstrong, M and Baron, A (1998) *Performance Management: The New Realities*, London, CIPD

Armstrong, M and Baron, A (2004) *Performance Management: Performance Management in Action*, London, CIPD

Armstrong, M and Murlis, H (1994) *Reward Management*, London, Kogan Page

Beer, M and Ruh, R A (1976) Employee growth through performance management, *Harvard Business Review*, July–August, pp 59–66

Bernardin, H J and Buckley, M R (1981) Strategies in rater training, *Academy of Management Review*, **6**, pp 205–12

Bevan, S and Thompson, M (1991) Performance management at the crossroads, *Personnel Management*, November, pp 36–39

Chell, E (1992) *The Psychology of Behaviour in Organisations*, Basingstoke, Macmillan

Coens, T and Jenkins, M (2002) *Abolishing Performance Appraisals: Why they backfire and what to do instead*, San Francisco CA, Berrett-Koehler

Drucker, P (1955) *The Practice of Management*, London, Heinemann

e-reward (2005) *Survey of Performance Management Practice*, Stockport, e-reward

Flanagan, J C (1954) The critical incident technique, *Psychological Bulletin*, **51**, pp 327–58

Fletcher, C (1993) Appraisal: an idea whose time has gone? *Personnel Management*, September, pp 34–37

Fowler, A (1990) Performance management: the MBO of the '90s? *Personnel Management*, July, pp 47–54

Hampson, S E (1982) *The Construction of Personality*, London, Routledge and Kegan Paul

Hartle, F (1995) *Transforming the Performance Management Process*, London, Kogan Page

Hedge, L M, Borman, W C and Birkeland, S A (2001) History and development of multisource feedback as a methodology, in D W Bracken, C W Timmwreck and A H Church (eds), *Handbook of Multisource Feedback*, San Francisco CA, Jossey-Bass

Humble, J (1972) *Management by Objectives*, London, Management Publications

Institute of Personnel Management (1992) *Performance Management in the UK: An analysis of the issues*, London, IPM

Koontz, H (1971) *Appraising Managers as Managers*, New York, McGraw-Hill

Latham, G P and Wexley, K N (1977) Behavioural observation scales, *Personnel Psychology*, **30**, pp 255–68

Lazer, R I and Wikstrom, W S (1977) *Appraising Managerial Performance: Current Practices and New Directions*, New York, The Conference Board

Long, P (1986) *Performance Appraisal Revisited*, London, Institute of Personnel Management

McGregor, D (1957) An uneasy look at performance appraisal, *Harvard Business Review*, May–June, pp 89–94

Murphy, K R and Balzer, W K (1989) Rater errors and rating accuracy, *Journal of Applied Psychology*, **74** (4), pp 619–24

Plachy, R J and Plachy, S J (1988) *Getting Results From Your Performance Management and Appraisal System*, New York, AMACOM

Rowe, K (1964) An appraisal of appraisals, *Journal of Management Studies*, **1** (1), pp 1–25

Smith, P C and Kendall, L M (1963) Retranslation of expectations: an approach to the construction of unambiguous answers for rating scales, *Journal of Applied Psychology*, 47, pp 853–85

Sparrow, P (2008) Performance management in the UK, in A Varma, P S Budhwar and A DeNisi (eds), *Performance Management Systems: A global perspective*, Abingdon, Routledge

Sulsky, L M and Balzer, W K (1988) The meaning and measurement of performance rating accuracy: some methodological and theoretical concerns, *Journal of Applied Psychology*, 73, pp 497–506

Taylor, F W (1911) *Principles of Scientific Management*, New York, Harper

Warren, M (1972) Performance management: a substitute for supervision, *Management Review*, October, pp 28–42

The conceptual framework

03

Performance management concepts explain its theoretical basis and how it should work. They provide a framework within which performance processes can be developed, operated and evaluated.

This chapter examines the following concepts:

- The meaning of performance and what determines it
- Factors influencing performance
- Underpinning theories
- Performance management and the psychological contract
- Performance management values

The meaning of performance

If you can't define performance you can't measure or manage it. It was pointed out by Bates and Holton (1995) that: 'Performance is a multidimensional construct, the measurement of which varies depending on a variety of factors'. They also stated that it is important to determine whether the measurement objective is to assess performance outcomes or behaviour.

Latham *et al* (2007) emphasized that an appropriate definition of performance is a prerequisite for feedback and goal setting processes. They stated that a performance theory is needed which stipulates:

- the relevant performance dimensions;
- the performance standards or expectations associated with different performance levels;

- how situational constraints should be weighed (if at all) when evaluating performance;
- the number of performance levels or gradients;
- the extent to which performance should be based on absolute or comparative standards.

There are different views on what performance is. It could just mean outcomes – the results obtained. Or it could mean behaviour – how the results were obtained. Or it could be both results and behaviour.

Performance as outcomes

Kane (1996) argued that performance 'is something that the person leaves behind and that exists apart from the purpose'. Bernadin *et al* (1995) were concerned that:

> Performance should be defined as the outcomes of work because they provide the strongest linkage to the strategic goals of the organisation, customer satisfaction, and economic contributions.

Performance as behaviour

Campbell (1990) explained that: 'Performance is behaviour and should be distinguished from the outcomes because they can be contaminated by systems factors'. Aguinis (2005) was positive that: 'performance is about behaviour or what employees do, and not about what employees produce or the outcomes of their work'.

Campbell *et al* (1993) focused on the measurement of performance which they defined as behaviour or action relevant to the attainment of the organization's goals that can be scaled, that is, measured. They suggested that performance is multidimensional and that each dimension is characterized by a category of similar behaviour or actions. The components consist of: (1) job-specific task proficiency, (2) non-job specific proficiency (eg organizational citizenship behaviour), (3) written and oral communication proficiency, (4) demonstration of effort, (5) maintenance of personal discipline, (6) facilitation of peer and team performance, (7) supervision/leadership and (8) management/administration.

Borman and Motowidlo (1993) put forward the notion of contextual performance which covers non-job specific behaviours such as cooperation, dedication, enthusiasm and persistence and is differentiated from task performance covering job specific behaviours. As Fletcher (2001) mentioned, contextual performance deals with attributes that go beyond task competence and which foster behaviours that enhance the climate and effectiveness of the organization.

Performance as both outcomes and behaviour

It can be argued that a more comprehensive view of performance is achieved if it is defined as embracing both behaviour and outcomes. When people are said to be performing well it does not solely refer to how well they behave. It also covers the results they deliver. The *Oxford English Dictionary* defines performance as: 'The accomplishment, execution, carrying out, working out of anything ordered or undertaken.' This refers to outputs/outcomes (accomplishment) as well as behaviours (carrying out the work). As Brumbach (1988) put it:

> Performance means both behaviours and results. Behaviours emanate from the performer and transform performance from abstraction to action. Not just the instruments for results, behaviours are also outcomes in their own right – the product of mental and physical effort applied to tasks – and can be judged apart from results.

Defining performance like this leads to the conclusion that when managing the performance of individuals and teams both inputs (behaviour) and outputs (results) need to be considered. This was supported by Aguinis (2005) who in spite of stating that performance was concerned solely with behaviour later suggested that performance management was about measuring results as well as behaviours.

This is the mixed model of performance management which covers competency levels and achievements as well as objective setting and review. And it is this model which research (eg Armstrong and Baron, 2004) has shown to be the one which is now interesting many organizations. Levels of individual performance are affected by a number of factors as discussed overleaf.

Factors influencing performance

Four major influences on overall performance were identified by Harrison (1997):

- *the learner*, who needs the right level of competence, motivation, support and incentives in order to perform effectively;
- *the learner's work group*, whose members will exercise a strong positive or negative influence on the attitudes, behaviour and performance of the learner;
- *the learner's manager*, who needs to provide continuing support and act as a role model, coach and stimulator related to performance;
- *the organization*, which may produce barriers to effective performance if there is no powerful, cohering vision; ineffective structure, culture or work systems; unsupportive employee relations policy and systems, or inappropriate leadership and management style.

The specific factors affecting performance are described below.

Factors affecting individual performance

Vroom (1964) suggested that performance is a function of ability and motivation as shown in the formula: Performance = f(Ability × Motivation). The effects of ability and motivation on performance are not additive but multiplicative. People need both ability and motivation to perform well and if either ability or motivation is zero there will be no effective performance.

A formula for performance was produced by Blumberg and Pringle (1982) which emphasized the importance of the organizational context. Their equation was:

Performance = Individual Attributes × Work Effort × Organizational Support

A variation on the above was offered by McCloy *et al* (1994). They proposed that a combination of three factors enables some people to perform at higher levels than others:

1 *Declarative knowledge* (about facts concerning task requirements and goals).

2 *Procedural knowledge* (a combination of knowing what to do and how to do it).

3 *Motivation* (level and persistence of effort).

Research carried out by Bailey *et al* (2001) focused on another factor affecting performance – participation. They noted that 'organizing the work process so that non-managerial employees have the opportunity to contribute discretionary effort is the central feature of a high-performance work system'. (This was one of the earlier uses of the term discretionary effort.)

The 'AMO' formula put forward by Boxall and Purcell (2003) is a combination of the Vroom and Bailey *et al* ideas. This model states that performance is a function of Ability + Motivation + Opportunity to Participate (note that the relationship is additive not multiplicative).

These formulas focus mainly on individual performance but systems factors are also important.

Systems factors

Individual performance is influenced by systems factors as well as person factors (Cardy and Dobbins, 1994). Systems theory as formulated by Miller and Rice (1967) states that organizations should be treated as open systems which transform inputs into outputs within the environments (external and internal) upon which they are dependent. Systems theory is the basis of the input–process–output–outcome model of managing performance which assesses the entire contribution that an individual makes within the system in carrying out his or her allotted tasks. Inputs are the skills and knowledge that an individual brings to a job. Process is how people actually perform their jobs. Outputs are the results of performance expressed in quantified terms such as sales volume, income generated or units of production and outcomes are a visible effect which is the result of effort but cannot necessarily be measured in quantified terms. The input–process–output–outcome model of managing performance is important first, because it provides the basis for measuring performance and second, because all the factors that influence performance, including the system and the context, can be taken into account when assessing it.

Systems factors include the support people get from the organization and other factors outside the control of individuals. Jones (1995) proposed that the aim should be to 'manage context not performance' and went on to explain that:

In this equation, the role of management focuses on clear, coherent support for employees by providing information about organization goals, resources, technology, structure, and policy, thus creating a context that has multiplicative impact on the employees, their individual attributes (competency to perform), and their work effort (willingness to perform). In short, managing context is entirely about helping people understand; it is about turning on the lights.

It was emphasized by Deming (1986) that differences in performance were largely due to systems variations. Gladwell (2008) also argued that success isn't primarily down to the individual, but to the context in which he or she worked. Coens and Jenkins (2002) made the following comments on the impact of systems.

An organizational system is composed of the people who do the work but far more than that. It also includes the organization's methods, structure, support, materials, equipment, customers, work culture, internal and external environments (such as markets, the community, governments), *and* the interaction of these components. Each part of the system has its own purpose but at the same time is dependent on the other parts....

Because of the interdependency of the parts, improvement strategies aimed at the parts, such as appraisal, do little or nothing to improve the system... Individual performance is mostly determined by the system in which the work is done rather than by the individual's initiative, abilities and efforts...

Because of these effects and the low yield benefit of improving the parts, it makes little sense to design organizational improvement systems around appraisal while the leveraging power of improving the system is ignored... The myopic focus on *individual* improvement equates to a religious dogma that is manifested through the rituals and rites of ranking and rating.

However, Coens and Jenkins also stated that: 'We do not advocate abandoning all strategies aimed at individual improvement, personal development and goal attainment. When combined with serious efforts toward improving the system and work environment, such initiatives can significantly bolster organizational transformation'.

Contextual factors

Systems operate within the context of the organization. Nadler and Tushman (1980) observed that:

> The manager needs to understand the patterns of behaviour that are observed to predict in what direction behaviour will move (particularly in the light of management action) and to use this knowledge to control behaviour over the course of time. Effective managerial action requires that the manager be able to diagnose the situation he or she is working in.

This point should be extended to include the people managers manage – they equally want to know and are entitled to know the situation *they* are working in.

The situation or context in which people work and the way performance can be measured can be described in terms of systems theory as explained earlier. More specifically, the context includes the organizational culture, the employee relations climate, the people involved and the internal environment in terms of the organization's structure, its size and its technology and working practices.

Organizational culture

Organizational culture is the pattern of shared beliefs, norms and values in an organization which shape the way people act and interact and strongly influence the ways in which things get done. From the performance management viewpoint one of the most important manifestations of organizational culture is management style. This refers to the ways in which managers behave in managing people and how they exercise authority and use their power. If the prevailing management style in a command and control type structure is autocratic, directive, task-orientated, distant and tough, then a 'caring and sharing' philosophy of performance management is not likely to work, even if it were felt to be desirable, which is unlikely. Alternatively, a non-directive, participative and considerate style is more likely to support a 'partnership' approach to performance management, with an emphasis on involvement, empowerment and ownership.

It is vital to take account of cultural considerations when developing and implementing performance management. The aim must be to achieve a high degree of fit between the performance management processes and the corporate culture when the latter is embedded and appropriate. However, performance management is one of the instruments that can be used in a cultural change programme where the focus is on high performance, engagement, commitment and involvement.

Employee relations climate

The employee relations climate of an organization represents the perceptions of employees and their representatives about the ways in which relationships between management and employees are maintained. It refers to the ways in which formal or informal employee relations are conducted and how the various parties (managers, employees and trade unions or staff associations) behave when interacting with one another. The climate can be good, bad or indifferent according to perceptions about the extent to which:

- the parties trust one another;
- management treats employees fairly and with consideration;
- management is open and honest about its actions and intentions;
- harmonious relationships exist; management treats employees as stakeholders;
- employees are committed to the interests of the organization;
- what management does is consistent with what it says it will do.

Clearly, a good climate will be conducive to the design and operation of effective performance management processes as long as these are developed jointly by the stakeholders and take account of the interests of all involved. An improved employee relations climate may also result from pursuing the development and implementation of performance management in accordance with the ethical principles set out in Chapter 1.

People

Performance management processes will vary in accordance with the composition of the workforce. For example, a firm employing mainly knowledge workers is likely to adopt a different approach from a manufacturing firm. Within the organization, approaches may vary between different groups of employees. In the Victoria and Albert Museum, for example, it is recognized that the way in which objectives are agreed by a curator will be different from how the standards of performance are agreed for security guards.

Organization structure

A hierarchical or functional structure with well-defined layers of authority is more likely to support a directive, top-down approach to setting objectives and reviewing performance. A flatter, process-based structure will encourage more flexible participative approaches with an emphasis on teamwork and the management of performance by self-directed teams.

A structure in which responsibility and authority are devolved close to the scenes of action will probably foster a flexible approach to performance management. A highly centralized organization may attempt to impose a monolithic performance management system, and fail.

Technology and working practices

There is no conclusive evidence that advanced technology and working practices are associated with sophisticated approaches to performance management. But it is reasonable to assume that high technology firms or sophisticated organizations are more likely to innovate in this field. Another aspect of work practices is the extent to which the work is computer or machine controlled, or routine. Computerized performance monitoring provides an entirely different method of measuring performance which is related directly to outputs and/or errors. As Bates and Holton (1995) noted as a result of their research, this can have detrimental effects by transforming a helpful supervisory style into one that is more coercive. But research conducted by Earley (1986) found that employees trusted feedback from a computer more than feedback from a supervisor. He claimed that performance management could have a greater impact on performance because of higher self-efficacy (ie the individual's self-belief that he or she will be able to accomplish certain tasks).

Bureaucratic methods of working may also affect the design and operation of performance management. Organizations that function as bureaucracies, appropriately or inappropriately, are more likely to have a formalized performance management system. The system may be centrally controlled by HR and the emphasis will be on the annual appraisal carried out in accordance with strictly defined rules. The appraisal may be a top-down judgemental affair referring to personality traits. Performance and potential will be rated.

Organizations which work flexibly with an emphasis on horizontal processes and teamwork are more likely to have a less formal process of performance management, leaving more scope for managers and teams to manage their own processes in accordance with agreed principles.

Size

Research carried out by Beaver and Harris (1995) into performance management in small firms came to the conclusion that:

> The performance management systems of large firms simply cannot be scaled down to fit the smaller enterprise which often exhibits a radically different management process and operation.

They described the management process in small firms as likely to be characterized by the highly personalized preferences, prejudices and attitudes of the firm's entrepreneur or owner, who will probably work close to the operating process.

The external environment

If the external competitive, business, economic and political environment is turbulent – which it usually is – organizations have to learn to respond and adapt rapidly. This will influence the ways in which business strategies and plans are developed and the sort of goals people are expected to achieve. Performance management has to function flexibly in tune with the constant changes in demands and expectations to which the organization is subject. A business which operates in a fairly steady state as far as its external environment is concerned (rare, but they do exist) can adopt more structured and orderly performance management systems.

Underpinning theories

Performance management practice is underpinned and explained by the theories summarized below. Goal theory has perhaps been the most influential because setting goals and assessing performance against the goals is such a significant part of a performance management system. But other theories are also relevant such as those relating to control and reinforcement which explain the fundamental mechanism of feedback, and expectancy theory which indicates how performance management can help to motivate people. Social learning theory links reinforcement and expectancy theory, and self-efficacy theory highlights the importance of helping people to believe in themselves and their ability to improve.

Goal theory

Goal theory as developed by Latham and Locke (1979) highlights four mechanisms that connect goals to performance outcomes: (1) they direct attention to priorities; (2) they stimulate effort; (3) they challenge people to bring their knowledge and skills to bear to increase their chances of success and (4) the more challenging the goal, the more people will draw on their full repertoire of skills. This theory underpins the emphasis in performance management on setting and agreeing goals against which performance can be measured and managed.

Robertson *et al* (1992) on goal theory

Goals inform individuals to achieve particular levels of performance, in order for them to direct and evaluate their actions; while performance feedback allows the individual to track how well he or she has been doing in relation to the goal so that, if necessary, adjustments in effort, direction or possibly task strategies can be made.

Expectancy theory

Expectancy theory as originally formulated by Vroom (1964) states that effort (motivation) depends on the extent to which people expect that rewards will follow effort and that the reward is worthwhile.

Performance management is concerned with influencing behaviour to achieve better results. It operates in line with expectancy theory by defining the relationship between effort, achievement and reward thus motivating people and providing them with a sense of direction. Positive feedback provides a reward in the shape of the recognition of work well done. This is

FIGURE 3.1   Expectancy-based motivational model for performance

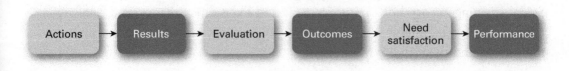

intrinsic motivation provided by the work itself which arises when work satisfies needs for accomplishment, provides opportunities for growth and the scope to use and develop abilities, and fosters self-belief.

An expectancy-based motivational model for individual performance improvement was devised by DeNisi and Pritchard (2006). It is based on the belief that people allocate energy to actions in a way that will maximize their anticipated need satisfaction. The sequence is illustrated in Figure 3.1.

The key for performance management is to ensure that evaluations and outcomes are structured so that employees will focus their actions in the ways desired by the organization, resulting in the kind of performance that is needed and appropriate rewards. The stronger the links between each element in the motivation process, the greater will be the motivation of employees to improve their performance. The process should aim to strengthen the perceived connection between actions and outcomes.

Control theory

Control theory focuses attention on feedback as a means of shaping behaviour. As people receive feedback they appreciate the discrepancy between what they are doing and what they are expected to do and take corrective action to overcome the discrepancy. Feedback is recognized as a crucial part of performance management processes.

Reinforcement theory

Reinforcement theory (Hull, 1951) states that successes in achieving goals and rewards act as positive incentives and reinforce the successful behaviour which is repeated the next time a similar need arises. Positive feedback therefore provides for positive reinforcement. Constructive feedback can also reinforce behaviours which seek alternative means of achieving goals.

Social learning theory

Social learning theory as formulated by Bandura (1977) combines aspects of reinforcement and expectancy theory. It recognizes the significance of the basic concept of reinforcement as a determinant of future behaviour but also emphasizes the importance of internal psychological factors, especially expectations about the values of goals and the ability of individuals to reach them.

Self-efficacy theory

Self-efficacy theory as also developed by Bandura (1982) indicates that self-motivation will be directly linked to the self-belief of individuals that they will be able to accomplish certain tasks, achieve certain goals or learn certain things. An important aim of performance management is to increase self-efficacy by giving individuals the opportunity to consider and discuss with their managers how they can do more. But the onus is on managers to encourage self-belief in the minds of those with whom they discuss performance and development.

Performance management and the psychological contract

The psychological contract is the set of reciprocal but unwritten expectations which exist between individual employees and their employers. A psychological contract is implied and inferred rather than stated and agreed. It cannot necessarily be spelt out in detail because it evolves over time. But performance management processes can be used to ensure that performance expectations are agreed and reviewed regularly. And this should contribute to the clarification of the psychological contract and the employment relationship.

Performance management values

Performance management values are based on the ethical principles of respect for the individual, mutual respect, procedural fairness and transparency as defined by Winstanley and Stuart-Smith (1996). The values refer to beliefs that:

- the management of the organization has the overriding responsibility for creating the conditions in which high performance is achievable;

- everyone is concerned with the improvement of performance; it is the joint responsibility of managers and their teams and they are mutually dependent on one another to attain this purpose;

- people should be valued for what they are as well as what they achieve;

- the needs of individuals as well as those of the organization must be recognized and respected;

- individuals should be given the opportunity to express their views about the objectives they are expected to achieve;

- individuals should understand and agree to the measures used to monitor their performance and should be able to track their own performance against those measures;

- individuals have the right to obtain feedback on their performance and to comment on that feedback;

- individuals should know how and why decisions affecting them emerging from performance reviews have been made, and should have the right to appeal against those decisions;

- the focus should be on developing performance rather than merely managing it – priority should therefore be given to the developmental aspects of performance management.

There are, however, two overriding values. First, the values set out above and any others that are believed to be important should not be imposed by management. They should be debated with managers, employees and employee representatives in order to obtain general agreement and understanding that these are the things that matter. Second there should be a process of what Boyett and Conn (1995) call 'reality checking'. This means finding out if behaviour is consistent with espoused values and if not, what needs to be done – change the behaviour or change the value.

References

Aguinis, H (2005) *Performance Management*, Upper Saddle River NJ, Pearson Education

Armstrong, M and Baron, A (2004) *Managing Performance: Performance Management in Action,* London, CIPD

Bailey, T, Berg, P and Sandy, C (2001) The effect of high performance work practices on employee earnings in the steel, apparel and medical electronics and imaging industries, *Industrial and Labor Relations Review*, 54 (2A), pp 525–43

Bandura, A (1977) *Social Learning Theory*, Englewood Cliffs NJ, Prentice-Hall

Bandura, A (1982) Self-efficacy mechanism in human agency, *American Psychologist*, 37, pp 122–47

Bates, R A and Holton, E F (1995) Computerized performance monitoring: a review of human resource issues, *Human Resource Management Review*, Winter, pp 267–88

Beaver, G and Harris, L (1995) Performance management and the small firm: dilemmas, tensions and paradoxes, *Journal of Strategic Change*, 4, pp 109–19

Bernadin, H K, Kane, J S, Ross, S, Spina, J D and Johnson, D L (1995) Performance appraisal design, development and implementation, in G R Ferris, S D Rosen, and D J Barnum (eds), *Handbook of Human Resource Management*, Cambridge MA, Blackwell

Blumberg, M and Pringle, C (1982) The missing opportunity in organizational research: some implications for a theory of work performance, *Academy of Management Review*, 7 (4), pp 560–69

Borman, W C and Motowidlo, S J (1993) Expanding the criterion domain to include elements of contextual performance, in N Schmitt and W C Borman (eds), *Personnel Selection in Organizations*, San Francisco, Jossey-Bass

Boxall, P F and Purcell, J (2003) *Strategy and Human Resource Management*, Basingstoke, Palgrave Macmillan

Boyett, J H and Conn, H P (1995) *Maximum Performance Management*, Oxford, Glenbridge Publishing

Brumbach, G B (1988) Some ideas, issues and predictions about performance management, *Public Personnel Management*, 17 (4), pp 387–402

Campbell, J P (1990) Modeling the performance prediction problem in industrial and organizational psychology, in M P Dunnette and L M Hugh (eds), *Handbook of Industrial Psychology*, Cambridge MA, Blackwell

Campbell, J P, McCloy, R A, Oppler, S H and Sager, C E (1993) A theory of performance, in N Schmitt and W Borman, eds, *Personnel Selection in Organizations*, San Francisco, Jossey-Bass

Cardy, R L and Dobbins, G H (1994) *Performance Appraisal: Alternative Perspectives*, Cincinnati OH, South-Western Publishing

Coens, T and Jenkins, M (2002) *Abolishing Performance Appraisals: Why they backfire and what to do instead*, San Francisco, Berrett-Koehler

Deming, W E (1986) *Out of the Crisis*, Cambridge MA, Massachusetts Institute of Technology Centre for Advanced Engineering Studies

DeNisi, A S and Pritchard, R D (2006) Performance appraisal, performance management and improving individual performance: a motivational framework, *Management and Organization Review*, 2 (2), pp 253–77

Earley, D C (1986) Computer-generated performance feedback in the magazine industry, *Organisation Behaviour and Human Decision Processes*, 41, pp 50–64

Fletcher, C (2001) Performance appraisal and management: the developing research agenda, *Journal of Occupational and Organizational Psychology*, 74 (4), pp 473–87

Gladwell, M (2008) *Outliers: The story of success*, London, Allen Lane

Harrison, R (1997) *Employee Development*, London, IPM

Hull, C (1951) *Essentials of Behaviour*, New Haven CT, Yale University Press

Jones, T W (1995) Performance management in a changing context, *Human Resource Management*, 34 (3) pp 425–42

Kane, J S (1996) The conceptualization and representation of total performance effectiveness, *Human Resource Management Review*, Summer, pp 123–215

Latham, G P and Locke, E A (1979) Goal Setting – a motivational technique that works, *Organizational Dynamics*, Autumn, pp 442–47

Latham, G, Sulsky, L M and Macdonald, H (2007) Performance management, in P Boxall, J Purcell and P Wright (eds), *Oxford Handbook of Human Resource Management*, Oxford, Oxford University Press

McCloy, R A, Campbell, J P and Cudeck, R (1994) A confirmatory test of performance determinants, *Journal of Applied Psychology*, 79, pp 493–505

Miller, E and Rice, A (1967) *Systems of Organization*, London, Tavistock

Nadler, D A and Tushman, M (1980) A congruence model for diagnosing organizational behaviour, in R H Miles (ed) *Resource Book in Macro-Organizational Behaviour*, Santa Monica CA, Goodyear Publishing

Robertson, I T, Smith, M and Cooper, C L (1992) *Motivation*, London, Institute of Personnel and Development

Vroom, V (1964) *Work and Motivation*, New York, Wiley

Winstanley, D and Stuart-Smith, K (1996) Policing performance: the ethics of performance management, *Personnel Review*, 25 (6), pp 66–84

Issues in performance management

04

The many-faceted nature of performance was commented on as follows by Cascio (2010):

> It is an exercise in observation and judgement, it is a feedback process, it is an organizational intervention. It is a measurement process as well as an intensely emotional process. Above all, it is an inexact, human process.

As a human process, performance management can promise more than it achieves. Coens and Jenkins (2002) delivered the following judgement:

> Throughout our work lives, most of us have struggled with performance appraisal. No matter how many times we redesign it, retrain the supervisors, or give it a new name, it never comes out right. Again and again, we see supervisors procrastinate or just go through the motions, with little taken to heart. And the supervisors who do take it to heart and give it their best mostly meet disappointment.

Shields (2007) argued that: 'Ill-chosen, badly designed or poorly implemented performance management schemes can communicate entirely the wrong messages as to what the organization expects from its employees.'

The chapter starts with a discussion of the fundamental problems and continues by examining the individual factors affecting performance, the design of the system, its implementation, and its operation, especially the role of line managers. Consideration is then given to ways of dealing with the issues and the concept of evidence-based performance management.

The fundamental problems

Duncan Brown (2010) remarked that:

> The problems [of performance management] are... not of ambition or intent, but rather practice and delivery. Low rates of coverage and even more frequently low quality conversations and non-existent follow-up are commonplace, in the wake of uncommitted directors, incompetent line managers, uncomprehending employees and hectoring HR with their still complex and bureaucratic HR processes.

On the basis of the Bath University research, Hutchinson and Purcell (2003) noted that: 'Performance appraisal is an area in which front line managers have traditionally had direct involvement with their staff, and provides a good example of the key role these managers have to play in their delivery of HR policies.' They also commented that:

> Looking at the sample of employees interviewed over the two years, we found that performance appraisal was rated as the least effective HR policy (in terms of levels of satisfaction) after pay, and in a fair number of organizations it was the least favourite HR activity. The reasons given were numerous, and included the views that the measurements and targets were felt to be unclear and/or not relevant, and that the system was too complicated and time consuming. Many of the problems could be directly linked to the behaviour of managers, as the interviews with employees revealed.

Performance management issues in the UK as listed by Sparrow (2008) include:

- the ability to produce higher levels of employee engagement as opposed to just more self-awareness or measurement accuracy;
- the level of alignment between rewards (in their fullest sense) produced by the performance management system, and the varied needs of diverse employee segments, who may be working to very different psychological contracts;
- the extent to which stand alone performance management systems contribute directly to value creation in the organization or rather serve more to protect value by managing only marginal risks (extremely high or low performance, the identification and management of which may well be handled through other processes such as business

performance modifications, team socialization processes or talent management/calibration exercises).

According to Pulakos *et al* (2008) the main problems with performance management in the US are:

- Performance management is regarded as an administrative burden to be minimized rather than an effective strategy to obtain business results.
- Managers and employees are reluctant to engage in candid performance discussions.
- Judgement and time factors impede accurate performance assessments.

A survey by WorldatWork and Sibson (2010) established that the top three performance management challenges reported by respondents were (1) managers lack courage to have difficult performance discussions (63 per cent); (2) performance management is viewed as an 'HR process' instead of as a 'business critical process' (47 per cent); and (3), that they experienced poor goal setting (36 per cent). They also noted that: 'Too much attention has been placed on the design of a [performance management] system and not enough on how it works when implemented'.

The e-reward 2014 survey of performance management found that the three major concerns of respondents – all about line managers – were:

1 The lack of line managers with the skills required to carry out performance management effectively.

2 Line managers who don't discriminate sufficiently when assessing performance.

3 Line managers who were reluctant to conduct performance management reviews.

However, the respondents made many sound suggestions on how to deal with these problems and a selection of these is given towards the end of this chapter.

Individual factors

As Coens and Jenkins (2002) claimed: 'An organization, because it is a system, cannot be significantly improved by focusing on individuals'. In any case, as noted by Banks and May (1999), the traditional approach to performance management is appropriate for static jobs in which work processes are also static and easily observable. But, as explained by Gruman and Saks (2011) contemporary jobs are much less static – the definition of a job and what represents good performance is more variable. As they also commented: 'Because of the dynamic, multi-faceted nature of modern jobs, in the contemporary work environment achieving increments in performance often involves less "management" of performance than "facilitation" of performance'. The influence of contextual and system factors was discussed in Chapter 3.

System design

It was observed by Lee (2005) that:

> Most traditional performance appraisal schemes are fundamentally flawed as they are counterproductive by design. The stated purpose of these systems is to measure and rate past performance when, in reality, the goal of any performance management system should be performance enhancement... No one has the power to alter the past, so it is far wiser to direct attention and efforts to the future.

This highlights two basic performance management design issues:

- *The extent to which the system should be forward-looking.*
  A forward-looking approach is fundamental to the concept of performance management. It is what distinguishes it from traditional performance appraisal. Although past performance will be analysed, the only reason for doing this is to identify any areas where future performance can be enhanced and how this should be done.

- *The extent to which the system should focus on performance enhancement.* As indicated above, this should be the main purpose of performance management. It does not exist simply to inform performance pay decisions or to identify underperforming people.

The other main design issues are:

1 *The form and content of the performance agreement.* The performance agreement provides the basis for managing performance. At the design stage consideration has to be given to what type of goals are required

and how they should be set as well as the use of performance improvement and personal development plans.

2 *The alignment of individual and organizational goals.* The process of strategic alignment at individual levels starts with the definition of a role profile in which the key result areas for individuals are referenced to the key result areas for the organization associated with its strategic goals. It continues by cascading and integrating goals and, sometimes, through the use of a balanced scorecard. But for reasons given in Chapter 5 it is not a simple process.

3 *Whether or not ratings should be used and if so, in what form.* There are arguments for and against ratings and if ratings are used there are a number of different configurations (this is discussed in Chapter 9).

4 *The link between performance management and performance pay.* Performance management and performance pay are often associated but there are arguments for keeping them separate (see Chapter 17).

5 *How performance management should be documented.* The temptation is to design elaborate documentation. But the aim should be to keep it simple (see Chapter 19).

System operation

Performance management can be modelled convincingly as a system but in practice the acts or failures to act of fallible human beings prejudice the effectiveness of the system. Pearce and Porter (1986) described performance appraisal as 'one of the most emotionally charged activities in business life'.

Dealing with performance management issues

To deal with operational issues respondents to the e-reward (2014) survey on performance management emphasized the importance of doing the following:

- 'Train, communicate, evaluate performance management through employee engagement surveys, have HR business partners work with line managers, organize round tables (calibration), provide details of expected competency levels per job type/level, clarify that good is acceptable (not everyone can be a star), encourage ongoing performance management, it's more than just an annual administrative hoop – it's a powerful management tool.'

- 'Keep it very, very simple, be able to translate strategy to individual goals and give people a clear line of sight, ensure all people managers are capable to deliver performance management, ie have a performance dialogue (this is the key!) at any time and not just at the annual review.'

- 'Focus on the positives, create a culture of continual performance management rather than restricting it to an annual appraisal (to avoid surprises when it comes to ratings and encourage individuals to focus on performance throughout the year). Make a performance management system open and available all year round (rather than releasing an appraisal at certain set times of the year). Analyse the data on performance ratings, to see trends, highlight areas for improvement and ensure no discriminatory bias. Train.'

- 'Ensure the paperwork (hardcopy or e-) does not drive the process. The appraisal should be clearly aligned to the organization's strategic objectives and values. It is the conversation between the manager and employee that is most important. Managers need to be given the skills to manage difficult conversations and all staff need to know how to give and receive feedback.'

- 'Ensure the system isn't hampered by bureaucracy and tedious paperwork. Make it easy for all to actively engage with the system and put the focus on having quality open conversation between reviewer and reviewee.'

- 'Consistency – one scheme for all, make it about good conversations, not just a process.'

- 'Clear line of sight between objective setting, performance review and business goals. Regularly review and update in accordance with any changes in business needs.'

- 'Acknowledge any link to remuneration – if you don't, people will create their own links.'

- 'Stop trying to enforce a system which, from my 40 years' experience, no line managers really want to participate in.'

Methods of dealing with the issues are also considered in Chapters 22, 23 and 24.

Evidence-based performance management

Dealing with the issues set out above requires an evidence-based approach. Evidence-based performance management makes use of appropriate information derived from the analysis of surveys of current practice and the evaluation of the operation and impact of performance management processes. The aim is to ensure that informed decisions are made on any improvements required to performance management policy and practice. As Pfeffer and Sutton (2006) explained, evidence-based management 'features a willingness to put aside belief and conventional wisdom – the dangerous half-truths that many embrace – and replace these with an unrelenting commitment to gather the necessary facts to make more intelligent and informed decisions'.

References

Banks, C G and May, K E (1999) Performance management: the real glue in organizations, in A I Kraut and A K Korman (eds), *Evolving Practices in Human Resource Management*, San Francisco CA, Jossey-Bass

Brown, D (2010) 'Practice what we preach?' Posted by Reward Blogger, 6 December, London, CIPD

Cascio, W F (2010) *Managing Human Resources: Productivity, quality of work life, profits*, 8th edition, New York, McGraw-Hill Irwin

Coens, T and Jenkins, M (2002) *Abolishing Performance Appraisals: Why they backfire and what to do instead*, San Francisco CA, Berrett-Koehler

e-reward (2014) *Survey of Performance Management Practice*, Stockport, e-reward

Gruman, J A and Saks, A M (2011) Performance management and employee engagement, *Human Resource Management Review*, 21 (2), pp 123–36

Hutchinson, S and Purcell, J (2003) *Bringing Policies to Life: The vital role of front line managers in people management*, London, CIPD

Lee, C D (2005) Rethinking the goals of your performance management system, *Employment Relations Today*, 32 (3), pp 53–60

Pearce, J L and Porter, L W (1986) Employee responses to formal performance feedback, *Journal of Applied Psychology*, **71** (2), pp 211–18

Pfeffer, J and Sutton, R I (2006) Evidence-based management, *Harvard Business Review*, January, pp 62–74

Pulakos, E D, Mueller-Hanson, R A and O'Leary, R S (2008) Performance management in the US, in A Varma, P S Budhwar and A DeNisi (eds), *Performance Management Systems: A global perspective*, Abingdon, Routledge

Shields, J (2007) *Managing Employee Performance and Reward*, Port Melbourne, Cambridge University Press

Sparrow, P (2008) Performance management in the UK, in A Varma, P S Budhwar and A DeNisi (eds), *Performance Management Systems: A global perspective*, Abingdon, Routledge

WorldatWork and Sibson Study on the State of Performance Management (2010) Scottsdale AZ, WorldatWork

PART TWO
Performance management processes and skills

Setting goals

05

Setting goals is a key performance management activity. Goals define the direction people should take and provide the criteria needed to assess performance. They are the means through which the organization's strategies can be communicated to employees. Lawler *et al* (2012) observed that: 'Goals provide a very effective approach to directing individuals to support the business strategy of the organization and can translate strategies from an organizational objective to specific individual behaviours... It is hard to imagine an effective performance management scheme that does not utilize goals in some way'. A study by Longenecker (1997) established that eight in ten respondents to his survey suggested that the failure to have clear performance criteria negated the potential benefits of conducting an appraisal. Performance goals as a basis for performance planning and assessment were used by 83 per cent of the respondents to the e-reward 2014 survey of performance management.

A performance goal or objective (the terms are interchangeable) defines what someone has to accomplish. Goals for individuals can be agreed either as specific targets – eg 'reduce reject levels by 3 per cent within nine months', 'introduce x by y', or as quantified standards which indicate the conditions that exist when a task has been done well – eg 'performance will be up to standard when reject rates are maintained below 2 per cent'. They can also be laid down as collective goals in the form of a standard to be achieved by everyone working in the same area or on similar tasks, eg, in a call centre: 'responses to all incoming queries or complaints are made within two working days to the satisfaction of the customer', 'x per cent of cold calls should be converted into an order'.

In addition to performance goals, agreement may be reached on a development plan setting out goals for performance development including the expansion of knowledge and skills and changes in behaviour.

This chapter deals with setting performance goals under the following headings:

- The conceptual background
- Criteria for an effective performance goal
- How to set performance goals
- Strategic alignment (of goals)
- Critical success factors

The last two sections of the chapter cover the agreement of objectives for developing knowledge and skills and for enhancing levels of behavioural competency.

The conceptual background

The conceptual background to the use of goals in performance management is provided by goal theory (Latham and Locke, 1979) which states that people perform better when they have specific and challenging but reachable goals. Acceptance of goals is achieved when:

- people perceived the goals as fair and reasonable and trust their managers;
- individuals participate in goal setting;
- support is provided by the manager – a supportive manager does not use goals to threaten people but rather to clarify what is expected of them;
- people are provided with the resources required to achieve their goals;
- success is achieved in reaching goals which reinforces acceptance of future goals.

Locke and Latham (1990) held that the extent to which goals lead to high performance depends on participation, commitment, and other elements of the performance management process such as feedback.

There are benefits arising from goal setting but also problems as summed up by Latham and Locke (2006), listed in Table 5.1.

TABLE 5.1   Benefits and problems of goal setting

Benefits	Potential problems
• Gives a sense of purpose. • Provides an unambiguous basis for judging success. • Increases performance. • Is a means for self-management. • Increases subjective well-being.	• Lack of sufficient knowledge for goal attainment. • Goal conflict among group members. • Fear of risk-taking. • Ignoring non-goal dimensions of performance. • Demoralization because following success management may set higher, impossible goals.

SOURCE: Latham and Locke (2006)

Criteria for an effective performance goal

The criteria for an effective performance goal in the form of a target or standard are that it should be:

- *aligned:* consistent with the goals and values of the organization and supporting their achievement;

- *relevant:* consistent with the purpose of the role;

- *precise:* specific, clear and well-defined – Furnham (2004) recommended that performance should be defined with a focus on valued outcomes and that performance dimensions should therefore be 'functions combined with aspects of value such as quantity, quality, timeliness, cost effectiveness, need for supervision or interpersonal impact';

- *measurable:* related to quantified or qualitative performance measures or standards;

- *trackable:* progress towards achieving the goal can be monitored;

- *challenging:* to stimulate high standards of performance and to encourage progress;

- *achievable:* performance goals should be achievable but not too easily – account should be taken of any constraints which might affect the individual's capacity to achieve the goals; these could include lack of resources (money, time, equipment, support from other people), lack of experience or training, external factors beyond the individual's control;

- *agreed* by the manager and the individual concerned – the aim is to provide for the ownership, not the imposition, of goals, although there will be occasions where individuals have to be persuaded to accept a higher standard than they believe themselves to be capable of attaining and individual goals must be consistent with over-arching corporate goals;

- *time-related*: the time scale or date for reaching targets should be specified.

The acronym 'SMART' is often used to define a good performance objective or goal. Traditionally, S stands for specific (sometimes stretching), M for measurable, A for agreed, R for realistic and T for time-related. But as Chamberlin (2011) argued, the real aim of setting goals is for people to know (1) what they have to do, (2) when they've done it, (3) that they are able to do it, (4) why they have to do it (ie who for), (5) that it is something they should be doing, and (6) how they are progressing along the way. He criticized the conventional acronym and, following Blanchard (1989), suggested that the last three letters of the mnemonic should be amended to read A for attainable, R for relevant and T for trackable. Chamberlin attached particular importance to *relevant* – the goal has to be linked to the business and its customers. He also emphasized *trackable* because the important thing to do with performance goals is to monitor progress over time, ie track them. He rejected *time-related* because it did not convey this essential feature and was in any case covered already by *specific*.

How to set performance goals

The basis for performance goal setting is provided by definitions of key result areas contained in a role profile which spells out expected outcomes. It is important when agreeing goals to ask the question: 'How will we know that this goal has been achieved?' The answer is given by a key performance indicator which defines how information on what has happened will be obtained.

FIGURE 5.1   The performance goal setting sequence

Key performance indicators can be established for each key result area and these inform definitions of performance targets and standards. An example of this sequence for one of the key result areas of a plant production manager is shown in Figure 5.1.

The aim will be to reach agreement on a set of goals which meet the criteria for an effective goal listed earlier. Employees should participate fully in the process. This is important because it means that they are more likely to understand and accept what they are expected to do and are therefore more likely to do it. It is essential to ensure that organizational goals and the ways in which employees can help to translate them into action are understood.

Goal setting may start from a clean sheet. But it often doesn't. Goals may already exist having been set or reset at the beginning of the performance management cycle. However, at the end of the cycle they will need to be reconsidered in the light of an assessment of performance in meeting them over the review period and also any changes in demands or circumstances that have taken place. This will be a matter of updating and amendment covering the same ground as when starting from scratch, ie reviewing in turn key result areas and key performance indicators, performance targets, performance standards, behavioural indicators and learning goals, and changing or replacing them as necessary.

Managers should explain to individuals how their performance in achieving goals will be monitored and reviewed. It is important for the latter to know that there will be a fair and just process of measurement and assessment and that they will receive feedback on how they are doing. Guidance should also be given to individuals on how they can monitor their own performance by reference to key performance indicators.

Methods of defining key result areas, key performance indicators, performance targets, and performance standards are described below.

Key result areas

Key result areas or KRAs are the elements or core tasks of a role for which clear outputs or outcomes can be defined, each of which makes a significant contribution to achieving the overall purpose of the role. An output is a result which can be measured quantifiably, while an outcome is a visible effect which is the result of effort but cannot necessarily be measured in quantified terms. There are components in all jobs that are difficult to measure quantifiably as outputs.

As described by Shields (2007): 'In essence a KRA is a significant, distinct area of work activity or accountability, the achievement of which determines or indicates performance effectiveness or success'. A key result area may be described as an accountability – an aspect of the role for which the role holder is responsible (held to account for).

To achieve strategic alignment, the key result areas for a role should so far as possible take account of the key result areas and strategic goals of the organization (strategic alignment is considered in greater depth later in this chapter).

There are typically around five to six KRAs in a role. These should cover the range of important tasks that the role holder is expected to perform. For example, the key result areas for a plant production manager could be:

1 Achieve output targets.

2 Achieve productivity and cost targets.

3 Prepare and implement production schedules and plans showing time scales and resource allocation (people and plant).

4 Achieve quality standards and targets.

5 Achieve safety standards and targets.

6 Lead people and ensure that they are engaged with their work.

The key result areas for a quality control technician could be:

1 Conduct tests to establish the extent to which a range of food products meets quality standards.

2 Monitor the achievement of food hygiene standards and conduct tests to establish the extent to which company and national/international standards are being achieved for the range of products.

3 Recommend actions to remedy quality or hygiene problems identified by the tests.

4 Prepare replies for customer services to send to customers who have complained about the quality of any item in the product range.

5 Prepare regular reports summarizing test results and findings.

6 Contribute to reviews of how quality and hygiene standards can be improved.

The key result areas for a database manager could be:

1 Identify database requirements for all projects that require data management in order to meet the needs of internal customers.

2 Develop project plans collaboratively with colleagues to deliver against their database needs.

3 Implement project plans in accordance with defined criteria, within the predefined budget and within the agreed time scale.

4 Support underlying database infrastructure to ensure that the level of service delivery required is achieved.

5 Ensure security of the underlying database infrastructure through adherence to established protocols and develop additional security protocols where needed.

The following are other examples of key result area definitions:

- test new systems to ensure they meet agreed systems specifications;
- post cash to the nominal and sales ledgers in order to provide up-to-date and accurate financial information;
- dispatch the warehouse planned output so that all items are removed by carriers on the same day they are packed;

- ensure that management accounts are produced which provide the required level of information to management and individual managers on financial performance against budget and on any variances;
- prepare marketing plans which provide clear guidance on the actions to be taken by the production, marketing and sales departments;
- plan and implement sales campaigns to meet sales targets.

A key result area definition should be expressed in one sentence starting with an active verb. The content of the key result area definition should focus on the specific purpose of the activity rather than describing in detail the duties involved. Too many key result areas will be confusing and make it more difficult to plan, measure and control. The aim should be to focus on the five or six aspects of the job that really matter.

To assist with strategic alignment, managers should start by sharing with the individual the over-arching goals of the organization and the specific goals of their function or department. The relationship between these goals and those of the individual can then be discussed with an emphasis on establishing how the individual can support their achievement. Individuals can then be asked by their manager to answer questions such as:

- What do you think is the overall purpose of your job?
- What do you think are the most important things you have to do to achieve that purpose?
- What do you believe you are expected to achieve in each of these areas?
- How will you – or anyone else – know whether or not you have achieved them?
- How does what you are expected to do support the achievement of corporate/departmental goals?

The answers to these questions may need to be sorted out – initially they can result in a mass of jumbled information which has to be analysed so that the various activities can be distinguished and refined to the five or six key areas. This activity requires some skill which needs to be developed by training followed by practice. It is an area in which HR specialists can usefully coach managers and follow-up on a one-to-one basis after an initial training session.

Key result areas as defined in a role profile may be ongoing to a certain degree but requirements change and role profiles need to be reviewed regularly and as necessary, modified. This can take place at any time, but at the planning stage of the performance management cycle it is useful to review the role profile and the associated KRAs to ensure that they are up-to-date.

Key performance indicators

To provide the basis for setting goals and monitoring and reviewing perform-ance it is necessary to answer the question for each key result area: 'How will we know when the results specified in this area have been achieved?'. The answer to this question is known as a key performance indicator (KPI). A KPI may be a metric – a measure providing data which indicate in quanti-tative terms the outcome of an activity, for example, performance in terms of sales value, output (units produced), throughput (units processed), pro-ductivity, cost per unit of output, the volume of such things as customer complaints, defective components (rejects) or waste, or the speed with which orders are processed or enquiries dealt with.

Where the use of metrics is not possible it will be necessary to use a quali-tative KPI in the form of a statement which defines the conditions which exist when a job has been well done. The key performance indicators for the role of plant manager as described earlier could be:

1 Figures of production output and throughput.

2 Figures setting out productivity in terms of output per person and costs in terms of cost per unit of output.

3 Information showing that production schedules and plans are realistic and implemented effectively.

4 Quality control reports showing results against standards and targets.

5 Safety records showing frequency rate of accidents.

6 Results of employee engagement surveys.

Key performance indicators show how performance can be measured. But what gets measured is often what is easy to measure. It was asserted by Levinson (1970) that:

> The greater the emphasis on measurement and quantification, the more likely the subtle, non-measurable elements of the task will be sacrificed. Quality of performance frequently, therefore, loses out to quantification.

Performance targets

Performance targets define the quantifiable results to be attained in a key result area. They can be established by referring to the key performance indicators which will indicate the measures that can be used. Here are some examples of targets where a time frame exists:

- increase market share for product A by x per cent by end of financial year;
- reduce waiting lists by y per cent within six months;
- increase successful outcome of cold calls by z per cent by end-February next year;
- launch product B by end-October this year.

Targets can also be ongoing quantified performance requirements, for example:

- distribute management accounts to managers within three working days of the end of the accounting period;
- respond satisfactorily to 90 per cent of customer queries or complaints within 24 hours – the rest to be acknowledged within 24 hours and answered within three working days;
- complaints from customers should not exceed 1:1,000 transactions;
- job evaluation appeals should be held within five working days.

Performance standards

A performance standard describes the conditions that exist when a task is well done. It is defined in the form of a statement that performance will be up to standard if a specified result happens. The results expected can be defined in such terms as:

- the achievement of already defined operational norms related to administrative procedures, quality and continuous improvement requirements, customer or client satisfaction, levels of service to internal and external customers or good employment practices;
- the ability to meet deadlines;

- the extent to which backlogs are controlled;

- speed of activity or response to requests;

- change in the behaviour of employees, customers, clients and other people of importance to the organization;

- the reactions of clients, customers (internal and external) and outside bodies to the service provided;

- the degree to which behaviour supports core values in such areas as quality, care for people and teamworking.

Performance standards may be defined in a qualitative statement. Thus, if a key result area for a call centre agent is 'Deal with customer queries and complaints' the key performance indicator could be a sample of the recorded conversation with customers and the performance standard would be expressed as: 'Performance will be up to standard when callers are dealt with courteously at all times even when they are being difficult'. Here are more examples of performance standards:

- Performance will be up to standard when line managers obtain guidance on inventory control practice which makes a significant contribution to the achievement of inventory targets.

- Performance will be up to standard when proposals for new product development are fully supported by data provided from market research and product-testing programmes.

- Performance will be up to standard when data is consistently inputted to the database promptly and accurately.

Setting goals in practice

The description above of the process of setting goals provides a detailed guide for anyone involved in managing the design or operation of a performance management system. But in practice, it may be too complicated for the managers and individuals who use the system. At first, it needs to be presented to them as the basic performance management process in a much more straightforward way, free of jargon. The following is an example of how this process can be described in simpler language.

How to set goals

Our performance management system is based on goals – what someone in a job is expected to achieve. Every job has a number of key elements for each of which goals can be set. Goals can be described in two ways:

- *As a target* – a specific and measurable result to be achieved over a period of time. For example: 'Convert 10 per cent of cold calls into sales by year end'.

- *As a performance standard* – this describes the conditions that exist when a task is well done. It is used when the results expected cannot be quantified. For example: 'Performance will be up to standard when callers are dealt with courteously at all times even when they are being difficult'.

Goals are agreed between the manager and the job holder at the beginning of the performance management period. The manager provides feedback on how well the job holder has performed in achieving the agreed goals during the period and more formally in a performance review meeting at the end of the period.

The goal setting process

Goal setting involves a discussion between the manager and the job holder leading to an agreement of the answers to the following questions concerning the latter's job:

1 What is the overall purpose of the job?

2 What are the key activities the job holder has to carry out to attain that purpose? (No more than five or six.)

3 For each of these key activities, what is the job holder expected to achieve? (Express these in terms of goals or performance standards.)

4 How will we know that these goals or performance standards have been achieved?

But this is only a beginning. The terms used are meaningless unless they are illustrated by practical instances. Both managers and job holders should be trained in goal setting. The training should provide practice in defining role profiles, key result areas, key performance indicators and performance standards and goals. It is essential initially to get the basic goal setting process right by presenting it in an easily assimilated way. The training manual included in the web-based supporting material for this book provides guidance on doing this and a number of practical exercises.

Strategic alignment

Strategic alignment is concerned with integrating the performance goals of individuals with the strategic goals of the organization. Importantly, it can also mean aligning individual behaviours with the behavioural values of the organization, eg customer care. This can be done by ensuring that the organization's competency framework and individual competency require- ments reflect corporate values and that individual behaviour is assessed by reference to framework headings. Strategic alignment enables the meaning and significance of corporate goals and values to be communicated to employees.

The strategic alignment of performance goals starts with the definition of business goals and critical success factors as part of an organizational perform- ance management system. These provide the basis for defining the goals for which individuals are accountable.

As described below, it continues by cascading and integrating goals and, sometimes, through the use of a balanced scorecard. Perhaps the most prac- tical approach adopted by some respondents to the 2014 e-reward survey is for top management to define at the start of the performance management period the key corporate goals which should be taken into account when setting individual goals.

Cascading and integrating performance goals

Figure 5.2 illustrates the process of cascading corporate goals as affected by external and internal factors through functional and team goals down to those for individuals. Allowance is made for the upward flow of influence on each level of goal and a link between corporate and individual goals is included to show that these need to be directly aligned with one another.

The alignment of organizational and individual and team goals was referred to above as a process of 'cascading goals'. However, cascading should not be regarded as just an automatic top down process. There may be overarch- ing corporate goals, but people at each level should be given the opportunity to indicate how they believe they can contribute to the attainment of team and departmental goals. This is a 'bottom up' process and the views of em- ployees about what they believe they can achieve should be noted and, where appropriate, higher level goals amended to take account of them. An approach along these lines increases 'ownership' of the goals as well as providing a

FIGURE 5.2 Strategic alignment of goals

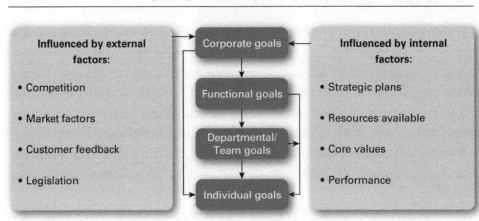

channel for upward communication on key issues affecting the achievement of business strategies. Of course there will be times when the overriding challenge has to be accepted, but there will also be occasions when the opinions of those who have to do the work will be well worth listening to. Figure 5.3 illustrates how goals can be aligned in a specific area.

The balanced scorecard

The aim of the concept of the balanced scorecard as originally formulated by Kaplan and Norton (1992, 1996) was to counter the tendency of companies to concentrate on short-term financial reporting. They emphasized that 'no single measure can provide a clear performance target or focus attention on the critical areas of the business. Managers want a balanced presentation of both financial and operational measures'. Their original concept of the scorecard required managers to answer four basic questions, which means looking at the business from four related perspectives as shown in Figure 5.4.

Some organizations have replaced the innovation and learning perspective with a broader people or human capital element.

Kaplan and Norton emphasized that the balanced scorecard approach 'puts strategy and vision, not control at the centre'. They suggested that while it defines goals, it assumes that people will adopt whatever behaviours and take whatever actions are required to achieve those goals.

FIGURE 5.3   Two-way process of aligning goals

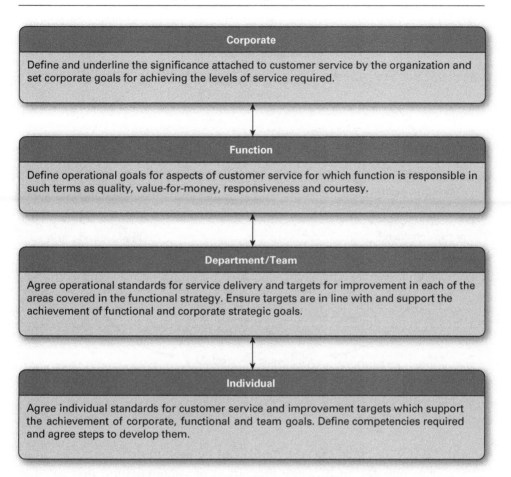

Although the balanced scorecard is often regarded as only operating at corporate level it is used for individuals by 17 per cent of the respondents to the e-reward 2014 survey of performance management. At Lloyds Banking Group it provides the framework for objective setting. Kaplan and Norton pointed out that it can help to align employees' individual performance with the overall strategy. They commented that:

> Many people think of measurement as a tool to control behaviour and to
> evaluate past performance. The measures on a balanced scorecard, however,
> should be used as the cornerstone of a management system that communicates
> strategy [and] aligns individuals and teams to the strategy.

FIGURE 5.4   The balanced scorecard

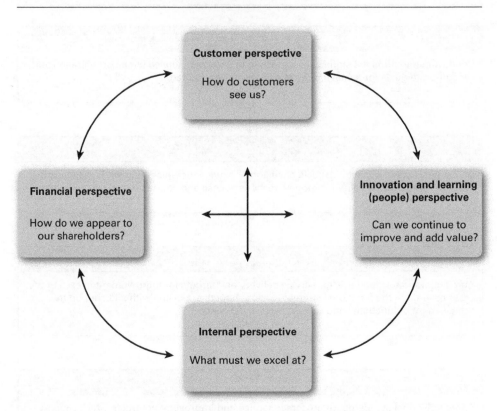

Shields (2007) observed that the model can be used to define strategic indicators and goals for each of the four areas of value creation that cascade down the organization:

> Goals that are transmitted from the apex to the base of the organization will thus serve to communicate strategic business goals throughout the whole organization to the point where the goals of the individual business units and individual employees coincide at all levels with the organization's strategic success factors... [It] offers a means of thorough-going strategic alignment and provides employees with a direct line of sight between the organization's goals and theirs.

But as Shields also noted: 'Its ambitious scope means that its implementation will necessarily take considerable time, resourcing and commitment'.

Strategic alignment issues

The strategic goal alignment procedures described above look deceptively straightforward. Everyone who writes or talks about performance management refers to the importance of alignment but they seldom refer to the practical difficulties of achieving it. Assuming that defined strategic goals exist and are communicated to those concerned with setting goals (a big assumption), the basic problem is that of translating generalized strategic goals into specific ones for individuals. It is hard to link a broad corporate goal of, say, increasing market share by x per cent, into goals relating to any key results area of a junior employee such as a data administrator. A corporate strategic goal may refer to specific improvements in performance in an area such as productivity. However, for people who are concerned with production or service delivery, productivity goals will be set or at least should be set whether or not they exist at a strategic level. The strategic alignment of individual goals is indeed important for anyone who is closely involved in achieving corporate strategic goals and who is concerned with setting the goals of subordinates, but the further people are away from the coal face the more difficult it is to achieve close alignment. This does not mean that it should not be attempted but there are limitations to the extent to which it can be applied rigorously throughout an organization. However, as mentioned earlier, alignment is an important process for communicating the meaning and significance of corporate performance goals and values to employees, often in a balanced scorecard format.

The alignment of individual behaviours with corporate values (an important aspect of alignment) does not present so many difficulties. Corporate values can be expressed as expected behaviours in terms relating, for example, to teamwork which can readily be aligned to a competency framework applied to individuals.

Critical success factors

The term critical success factor describes those aspects of a role that must go well to ensure success. Alternatively, the term 'role requirement' can be used which embraces both knowledge and skills and behavioural competency requirements as described below. The definition of critical success factors in these terms can provide the basis for setting the goals in a development plan (see Chapter 1).

Defining knowledge and skill requirements

Knowledge and skills requirements are defined by answering two questions:

1 What does the role holder need to know to perform this role well?

2 What should the role holder be able to do perform this role well?

The first question covers such areas as professional, scientific or technical knowledge, procedural knowledge and knowledge of the organization's products, processes, markets and customers. The second question covers skills in such areas as planning, problem solving, creative and analytical thinking, leading and working with people, communicating, selling, customer relations, management, administration, handling figures (numeracy) and operating plant or equipment.

Definitions of knowledge and skill requirements can lead to the agreement of learning goals. As defined by Seijts and Latham (2005): 'Learning goals are framed to focus attention on knowledge or skill acquisition'. They contrasted learning and performance goals as follows:

> The purpose of a learning goal is to stimulate one's imagination, to engage in discovery, and to 'think outside the box', whereas the purpose of a performance goal is to choose to exert effort, and to persist in the attainment of a desired goal or outcome using the knowledge one already possesses. Thus the behaviour of a person with a learning goal is to systematically search for new ideas, actively seek feedback, be reflective, and execute a specific number of ideas in order to test newly formed hypotheses. The resulting behaviour of a person with a performance goal is to focus on known ways to quickly implement knowledge and skills that have already been mastered.

Their research established that those with learning goals had higher commitment to their goals than did those with only performance goals. But they noted that to be successful both learning and performance goals are needed although they stressed that 'a performance goal should not be set until an employee has the knowledge to attain it'.

To define learning goals the question to be answered is: 'In what aspects of the role is there scope to improve performance by doing things differently or by doing new things?' The answer should specify what knowledge and skills need to be developed or acquired and what innovations should be considered. For example:

- Find ten ways of developing improved relationships with end-users of our products.
- Find out how the effectiveness of our computer controlled machining centre could be improved.
- Establish how the performance of our database management system could be improved.
- Develop project management skills.
- Learn about the use of social media for recruiting purposes.
- Develop interviewing skills.
- Develop skills in interpreting market research surveys.
- Improve report writing skills.
- Improve presentation skills.
- Understand more about how to increase employee engagement.

Defining competency requirements

Goals can be set in terms of what someone is expected to do to meet behavioural competency requirements which indicate the types of behaviour needed for the successful performance of a role and specify any necessary changes. Competency frameworks contain definitions of the behavioural competencies applicable to all employees in an organization. A list of typical competencies is provided in Chapter 1. An example of an element in a competency framework which sets out positive and negative performance indicators is given in Table 5.2.

Alternatively, behavioural competency requirements may be determined for individual roles and included in a role profile as in the following example for a database manager:

- Aim to get things done well and set and meet challenging goals, create own measures of excellence and constantly seek ways of improving performance.
- Analyse information from range of sources and develop effective solutions/recommendations.
- Communicate clearly and persuasively, orally or in writing, dealing with technical issues in a non-technical manner.

TABLE 5.2   Example of competency framework definition

Leadership	
Competency definition	Exercise leadership in order to deliver required results through people
Positive indicators	• Agrees clear team goals • Inspires team to achieve goals • Leads by example • Gives clear direction • Offers firm support and guidance • Lets people know that they are valued • Carries out thorough and helpful performance reviews • Takes an active interest in staff development
Negative indicators	• Fails to allocate tasks appropriately • Ignores contribution of individuals • Not interested in helping staff to improve their performance • Fails to clarify team goals and standards • Not interested in conducting performance reviews • Seldom if ever gives feedback • Adopts a 'command and control' approach • Does not win respect of team members

- Work participatively on projects with technical and non-technical colleagues.
- Develop positive relationships with colleagues as the supplier of an internal service.

Competency requirements should be aligned with the organization's core values. These values can include such concerns as quality, continuous improvement, customer service, innovation, care and consideration for people, environmental issues and equal opportunity. Discussions held when agreement on goals is being reached can define what these values mean as far as individual behaviour is concerned.

Setting competency goals may simply be a matter of ensuring that individuals are aware of the organization's competency framework and core values and are involved in a discussion of what that means for them followed by an agreement on how their behaviour will be reviewed under each heading. The same approach applies to the use of individual competency guidelines if they already exist in a role profile. If nothing exists, then managers can go through a checklist of competency headings and discuss with them how they apply in the individual's role and what should be done about them. To avoid over-complexity, the headings should be limited to four or five key items, for example, teamworking, customer focus, problem-solving, flexibility and leadership.

References

Blanchard, K H (1989) *The One Minute Manager – Live!* London, CareerTrack Publications

Chamberlin, J (2011) Who put the 'art' in SMART goals? *Management Services*, Autumn, pp 22–27

e-reward (2014) *Survey of Performance Management*, Stockport, e-reward

Furnham, A (2004) Performance management systems, *European Business Journal*, 16 (2), pp 83–94

Kaplan, R S and Norton, D P (1992) The balanced scorecard – measures that drive performance, *Harvard Business Review*, January–February, pp 71–79

Kaplan, R S and Norton, D P (1996) Using the balanced scorecard as a strategic management system, *Harvard Business Review*, January–February, pp 75–85

Latham, G P and Locke, E A (1979) Goal Setting – a motivational technique that works, *Organizational Dynamics*, Autumn, pp 442–47

Latham, G P and Locke, E A (2006) Enhancing the benefits and avoiding the pitfalls of goal setting, *Organizational Dynamics*, 35 (4), pp 332–40

Lawler, E E, Benson, G S and McDermott, M (2012) What makes performance appraisals effective? *Compensation & Benefits Review*, 44 (4), pp 191–200

Levinson, H (1970) Management by whose goals? *Harvard Business Review*, July–August, pp 125–34

Locke, E A and Latham, G P (1990) *A Theory of Task Setting and Goal Performance*, Englewood Cliffs NJ, Prentice Hall

Longenecker, C (1997) Why managerial performance appraisals are ineffective: causes and lessons, *Career Development International*, 2 (5), pp 212–18

Seijts, G H and Latham, G P (2005) Learning versus performance goals: when should each be used? *Academy of Management Executive*, 19 (1), pp 124–31

Shields, J (2007) *Managing Employee Performance and Reward*, Port Melbourne, Cambridge University Press

Providing feedback

Feedback to people on how they are doing is an important performance management activity. It is provided by managers informally during the year or formally at a performance review meeting. It can be given by subordinates or internal customers as part of a 360-degree feedback system (see Chapter 7). Or it can be something that individuals do for themselves. This chapter deals with feedback under the following headings:

- Feedback defined
- The nature of feedback
- Use of feedback
- How effective is feedback?
- What makes feedback effective?
- Guidelines on providing feedback
- Handling difficult conversations

Feedback defined

Feedback is the provision of information to people on how they have performed in terms of results, events, critical incidents and significant behaviours. Feedback can be positive when it tells people that they have done well, constructive when it provides advice on how to do better, and negative when it just tells people that they have done badly. Feedback reinforces effective behaviour and indicates where and how behaviour needs to change.

In systems engineering, feedback transmits information on performance from one part of a system to an earlier part of the system in order to generate corrective action or to initiate new action. In this respect performance management has the characteristics of a system in that it provides for information to be presented (feedback) to people on their performance, which helps them to understand how well they have been doing and how effective their behaviour has been. The aim is for feedback to promote this understanding so that appropriate action can be taken. This can be positive action taken to make the best use of the opportunities the feedback has revealed, or corrective action where the feedback has revealed that something has gone wrong.

Systems engineers design self-regulating systems that generate their own feedback and respond to this information of their own volition. The same principle can be applied in performance management – individuals can be encouraged to understand the performance measures that are available for them to use in order to provide their own feedback and to develop their own plans for performance development and improvement.

Such self-generated feedback is a highly desirable feature of a full performance management process but there will always be a need for managers and colleagues to provide feedback based on their own observations and understanding.

The nature of feedback

Feedback in performance management is positive in the sense that its aim is to point the way to further development and improvement. Feedback is helpful when it recognizes success and constructive when it identifies areas for improvement that can lead to effective action. It is negative and unhelpful when perceived failings are dwelt on as matters for blame. A positive approach is to treat mistakes or errors of judgement as opportunities for learning so that they are less likely to be repeated in the future.

Evidence-based performance management depends on feedback that relies on facts not opinions. It refers to results, events, critical incidents and significant behaviours that have affected performance in specific ways. It compares what has actually happened with what was supposed to have happened. It refers to agreed goals, success criteria and performance measures, and uses the latter to establish outcomes. The feedback should be presented in a way that enables individuals to recognize and accept its factual nature. Of course there will often be room for some interpretation of the facts but such interpretations should start from the actual situation as reported in the feedback not from the subjective views expressed by the provider of the feedback.

Use of feedback

Providing regular feedback as an important part of the continuous process of performance management was well described by Lee (2005) as follows:

The use of feedback in reviewing and developing performance (Lee, 2005)

Performance conversations should include a two-way exchange to ensure that the employee fully understands what is good, what is bad, and why the good performance is good and the bad is bad. With accurate descriptions of the nuances of performance the employee can better understand how his or her past actions or activities affected performance outcomes and how future efforts are likely to contribute to future performance. Accurate descriptions or diagnoses of performance are crucial, for understanding and improvement are possible only through timely feedback.

The longer the gap between performance events and performance feedback, the greater the challenge of remembering with clarity the character and quality of the performance events... two semi-annual or one annual performance conversation cannot manage performance alone. They might be effective in documenting some performance parameters but they are not likely to be effective in managing, regulating and improving performance. Good supervision with ample feedback is good performance management.

Lee also pointed out that: 'Although many people confuse the two, feedback and appraisal are fundamentally different things. Feedback is information-based, whereas the basis of appraisal is judgement or evaluation. Furthermore, feedback is an ongoing activity, and appraisal is periodic and event-based (annual).'

As London *et al* (2004) commented, feedback plays a key role, along with goal setting, in the self-regulation of performance. Feedback focuses attention on performance goals that are important to the organization, helps discover errors, maintains goal direction, influences new goals, provides information on performance capabilities and on how much more effort/energy is needed to achieve goals, and provides positive reinforcement for goal accomplishments.

How effective is feedback?

Research on performance appraisal feedback suggests that when individuals receive negative feedback they are often discouraged rather than motivated to improve. Kluger and DeNisi (1996) cautioned that not all feedback interventions result in improvements. In their meta-analysis based largely on performance appraisal feedback research they concluded that, in over a third of the cases, feedback actually resulted in less effective performance. The analysis suggested that there may be many factors that influence how individuals react to feedback affecting who will improve following feedback and who will not.

What makes feedback effective?

DeNisi and Kluger (2000) commented that feedback interventions are more likely to be effective if they keep the employee's attention focused on objectives at the task performance level and least likely to be effective if they are applied at a personal level.

Research by Gray (2001) identified two factors that influenced how receivers valued their feedback: (1) the extent to which the feedback was trustworthy, and (2) the extent to which it was constructive.

Guidelines on providing feedback

1 *Build feedback into the job.* To be effective, feedback should be built into the job or provided soon after the activity has taken place.

2 *Provide feedback on actual events.* Feedback should be given on actual results or observed behaviour. It should be backed up by evidence. It should not be based on supposition about the reason for

the behaviour. You should, for example, say: 'We have received the following complaint from a customer that you have been rude, would you like to comment on this?', rather than: 'You tend to be aggressive.'

3 *Describe, don't judge.* The feedback should be presented as a description of what has happened; it should not be accompanied by a judgement. If you start by saying: 'I have been informed that you have been rude to one of our customers; we can't tolerate that sort of behaviour,' you will instantly create resistance and prejudice an opportunity to encourage improvement.

4 *Refer to and define specific behaviours.* Relate all your feedback to specific items of behaviour. Don't indulge in transmitting general feelings or impressions. When commenting on someone's work or behaviour define what you believe to be good work or effective behaviour with examples.

5 *Emphasize the 'how' not the 'what'.* Focus attention more on how the task was tackled rather than on the result.

6 *Ask questions.* Ask questions rather than make statements: 'Why do you think this happened?'; 'On reflection is there any other way in which you think you could have handled the situation?'; 'How do you think you should tackle this sort of situation in the future?'

7 *Select key issues.* There is a limit to how much criticism anyone can take. If you overdo it, the shutters will go up and you will get nowhere. Select key issues and restrict yourself to them.

8 *Focus.* It is a waste of time to concentrate on areas that the individual can do little or nothing about. Focus on aspects of performance the individual can improve.

9 *Provide positive and constructive feedback.* People are more likely to work positively at improving their performance and developing their skills if they feel empowered by the process. Provide feedback on the things that the individual did well in addition to areas for improvement. Focus on what can be done to improve rather than on criticism.

10 *Ensure feedback leads to action.* Feedback should indicate any actions required to develop performance or skills.

The advice given by CEMEX on delivering feedback is given in Appendix B.

Handling difficult conversations

Many managers find it difficult to provide negative feedback – to criticize their subordinates – especially in a formal or semi-formal meeting. They worry in case the employee reacts badly and an unpleasant situation arises.

Minimizing the problem

This problem can be minimized if the steps given below are followed by managers before and during a feedback or review meeting.

1 Keep in touch with the members of their team. If they see that managers are approachable and ready to listen they are more likely to come to you with their problems. It is far better to nip the problems in the bud, wherever possible, rather than waiting for them to become more entrenched or complicated.

2 Get to know each individual in order to anticipate possible behaviour.

3 Do not wait until a formal review meeting. They should have a quiet word at the first sign something is going wrong.

4 If they have to hold a formal meeting, get the facts in advance – what happened, when and why?

5 Plan the meeting on the basis of the facts and what they know about the individual. Define what they want to achieve.

6 Set the right tone from the start of the meeting – adopt a calm, measured, deliberate but friendly approach.

7 Begin the conversation by explaining the purpose and structure of the meeting, indicating to the individual what the issue is, using their knowledge of the situation and giving specific examples.

8 Focus on the issue and not the person.

9 Ask for an explanation. Ask unloaded questions to clarify the issues and explore them together.

10 Listen to what the individual has to say – he or she may need to let off steam.

11 Keep an open mind and don't jump to conclusions.

12 Acknowledge the individual's position and any mitigating circumstances.

13 If new evidence emerges, adjourn the meeting if this feels appropriate.

14 Ask the employee for proposals to resolve the situation, discuss the options and if possible agree on action by the individual, the manager or jointly.

15 If agreement cannot be reached, managers may have to define the way forward, with reasons – they are in charge!

Dealing with difficult situations

With the best will in the world you may get a negative reaction from an individual – ranging from sullen silence to open hostility, even rage. To deal with this sort of difficult situation managers should adopt the approach set out below.

1 Maintain control of the meeting.

2 Put clear boundaries in place and ensure that the conversation keeps within them.

3 Remain calm at all times – never respond to anger with anger.

4 Use questioning techniques to clarify the facts.

5 Be firm and restate their position as necessary.

6 Decide what tactics are working and if they need to change their approach. Know when to expand a conversation by seeking clarification and gaining understanding and when to restrict it.

7 Decide if and when they need to adjourn for a break to allow either party to consider their position or to cool things down.

8 Stay clear of emotive language and don't respond to manipulative behaviour.

9 Allow people to have their say and listen to them, but make it clear that rudeness or any other form of unacceptable behaviour will not be tolerated. Terminate the meeting before things get out of hand.

10 If, in spite of the facts, the individual is in denial, restate the evidence, indicate what happens next (possibly another meeting after a cooling off period) and close the meeting.

References

DeNisi, A S and Kluger, A N (2000) Feedback effectiveness: Can 360-degree appraisals be improved? *Academy of Management Executive*, **21** (1), pp 129–39

Gray, A (2001) Individual differences in 360-degree feedback, in *The Feedback Project*, Roehampton, University of Surrey

Kluger, A N and DeNisi, A (1996) The effects of feedback interventions on performance: A historical review, a meta-analysis, and a preliminary feedback theory, *Psychological Bulletin*, **119**, pp 254–284

Lee, C D (2005) Rethinking the goals of your performance management system, *Employment Relations Today*, **32** (3), pp 53–60

London, M, Mone, E M and Scott, J C (2004) Performance management and assessment: methods for improved rater accuracy and employee goal setting, *Human Resource Management*, **43** (4), pp 319–36

360-degree feedback

07

360-degree feedback, also known as multi-source feedback, aims to provide for a more accurate and balanced assessment of performance and behaviour. This chapter covers the practice of 360-degree feedback under the following headings:

- 360-degree feedback defined
- Use of 360-degree feedback
- Methodology
- 360-degree feedback and appraisal
- Effectiveness of 360-degree feedback
- Introducing 360-degree feedback

360-degree feedback defined

360-degree feedback is the assessment and feedback of someone's performance by a number of people who will include their manager and their subordinates and may additionally include colleagues and customers.

360-degree feedback was defined by Ward (1997) as: 'The systematic collection and feedback of performance data on an individual or group derived from a number of the stakeholders on their performance'. Assessments take the form of ratings against various performance dimensions (see Figure 7.1).

FIGURE 7.1   360-degree feedback

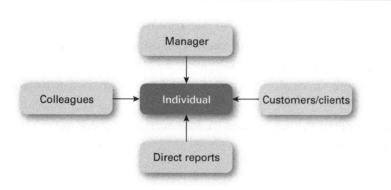

London and Beatty (1993) suggested that 360-degree feedback can become a powerful organizational intervention to increase awareness of the importance of aligning leader behaviour, work unit results, and customer expectations. It recognizes the complexity of management and the value of inputs from various sources – it is axiomatic that managers should not be assessing behaviours they cannot observe, and the leadership behaviours of subordinates may not be known to their managers. It also directs attention to important performance dimensions which may hitherto have been neglected by the organization. The Feedback Project (2001) listed the following benefits of 360-degree feedback:

- Increased employee self-awareness.
- Enhanced understanding of behaviours needed to increase individual and organizational performance.
- The creation of development activities that are more specific to the employee.
- Increased involvement of employees at all levels in the hierarchy.
- Increased devolution of self-development and learning to employees.

Use of 360-degree feedback

360-degree feedback was used by only 19 per cent of the respondents to the 2014 e-reward performance management survey, mainly for managers.

Research conducted by Handy *et al* (1996) found that typically, it forms part of a self-development or management development programme. It serves a number of purposes – 71 per cent of the 45 organizations covered by the e-reward survey used it solely to support learning and development, 23 per cent used it to support a number of HR processes such as appraisal, resourcing and succession planning, and 6 per cent used it to support pay decisions.

An example of the application of 360-degree feedback in CEMEX is given in Appendix B.

360-degree feedback – methodology

360-degree feedback processes typically obtain data from questionnaires which measure from different perspectives the behaviours of individuals against a list of competencies. In effect, they ask for an evaluation: 'how well does X do Y?' The competency model may be one developed within the organization or the competency headings may be provided by the supplier of a questionnaire. A typical questionnaire may cover aspects of performance such as leadership, teamwork, openness to new ideas, valuing other people's opinions and readiness to recognize achievements.

Ratings

Ratings are given by the generators of the feedback on a scale against each heading. This may refer both to importance and performance. For example, the importance of each item could be rated on a scale of 1 (not important) to 6 (essential), and performance could be rated on a scale of 1 (weak in this area) to 6 (outstanding).

Feedback ratings are often accompanied by managers' self-ratings on the same items on which they are rated by their subordinates, peers, and customers. Self-ratings help focus the manager's attention on the results and build motivation in establishing the direction of self-development efforts.

An analysis of the results may be presented as a profile, an example of which is shown in Figure 7.2.

FIGURE 7.2 Example of 360-degree profile

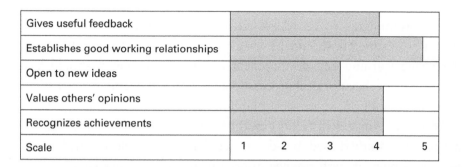

	1	2	3	4	5
Gives useful feedback					
Establishes good working relationships					
Open to new ideas					
Values others' opinions					
Recognizes achievements					
Scale	1	2	3	4	5

Data processing

Questionnaires are normally processed with the help of software usually provided by external suppliers. This enables the data collection and analysis to be completed swiftly, with the minimum of effort and in a way which facilitates graphical as well as numerical presentation.

Feedback

The feedback is often anonymous and may be presented to the individual (most commonly), to the individual's manager or to both the individual and the manager.

Action

The action generated by the feedback will depend on the purposes of the process, ie development, appraisal or pay. If the purpose is primarily developmental, the action may be left to individuals as part of their personal development plans, but the planning process may be shared between individuals and their managers if they both have access to the information. Coaches from inside or, commonly, outside the organization can review the feedback with the individual and discuss its implications and any development activities that may therefore be appropriate.

Even if the data only goes to the individual it can be discussed in a performance review meeting so that joint plans can be made, and there is much to be said for adopting this approach.

360-degree feedback and appraisal

An important issue to be addressed in developing a 360-degree feedback system is whether it should be used purely for development purposes (ie identifying learning and development needs) or whether it should be also used as part of the appraisal process (contributing to overall ratings and decisions on promotion, succession planning, pay or even retention). Research by Warr and Ainsworth (1999) established that 100 per cent of the organizations they studied used 360-degree feedback for development, 50 per cent used it as part of performance appraisal and only 7 per cent used it for determining pay.

Incorporating 360-degree feedback into appraisal can be attractive to organizations because they feel that (1) it makes the maximum use of the data it provides so that they get their money's worth, (2) it widens the base of opinion and (3) offers a broader assessment of performance.

As noted by Fletcher (1998) the shift in the late 1990s from using 360-degree feedback for developmental purposes to making it part of the appraisal process took place because of the perceived failings of conventional top-down appraisals. These were often seen to be limited because they reflect the perspective of only one person and ratings have been shown to be prone to bias. Also, top down appraisals too often appeared to achieve little behavioural change.

According to Fletcher, including 360-degree feedback in appraisals seems to offer a solution to some of these problems. In theory, multiple levels and sources of data should lead to a more objective picture of an individual's contribution, strengths and development needs. It should consequently promote higher levels of trust in the fairness of the process. This in turn should make it more likely that changes in behaviour will ensue. Making feedback part of appraisal also indicates that the organization takes it seriously.

But as Fletcher pointed out, there are problems. People giving the ratings may be less inclined to be honest if they know that they can affect pay decisions or have negative effects on the person concerned. His research at Shell showed that when the purpose of ratings became evaluative rather than developmental, up to 35 per cent of those giving the ratings change their assessments – and the changes could be in either direction. Furthermore, there is no guarantee that assessments by subordinates and peers may be free of bias. Fletcher concluded that his research findings should make people wary of grafting it onto appraisal systems. However, he did comment: 'This is not to say that it can't be used successfully, but it does need to be handled with care.'

Earlier research by Pollack and Pollack (1996) showed that the collection of 360-degree feedback data and the associated feedback process is more likely to be effective when the system is for developmental rather than appraisal purposes. Fletcher (1998) reported that organizations introducing 360-degree feedback for appraisal purposes have, in many cases, dropped it within two years. It was noted by Silverman *et al* (2005) that raters in one organization they studied resisted using feedback for appraisal purposes either because they were concerned about the impact their ratings would have on the receiver's pay or they were worried about confidentiality. They commented that there was a substantial amount of research, eg Handley (2001), which showed that raters tended to be more lenient when feedback was associated with appraisal. As they emphasize: 'The findings strongly suggest that linking 360-degree feedback to administrative decisions can contaminate the whole process'. There is also a legal aspect to this: if anonymous ratings lead to administrative actions such as demotion or even termination such actions may be difficult to support if challenged legally.

Effectiveness of 360-degree feedback

Research has produced varied conclusions about the effectiveness of 360-degree feedback. According to Bailey and Fletcher (2002) its benefits have been largely untested but rely on a number of assumptions – that individuals learn how effective task performance can be described, gain insight into how it is demonstrated and build the accuracy of self-perception and subsequent corrective behaviours. Their study of 104 managers receiving feedback on 50 behaviours over two years in an automobile breakdown service organization showed mixed benefits. The positive findings were that on average, self-raters, first and second level subordinates and bosses all saw improvements in competencies, development needs were perceived to decrease and there were dramatic changes in the perceptions of first and second level subordinates in terms of the association of self and other ratings. Self-perceptions also became a more accurate predictor of actual appraisal scores over time. On the negative side, greater similarities in scores between peers, self and individual levels largely resulted from subordinates altering their assessment of target managers – the managers' self-perceptions did not change much over time.

Warr and Ainsworth (1999) reported that many organizations which have implemented 360-degree feedback said that it was a success. Indeed, short-term indicators of success were typically cited as being the initial resistance of employees changing to acceptance and the fact that employees became willing to set aside time for use of the system. Longer-term success was typically viewed as the system being rolled out across the organization; receivers reporting behavioural change as a result of the feedback, 360-feedback ideas becoming part of the employees' thinking about their development, and increased alignment between 360-degree processes and organizational strategy.

Mixed results were observed by Silverman *et al* (2005). In one of their case studies (a brewing company) they noted that:

> The 360-degree feedback process had not been effective in changing behaviour or performance and there was some concern that it may even have caused more harm than good. There were particular worries about having raised expectations regarding what was possible for individuals after the feedback had been given and then not being able to provide the resources for this activity.

In a local authority, receivers found it difficult to cite concrete examples of behavioural change that could be attributed to the 360-degree feedback itself. However in a case researched by Silverman *et al* (a government office) it was established that 94 per cent of receivers had taken some action on the basis of the feedback and that there was evidence of positive, observable changes in behaviour. But feedback had more impact on some receivers than others. Another research project in a government office conducted by Morgan *et al* (2005) revealed a more negative situation. The findings were that at an organizational level the use of 360-degree feedback as a performance management tool failed to develop the awareness anticipated. Neither was it found to be aligned with other development plans or the organization's core competencies. At an individual level some individuals believed that they achieved little from the process overall.

Frisch (2001) commented that anonymous feedback is not necessarily a good thing: 'What happens in highly political, "out for yourself" organizational cultures is that anonymous feedback becomes an opportunity to get even or "take shots". Feedback that taps into power struggles and turf disputes can be personally damaging and yet hide behind the anonymity of the process.'

Maurer *et al* (2002) established that actual feedback ratings had only very weak relationships with subsequent involvement in development activity. What they found to be more important in predicting the uptake of development activity was a work environment in which employees are supportive of skills development and the extent to which those involved believed that they could improve their skills.

Table 7.1 summarizes some advantages and disadvantages of using 360-degree feedback.

TABLE 7.1   360-degree feedback – advantages and disadvantages

Advantages	Disadvantages
• Individuals get a broader perspective of how they are perceived by others than previously possible. • It gives people a more rounded view of their performance. • Increased awareness of and relevance of competencies. • Increased awareness by senior management that they too have development needs. • Feedback is perceived as more valid and objective, leading to acceptance of results and actions required.	• People do not always give frank or honest feedback. • People may be put under stress in receiving or giving feedback. • Lack of action following feedback. • Over-reliance on technology. • Too much bureaucracy. • Can be time-consuming and resource intensive.

The disadvantages can be reduced if not eliminated by careful design, involving stakeholders in the development programme, communication, training and follow-up.

Introducing 360-degree feedback

360-degree feedback is not an easy option. Silverman *et al* (2005) identified the following implementation issues which need to be addressed:

- The mission and scope of the use of 360-degree feedback is not clearly defined.
- There is an inadequate explanation of the whole process which leads to a lack of understanding of why it is used.
- Organizational readiness for feedback is not evident.
- Sufficient resources are not made available. Unrealistic promises are made at the implementation stage which leads to cynicism later on.
- The outcomes are not evaluated.

Guidelines produced by London and Beatty (1993) focus on 360-degree feedback as an operational procedure in the day-to-day activities of the organization. Their emphasis is on employee involvement at every stage – including development of job studies, identification and definition of areas for feedback and the design of feedback mechanisms. Implementation may require the study of specific organizational circumstances in relation to user acceptance and the ways in which 360-degree feedback may be of greatest short-term and long-term benefit for overall improvement of managerial competence.

Steps required

To develop and implement 360-degree feedback the following steps need to be taken:

1 *Define objectives* – it is important to define exactly what 360-degree feedback is expected to achieve. It will be necessary to spell out the extent to which it is concerned with personal development, appraisal or pay.

2 *Decide on recipients* – who are to be at the receiving end of feedback. This may be an indication of who will eventually be covered after a pilot scheme.

3 *Decide on who will give the feedback* – the individual's manager, direct reports, team members, other colleagues or internal and external customers. A decision will also have to be made on whether

HR staff or outside consultants should take part in helping managers make use of the feedback. A further decision will need to be made on whether or not the feedback should be anonymous (it usually is).

4 *Decide on the areas of work and behaviour on which feedback will be given* – this may be in line with an existing competency model or it may take the form of a list of headings for development. Clearly, the model should fit the culture, values and type of work carried out in the organization. But it might be decided that a list of headings or questions in a software package would be acceptable, at least to start with.

5 *Decide on the method of collecting the data* – the questionnaire could be designed in-house or a consultant's or software provider's questionnaire could be adopted, with the possible option of amending it later to produce better fit.

6 *Decide on data analysis and presentation* – again, the decision is on developing the software in-house or using a package. Most organizations installing 360-degree feedback do, in fact, purchase a package from a consultancy or software house. But the aim should be to keep it as simple as possible.

7 *Plan initial implementation programme* – it is desirable to pilot the process, preferably at top level or with all the managers in a function or department. The pilot scheme will need to be launched with communications to those involved about the purpose of 360-degree feedback, how it will work and the part they will play. The aim is to spell out the benefits and, as far as possible, allay any fears. Training in giving and receiving feedback will also be necessary.

8 *Analyse outcome of pilot scheme* – the reactions of those taking part in a pilot scheme should be analysed and necessary changes made to the process, the communication package and the training.

9 *Plan and implement full programme* – this should include briefing, communicating, training and support from HR and, possibly, the external consultants.

10 *Monitor and evaluate* – maintain a particularly close watch on the initial implementation of feedback but monitoring should continue. This is a process which can cause anxiety and stress, or produce little practical gain in terms of development and improved performance for a lot of effort.

360-degree feedback – criteria for success

- It has the active support of top management who themselves take part in giving and receiving feedback and encourage everyone else to do the same.

- There is commitment everywhere else to the process based on briefing, training and an understanding of the benefits to individuals as well as the organization.

- There is real determination by all concerned to use feedback data as the basis for development.

- Questionnaire items fit or reflect typical and significant aspects of behaviour.

- Items covered in the questionnaire can be related to actual events experienced by the individual.

- Comprehensive and well-delivered communication and training programmes are followed.

- No one feels threatened by the process – this is usually often achieved by making feedback anonymous and/or getting a third party facilitator to deliver the feedback.

- Feedback questionnaires are relatively easy to complete (not unduly complex or lengthy, with clear instructions).

- Bureaucracy is minimized.

References

Bailey, C and Fletcher, C (2002) The impact of multiple source feedback on management development; findings from a longitudinal study, *Journal of Organizational Behaviour*, **23** (7), pp 853–67

e-reward (2014) *Survey of Performance Management*, Stockport, e-reward

The Feedback Project (2001) *360-Degree Feedback: Best practice guidelines*, Roehampton, University of Surrey

Fletcher, C (1998) Circular argument, *People Management*, 1 October, pp 46–49

Frisch, M H (2001) Going around in circles with '360' tools: have they grown too popular for their own good? *Human Resource Planning*, **24** (2), pp 7–8

Handley, C (2001) Feedback skills, in *The Feedback Project*, Roehampton, University of Surrey

Handy, L, Devine, M and Heath, L (1996) *360-degree Feedback: Unguided Missile or Powerful Weapon?* Berkhamsted, Ashridge Management Group

London, M and Beatty, R W (1993) 360-degree feedback as competitive advantage, *Human Resource Management*, **32** (2/3), pp 353–72

Maurer, T, Mitchell, D and Barbiette, F (2002) Predictors of attitudes towards a 360-degree feedback system and involvement in post-feedback management development activity, *Journal of Occupational and Organizational Psychology*, **75**, pp 87–107

Morgan, A, Cannan, K and Culinane, K (2005) 360-degree feedback: a critical enquiry, *Personnel Review*, **34** (6), pp 663–80

Pollack, D and Pollack, L (1996) Using 360-degree feedback in performance appraisal, *Public Personnel Management*, **25** (4), pp 507–28

Silverman, M, Kerrin, M and Carter, A (2005) *360-degree Feedback: Beyond the spin*, Brighton, Institute for Employment Studies

Ward, P (1997) *360-Degree Feedback*, London, Institute of Personnel and Development

Warr, P and Ainsworth, E (1999) 360-degree feedback: some recent research, *Selection and Development Review*, **15** (3), pp 302–16

Conducting performance reviews

08

Performance management is a continuous process which involves both formal and informal reviews. As Plachy and Plachy (1988) explained: 'Performance review occurs whenever a manager and an employee confirm, adjust, or correct their understanding of work performance during routine work contacts'. This chapter covers:

- The process of reviewing performance
- Informal reviews
- Formal reviews

The process of reviewing performance

Performance can be reviewed formally or informally. Informal reviews provide the means to manage performance throughout the year. An informal and continuous approach is the best way to manage performance.

But it is still useful to have a formal review once or twice yearly. It is a focal point for the consideration of key performance and development issues and provides the basis for performance and development planning and agreements.

Informal reviews

Performance is reviewed informally as it occurs by the individual as well as the manager when comparisons are made between what happened with what was planned to happen. Informal feedback can take place whenever a manager comments on a piece of work or an action taken by an individual at work: 'Well done'; 'That's exactly what I wanted'; 'Could we discuss another way of doing this next time?'; 'Something seems to be going wrong. Let's discuss why and what can be done about it.'

Whenever appropriate, managers meet individual members of their teams to provide feedback, initiate coaching or other learning activities and agree on revised goals or any corrective action required. The outcome of such meetings may not be formally documented unless action to deal with poor performance through a capability procedure is invoked. However, managers may take notes for reference when preparing to conduct a formal review meeting.

Formal reviews

Formal reviews are meetings in which performance is analysed more systematically. They enable the five primary performance management elements of agreement, measurement, feedback, reinforcement and dialogue to be put to good use.

Their purposes are as follows:

- *Planning* – to provide the basis for re-formulating the performance agreement and the performance and development plans incorporated in it.

- *Motivation* – to provide positive feedback, recognition, praise and opportunities for growth; to clarify expectations; to empower people by encouraging them to take control over their own performance, learning and development.

- *Learning and development* – to provide a basis for self-managed learning and the development through coaching and other learning activities of the abilities relevant both to the current role and any future role the employee may have the potential to carry out.

- *Communication* – to serve as a two-way channel for communication about roles, expectations (objectives and competency requirements), relationships, work problems and aspirations.

- *Assessment* – to review how well individuals have performed their jobs.

The most common practice is to have one annual review – 65 per cent of respondents to the survey conducted by Armstrong and Baron (2004) did this. Twice-yearly reviews were held by 27 per cent of the respondents. These reviews led directly into the conclusion of a performance agreement (at the same meeting or later).

Preparing for formal review meetings

Review meetings are likely to be more effective if both parties – the manager and the individual – have prepared for them carefully. The extent to which detailed preparation is needed will vary according to the type of review. More care would need to be taken for a formal annual review and the approach suggested below is aimed at such occasions. But the same principles would apply, albeit less formally, to interim reviews.

Preparation by the manager

The manager should initiate the main formal review meeting by letting the individual know some time in advance (two weeks or so) when it is going to take place. A period of about two uninterrupted hours should be allowed for the meeting.

The manager should discuss with the individual the purpose of the meeting and the points to be covered. The aim should be, as far as possible, to emphasize the positive nature of the process and to dispel any feelings of trepidation on the part of the individual. The manager should also suggest that the individual prepares for the meeting along the lines described below.

The basis for preparation by managers should be the objectives, standards, competency requirements and plans agreed at the last main review as amended during the year. Achievements should be assessed by the application of appropriate performance measures. Any other evidence of good or not so good performance should also be assembled. Reference should be made to any notes made during or following interim review meetings about the individual's performance. Alterations to the individual's role since the last review should be noted. Consideration should be given to any changes in internal organizational, divisional or departmental circumstances which may have affected the definition and achievement of objectives. External pressure which may have affected performance and outcomes should also be noted. A preparation checklist is given in the performance management toolkit in Appendix A.

Preparation by the individual

Individuals should prepare for the meeting by carrying out a process of self-assessment. This involves them in reviewing their own performance, using a structured approach, as the basis for discussions with their managers in review meetings. On the whole people are surprisingly realistic when they do this, as long as their assessment is not going to contribute directly to a performance-related pay decision. In fact, some people underestimate themselves, which makes it even easier for their manager to take a positive approach.

Self-assessment involves analysing performance and identifying successes and any problems in achieving goals. Individuals may attribute any problems to lack of skill or experience and should be encouraged to be specific so that a personal development plan can be prepared. They may also comment on a lack of adequate support from their manager or colleagues, insufficient resources, unattainable objectives or any other factor beyond their control that they believe has affected their performance. The structure for self-assessment can be provided by a self-assessment checklist which is given to individuals before the review meeting. An example is provided in the performance management toolkit in Appendix A.

The main advantage of using a self-assessment approach is that it reduces defensiveness by allowing individuals to take the lead in reviewing their own performance rather than having their managers' judgements thrust upon them. It therefore helps to generate a more positive and constructive discussion during the review meeting, which can focus on joint problem-solving rather than attaching blame. In addition, it encourages people to think about their own development needs and how they can improve their own performance and provides for a more balanced assessment because it is based on the views of both the manager and the individual rather than those of the manager alone.

Self-assessment can allow employees to take the lead but the aim of the review meeting remains that of achieving an agreed joint assessment and a development plan. Managers have therefore to contribute and, as necessary, add to the views expressed by employees. They should also be prepared to allow employees in effect to criticize them for lack of support, providing inadequate resources or setting unachievable standards. Many managers may be unwilling to accept such criticisms and many employees may be unwilling to make them for fear of their managers' reactions. Steps can be taken to overcome this problem by education, guidance and example, but realistically, this may be difficult.

There is still room for confrontation if managers bluntly disagree, and it may require considerable skill on their part to persuade employees to reconsider their self-assessment. This can be achieved by good reviewers, but it means taking care to handle the situation by asking further questions or presenting additional facts rather than simply expressing an adverse opinion which is unsupported by evidence. Although many people can be surprisingly realistic in assessing their own performance, some will overestimate their abilities and they need to be handled carefully.

Incorporating self-assessment as part of a performance management/review process is most likely to be successful when all concerned fully understand the purpose of self-assessment and both managers and employees understand their respective roles in the review meeting and how they should be carried out. Employees need guidance on how to carry out self-assessments and both managers and employees need training in conducting reviews based on self-assessment, especially on joint problem-solving methods.

Self-assessment is directed to the future motivation and development of the employee and should not be used simply as the basis for raking over past problems, although the analysis of any such problems will provide guidance on the way ahead. Clearly, self-assessments should not be taken into account when making pay, promotion or disciplinary decisions.

The formal review process

Formal reviews include an overview and analysis of performance since the last review, comparing results with agreed expectations and plans. In a sense, they are stocktaking exercises. Reference may be made to events which illustrate performance as discussed during the year (they shouldn't be brought up at a formal meeting for the first time). The level of performance achieved is assessed so that individuals know where they stand. In many cases it is rated. Formal reviews are usually documented on paper or recorded on a computer. They can provide the basis for decisions on inclusion in talent management development programmes, training, performance and development plans, promotion, performance pay, and action to deal with poor performance (although the last is best carried out at the time rather than waiting for an annual review).

All this happens on a one-to-one basis – a get-together of the manager and the individual. This should be a conversation involving dialogue and joint analysis of performance. It should be constructive and forward-looking, not a top-down judgemental affair.

As described by Strebler *et al* (2001) performance reviews should:

- have clear aims and measurable success criteria;
- focus on clarity and performance improvement;
- provide employees with a clear 'line of sight' between their performance goals and those of the organization;
- be closely allied to a clear and adequately resourced training and development programme;
- explain clearly how any direct link to reward takes place.

The review should be rooted in the reality of the employee's performance. It is concrete, not abstract and it allows managers and individuals to take a positive look together at how performance can be developed in the future and how any problems in achieving goals and meeting performance standards can be resolved. Individuals should be encouraged to assess their own performance and become active agents for change in developing that performance. Managers should be encouraged to adopt their proper enabling role; coaching and providing support and guidance.

There should be no surprises in a formal review if performance issues have been dealt with as they should have been – as they arise during the year. Traditional appraisals are often no more than an analysis of where those involved are now, and where they have come from. This static and historical approach is not what performance management is about. The true role of performance management is to look forward to what needs to be done by people to achieve the purpose of the job, to meet new challenges, to make even better use of their knowledge, skills and abilities, to develop their capabilities by establishing a self-managed learning agenda and to reach agreement on any areas where performance needs to be developed and how that development should take place. This process also helps managers to improve their ability to lead, guide and develop the individuals and teams for whom they are responsible.

A problem-solving approach should be adopted. This approach enables the review to be constructive. It focuses on the identification and exploration of any significant problems facing the employee and on encouraging the employee to think through the issues involved. The manager will provide feedback, but this is constructive feedback in that it is aimed at helping the employee to work out for himself or herself what needs to be done, with the manager's support.

Managers comment on and, sometimes, add to the individual's self-assessment. They should avoid confrontation, ie total disagreement with the individual's opinions and should preferably ask exploratory questions such as the following:

- Why do you feel like that?
- Why do you think that happened?
- Have you taken into account such and such an event?
- The information I have is that you have not consistently achieved the performance standard for this particular task we agreed last year. Here are some examples. How did this happen?
- Do you think there are any other causes of this problem?
- Do you think you have contributed to this problem?
- Are there any other issues or problems you have not mentioned?
- How are *we* going to make sure that this problem does not occur again in the future?

Twelve golden rules for conducting a review meeting

There are twelve golden rules for conducting formal performance review meetings.

1 Be prepared

Managers should prepare by referring to a list of agreed goals and their notes on performance throughout the year. They should form views about the reasons for success or failure and decide where to give praise, which performance problems should be mentioned and what steps might be undertaken to overcome them. Thought should also be given to any changes that have taken place or are contemplated in the individual's role and to work and personal objectives for the next period. Individuals should also prepare in order to identify achievements and problems, and to be ready to assess their own performance at the meeting. They should also note any points they wish to raise about their work and prospects.

2 Work to a clear structure

The meeting should be planned to cover all the points identified during preparation. Sufficient time should be allowed for a full discussion – hurried meetings will be ineffective. An hour or two is usually necessary to get maximum value from the review.

3 Create the right atmosphere

A successful meeting depends on creating an informal environment in which a full, frank but friendly exchange of views can take place. It is best to start with a fairly general discussion which aims to put the individual at ease and create a non-threatening atmosphere and which covers the purpose of the meeting, emphasizing that it is a joint affair before getting into any detail.

4 Provide good feedback

Individuals need to know how they are getting on. Feedback needs to be based on factual evidence and careful thought should be given to what is said and how it is said so that it motivates rather than demotivates people. Techniques of giving feedback – a key aspect of the meeting – are described at the end of this chapter.

5 Use time productively

The reviewer should test understanding, obtain information, and seek proposals and support. Time should be allowed for the individual to express his or her views fully and to respond to any comments made by the manager. The meeting should take the form of a dialogue between two interested and involved parties both of whom are seeking a positive conclusion.

6 Use praise

If possible, managers should begin with praise for some specific achievement, but this should be sincere and deserved. Praise helps people to relax – everyone needs encouragement and appreciation.

7 Let individuals do most of the talking

This enables them to get things off their chest and helps them to feel that they are getting a fair hearing. Use open-ended questions (ie questions that invite the individual to think about what to reply rather than indicating the expected answer). This is to encourage people to expand.

8 Invite self-assessment

This is to see how things look from the individual's point of view and to provide a basis for discussion – many people underestimate themselves. Ask questions such as:

- How well do you feel you have done?
- What do you feel are your strengths?
- What do you like most/least about your job?
- Why do you think that project went well?
- Why do you think you didn't meet that target?

9 Discuss performance not personality

Discussions on performance should be based on factual evidence, not opinion. Always refer to actual events or behaviour and to results compared with agreed performance measures. Individuals should be given plenty of scope to explain why something did or did not happen.

10 Encourage analysis of performance

Don't just hand out praise or blame. Analyse jointly and objectively why things went well or badly and what can be done to maintain a high standard or to avoid problems in the future.

11 Don't deliver unexpected criticisms

There should be no surprises. The discussion should only be concerned with events or behaviours which have been noted at the time they took place. Feedback on performance should be immediate. It should not wait until the end of the year. The purpose of the formal review is to reflect briefly on experiences during the review period and on this basis to look ahead.

12 Agree measurable objectives and a plan of action

The aim should be to end the review meeting on a positive note.

Problems with formal performance reviews

Conducing satisfactory performance reviews requires considerable skill. It is hardly surprising that many managers and, indeed, employees generally find it difficult. Three main sources of difficulty in conducting reviews were identified in one of the earliest articles on performance management by Beer and Ruh (1976):

1 The quality of the relationship between the manager and the individual – unless there is mutual trust and understanding the perception of both parties may be that the performance review is a daunting experience in which hostility and resistance are likely to emerge.

2 The manner and the skill with which the interview is conducted.

3 The review process itself – its purpose, methodology and documentation.

The golden rules set out above may sound straightforward and obvious enough but they will only function properly in a culture which supports this type of approach. This is why it is essential to get and keep top management support and to take special care in developing and introducing the system and in training managers *and* their staff.

References

Armstrong, M and Baron, A (2004) *Managing Performance: Performance Management in Action*, London, CIPD

Beer, M and Ruh, R A (1976) Employee growth through performance management, *Harvard Business Review*, July–August, pp 59–66

Plachy, R J and Plachy, S J (1988) *Getting Results From Your Performance Management and Appraisal System*, New York, AMACOM

Strebler, M T, Bevan, S and Robertson, D (2001) *Performance Review: Balancing objectives and content*, Brighton, Institute for Employment Studies

Assessing performance

09

Performance assessment is the analysis and evaluation by a manager of how well someone is doing. It generates information which can be used first, to identify learning and development needs, second, to guide decisions on performance improvement plans and third, to provide a means of indicating people with talent who may be included in a talent management process by, for example, being allocated to talent pools. Performance assessment can also inform merit or performance pay decisions, especially where the assessments result in ratings. It differs from performance appraisal in that it may not include ratings and is a continuous affair rather than an annual event, although formal assessments usually take place once or twice a year. Performance assessment is part of the review stage of the performance management cycle.

This chapter starts with an examination of the approaches to performance assessment and how these approaches operate in practice. It continues with a discussion of the process of analysing performance. This leads into a review of methods of assessment, namely: ranking, narrative assessments, rating and visual assessment.

Approaches to performance assessment

There are four approaches to performance assessment, namely: trait, results, behaviour and the combination of behaviour and results.

Trait approach

Traits are predispositions to behave in certain ways in a variety of different situations. They include abilities such as initiative, persistence, self-confidence, dependability, originality and influence. Traditional merit rating schemes tended to use traits as the main basis for assessment. But because trait assessment focuses on general attributes rather than specific behaviour it is likely to be based on subjective, unsupported judgements. People tend to make global assessments which may well be biased. The other problem with the trait approach is that traits remain fairly stable over a lifetime and the extent to which individuals can control them is limited. This reduces the scope for an assessment to be a basis for improving performance. For these reasons trait assessment in its original form is little used and the emphasis is now more on results-based and behaviour approaches.

Results approach

The results approach focuses on what employees achieve in terms of the measurable outputs and outcomes they produce. It is not concerned with behaviours – *how* results were attained. Instead, it concentrates on *what people* achieve. The assessment process compares results in the key result areas of a role against predetermined and agreed goals. The assessment of results is commonly used because it can provide a basis for performance pay decisions, especially when an overall rating of performance is made. But it cannot produce the information needed to analyse *why* performance was good or not so good and cannot therefore inform individual development plans.

Behaviour approach

The behaviour approach concentrates on how people carry out their work as evidenced by their behaviour rather than by their traits. It involves the assessment of behavioural competencies which are measurable aspects of a person's behaviour that result in effective or superior performance. As described in Chapter 1, competencies can be set out in an organization's competency framework while specific competencies can be defined for individual roles. An assessment system that ignores the results achieved by using competencies is incomplete but levels of competency may be difficult to measure.

Combined approach

The combined approach makes use of both results and behavioural assessments. Although it may start with a review of results, the emphasis should be on how those results were achieved.

Assessment in practice

The different bases for assessment used by the respondents to the e-reward 2014 survey of performance management were:

- Achievement against specific, agreed objectives or targets for individuals – 83 per cent.

- Qualitative assessment of an individual's behaviour in carrying out work – 58 per cent.

- Assessment of the individual's level of competency achieved by reference to a competency framework – 43 per cent.

- Achievement against defined job profile key result areas for individuals – 31 per cent.

- Achievements against broad-defined preset performance goals specific for individuals – 30 per cent.

- Achievement against performance goals that are driven by the company's business strategy – 19 per cent.

- Other – 1 per cent.

Analysing performance

In his seminal article 'An uneasy look at performance appraisal' Douglas McGregor (1957) suggested that the emphasis should be shifted from appraisal to analysis. The article was written a long time ago but its message is just as relevant today, and the persistence of the concept of top-down judgemental appraisal in many organizations suggests that there is still much to be learnt from McGregor in this area, as in a lot of others.

Douglas McGregor on analysing performance

This (the shift to analysis) implies a more positive approach. No longer is the subordinate being examined by the superior so that his weaknesses may be determined; rather he is examining himself in order to define not only his weaknesses but also his strengths and potentials... He becomes an active agent, not a passive 'object'.

McGregor was also the first commentator to emphasize that the focus should be on the future rather than the past in order to establish realistic targets and to seek the best means of reaching them.

The problem of performance analysis

Assessments require the ability to judge performance, and good judgement is a matter of using clear standards, considering only relevant evidence, avoiding bias and shunning projection (ascribing to other people one's own faults).

Most managers think they are good judges of people. One seldom if ever meets anyone who admits to being a poor judge, just as one seldom meets anyone who admits to being a bad driver, although accident rates suggest that bad drivers do exist and mistakes in selection, placement and promotion indicate that some managers are worse than others in judging people. Different managers will assess the same people very differently unless, with difficulty, a successful attempt to moderate their views is made. This is because managers assessing the same people will tend to assess them against different standards. Managers may jump to conclusions or make snap judgements if they are just required to appraise and rate people rather than to conduct a proper analysis of performance. Other problems include poor perception – not noticing things or events for what they are, selectivity – relying on partial data, noticing only things one wants to see and poor interpretation – putting one's own, possibly biased, slant on information. This can lead to what O'Malley (2003) refers to as Type I and Type II errors. A Type I error occurs when the conclusion is that there are no differences in employees' performance when there are. Conversely, a Type II error is concluding that there are differences when in fact there are none.

Overriding all these problems is the likelihood that managers and employees are unsure what good or poor performance looks like and cannot recognize either when they meet them. The notion of performance is a vague one: Is it simply *what* someone produces – their output? Or is it *how* they produce it – their behaviour? Or is it both? It is, in fact, both, but this is not recognized by everyone, which results in suspect analyses and assessments.

It is also the case that while managers may be able to recognize those who are extremely talented and, at the other extreme, those who are performing very badly, they may find it difficult to distinguish performance differences between the people lying between those extremes. Managers can in effect tell an individual that she has done exceptionally well and that she will therefore be included in the talent management programme, or they can inform another individual that he has not done very well and that they must discuss what needs to be done about it. The best that can be done for the others is to tell them that they are doing a perfectly acceptable job. This is not very encouraging by itself but can become more positive and acceptable if there is a discussion on how performance could be developed.

Coens and Jenkins (2002) issued another warning about performance analysis. They asserted that performance is largely driven by the system and questioned the ability of anyone to distinguish adequately an individual's performance from the situational constraints. They pointed out that: In a given year some people perform better and some worse. A single individual's performance may be better one year, worse the next and somewhere in the middle in the year following. These differences, however, may not be the result of some people trying harder or anything else significant. It may just be 'the random happenstance of events and factors that impact individual performance'. They therefore argued that: 'Rather than think we can rank or effectively rate people, we change our assumptions, we accept that while results are measurable, discrete differences in what can be directly attributable to individuals is not measurable. We may only be able to recognize, with a healthy scepticism, people who "stand out" in various settings, thereby warranting special attention'.

The approach to performance analysis

To tackle these problems it is necessary to:

- ensure that the concept of performance is understood by all concerned, managers and employees alike, which means appreciating what constitutes good and not so good performance and how it should be measured and analysed;

- encourage managers to define and agree standards and measures of effectiveness beforehand with those concerned as a basis for analysis;

- get managers to base their judgements on evidence (evidence-based performance management) rather than on opinion – the assessment of results should be founded on measurable or recognizable outcomes, and assessments of behaviour should be supported by illustrative examples in the shape of critical incidents;

- encourage and train people to avoid jumping to conclusions too quickly – they need to consciously suspend judgement until all the relevant data available has been analysed and then consider all aspects of performance in order to ensure that a balanced view is obtained;

- provide managers with practice in exercising judgements which enable them to find out for themselves where they need to improve their performance analysis techniques;

- accept that managers will find it relatively easy to recognize extremes of performance but difficult to discriminate between middle ranking people – this suggests that the more levels rating scales have above the basic three (exceeds expectations, meets expectations, does not meet expectations) the less accurate the intermediate ratings will be;

- ensure that managers recognize the limitations of performance analysis and assessment as spelt out by Coens and Jenkins.

Analysis provides the information for each of the forms of assessment described below which consist of ranking, overall or analytical narratives, rating and graphic rating scales.

Ranking

Ranking means placing employees in a rank order from best to worst. It is a simple comparative method which is easy to explain and conduct. The problem with ranking, as with other overall assessment systems, is that the notion of performance is vague. In the case of ranking it is therefore unclear what the resulting order of employees truly represents. And this sort of ranking is not really feasible unless fairly large numbers of employees are being assessed – what is the point of a manager with only two or three subordinates ranking them? Furthermore, employees are compared on the basis of only one factor (overall performance) which leaves no scope for analysis and therefore feedback, and there is no information on the relative difference between them. A more feasible method is to rank people according to performance rating scores although, as discussed below, there are problems with rating.

A forced ranking system may be adopted in which the rank order can be divided into percentiles, eg the top 20 per cent, the middle 70 per cent and the bottom 10. The aim is to place employees into categories such as high flyers (the top 20 per cent in this example), unacceptable (the bottom 10 per cent) or those performing at an acceptable but not exceptional level (the remaining 70 per cent). This classification can be used to identify those who are fast-tracked in a talent management programme, or those who may not survive. The distribution of performance rankings between the different groups may be called a vitality curve. The term 'forced ranking' is a bit of a misnomer. It implies that the rank order is enforced, which is not the case. The only forced provision in such a system is that the division of the rank order into different categories or percentiles is predetermined and everyone concerned has to be forced into one of those categories.

Forced ranking first achieved fame when it was used by Jack Welch at General Electric to identify high flyers and poor performers. He argued that 20 per cent of any group of managers were top performers, 70 per cent were average and 10 per cent were not worth keeping. The latter were 'let go', hence the terms 'rank and yank' or 'dead man's curve' for this procedure.

Supporters of forced ranking say it is a good way of weeding out unsatisfactory employees as well as identifying and rewarding the top players. But it doesn't always work. Arkin (2007) noted that 'before imploding, thanks to the actions of its own top performers, Enron used a complicated system to rank and yank its employees'. The 'rank and yank' approach may have its advocates, but Meisler (2003), in an article tellingly called 'Dead man's curve', thought that: 'For most people, – especially those with out-moded concepts of loyalty and job security – the prospect of Darwinian struggle at the work place is not a happy one'.

The following criticism of forced ranking was made by Pfeffer and Sutton (2006):

> We couldn't find a shred of evidence that it is better to have just a few alpha dogs at the top and treat everyone else as inferior. Rather, the best performance comes in organizations where as many people as possible are treated as top dogs. If you want people to keep working together and keep earning together, it is better to grant prestige to many rather than few, and to avoid big gaps between who gets the most rewards and kudos.

Research conducted by Garcia as reported in *Machine Design* (2007) established that in forced ranking systems individuals will care less about performing well on a given task and instead shift their focus to performing relatively better on a scale. Those ranked highest on the scale are more competitive and less cooperative than those ranked lower.

A further difficulty is that when an organization gets rid of the bottom 10 per cent a proportion of those in the average category will drop down automatically into the unsatisfactory category without any change to their level of performance. As Ed Lawler, quoted by Aguinis (2005) commented, if a prescribed percentage of employees is let go every year because they have been placed in the 'C' category, this will at some time cut into the 'bone' of the organization. Research by Meisler (2003) found that for this reason after about three iterations forced distribution systems became ineffective. A simulation by Scullen *et al* (2005) established that while there were improvements in performance in the first few years of the operation of forced ranking this drains away and eventually becomes zero. O'Malley (2003) described forced ranking as a 'gross method of categorising employees into a few evaluative buckets'.

A forced ranking approach will not work unless employees understand what is expected of them, there are fair procedures for reviewing and classifying levels of performance and employees trust their managers to use these procedures to assess their performance correctly. These are exacting requirements.

A mechanistic 'rank and yank' system will only create a climate of fear and will at best inhibit and at worst destroy any possibility that performance management is perceived and used as a developmental process. It is better to have good processes for identifying performance problems and helping underperformers to improve, coupled with effective capability procedures as described in Chapter 11.

Narrative assessment of overall performance

An overall assessment may be recorded in a narrative consisting of a written summary of views about the level of performance achieved. This method was adopted by 27 per cent of the respondents to the e-reward 2004 contingent pay survey. It at least ensures that managers have to collect their thoughts together and put them down on paper. But, the results can be bland, misleading and unhelpful from the viewpoint of deciding what should be done to develop talent or improve performance. Research on performance appraisal systems by Kay Rowe led her to produce the following picture of what they can look like:

Has tact and is loyal. Shows initiative and leadership. A good organizer with sound judgement. Expresses himself in speech and writing moderately well. Has potential.

Businesses with merit pay schemes may disagree with this overall approach. The majority (73 per cent) of the respondents to the e-reward 2004 contingent pay survey depended on performance ratings to indicate the size of an increase or whether there was to be an increase at all. Even those without such pay schemes like to follow the traditional path of summarizing performance by ratings 'for the record' although they are not always clear about what to do with the record.

Analytical performance management assessments

Narrative performance assessment can be made more meaningful if it is carried out within a framework. This could be provided on a 'what' and 'how' basis. The 'what' is the achievement of previously agreed goals related to the headings on a role profile. The 'how' is behaviour as described in competency frameworks. The results for each 'what and how' heading can be recorded following a joint analysis during a review meeting. A framework for such an analysis is shown in Figure 9.1.

FIGURE 9.1   Analytical narrative assessment framework

	Description	Comments	Agreed action
Key result area goals			
		.	
Competencies			

Managers need to be trained in how to use this framework and how well they do so should be checked so that if necessary guidance can be given on how they could do better.

The rating process

Rating involves an assessment by a reviewer of the level of performance of an employee expressed on a scale. The e-reward 2014 survey of performance management found that 77 per cent of respondents used ratings. Since the days of merit rating and then performance appraisal, rating still reigns supreme. To many people it was and is the ultimate purpose and the final outcome of performance appraisal. Academics, especially American academics, have been preoccupied with rating – what it is, how to do it, how to improve it, how to train raters – for the last 50 years. Many problems with rating have been identified but it doesn't seem to have occurred to them that these could readily be overcome if rating weren't used at all.

The theory of rating

The theory underpinning all rating methods is that it is possible as well as desirable to measure the performance of people on a scale accurately and consistently and categorize them accordingly. As DeNisi and Pritchard (2006) comment: 'Effective performance appraisal systems are those where the raters have the ability to measure employee performance and the motivation to assign the most accurate ratings'.

Murphy and Cleveland (1995) distinguished between judgement and ratings. A judgement is a relatively private evaluation of a person's performance in some area. Ratings are a public statement of a judgement evaluation which is made for the record. Wherry and Bartlett (1982) produced the following theory of the rating process:

- Raters vary in the accuracy of ratings given in direct proportion to the relevancy of their previous contacts with the person being rated.

- Rating items which refer to frequently performed acts are rated more accurately than those which refer to acts performed more rarely.

- The rater makes more accurate ratings when forewarned of the behaviours to be rated because this focuses attention on the particular behaviours.

- Deliberate direction to the behaviours to be assessed reduces rating bias.

- Keeping a written record between rating periods of specifically observed critical incidents improves the accuracy of recall.

Research conducted on rating has produced a number of findings which supplement this theory. Pulakos *et al* (2008) noted that ratings for decision-making (eg on performance pay) tend to be higher than ratings for development, which tend to be variable, reflecting both employee strengths and development needs. They also commented that if the system is used for decision-making, ratings are important. If a system is strictly developmental, there is less need for ratings and in fact they may detract from development. This is because employees tend to be more concerned about their 'score' than their understanding of their development needs. From a development perspective, narratives may provide more useful information than numerical ratings. Even when performance is rated against defined standards the ratings do not convey what the employee did or did not do in sufficient detail. Jawahar and Williams (1997) reported that performance evaluations such as ratings obtained for administrative purposes (eg pay or promotions) are more lenient than those for research, feedback or employee development purposes.

One of the issues concerning assessment is the degree to which receivers accept what the reviewer says about them. Research by Roberts (1994) indicated that acceptance is maximized when the performance measurement process is perceived to be accurate, the system is administered fairly, the assessment system doesn't conflict with the employee's values and when the assessment process does not exceed the bounds of the psychological contract. He suggested that to increase the acceptability of assessments reviewers should:

- Pay less attention to mechanics and place more emphasis on process.

- Avoid basing conclusions on a small number of instances.

- Learn to seek information on external factors that may influence performance.

- Document employee performance.

- Involve individuals in the process through a genuine invitation to participate.

- Appreciate that reviewers do not have all the relevant performance information and that the employee is an important source.

- Encourage self-appraisal.
- Provide regular informal feedback, bearing in mind that once a year performance appraisal is unlikely to meet employee feedback requirements.

Silverman *et al* (2005) reported that many studies have demonstrated that performance ratings become higher over time. This was confirmed by Fletcher (2001). Rather than indicating performance improvement, this could simply arise because raters become complacent or careless or both.

Strebler *et al* (2001) commented that: 'The psychometric properties of the rating process – ie whether achieved ratings are valid and a true measure of actual performance – is the most researched aspect of performance assessment'. Their research in a care organization established that people became focused around the review headings (a little like wasps around jam) for the sole purpose of getting points (and points mean prizes) rather than improving the quality of care they delivered.

Saffie-Robertson and Brutus (2021) established through their research that evaluators who are uncomfortable about the appraisal process tend to inflate their performance ratings.

Ratings can be made solely for overall performance or they can be analytical, dealing separately with the performance dimensions of goals and competencies before, usually, summarizing with an overall assessment.

Overall performance rating scales

Overall performance rating scales summarize the level of performance achieved by an employee. This is done by selecting the point on a scale (sometimes referred to as a 'performance anchor') which most closely corresponds with the view of the assessor on how well the individual has been doing. A rating scale is supposed to assist in making judgements and it enables those judgements to be categorized to summarize the judgement of overall performance.

Types of scales

Overall rating scales can be defined alphabetically (a, b, c etc), or numerically (1, 2, 3 etc). Initials (x for excellent etc) are sometimes used in an attempt to disguise the hierarchical nature of the scale. The alphabetical or numerical scale points may be described adjectivally, for example, a = excellent, b = good, c = satisfactory and d = unsatisfactory.

Alternatively, scale levels may be described verbally as in the following example:

- *Exceptional performance*: Exceeds expectations and consistently makes an outstanding contribution which significantly extends the impact and influence of the role.

- *Well-balanced performance*: Meets objectives and requirements of the role, consistently performs in a thoroughly proficient manner.

- *Barely effective performance*: Does not meet all objectives or role requirements of the role; significant performance improvements are needed.

- *Unacceptable performance*: fails to meet most objectives or requirements of the role; shows a lack of commitment to performance improvement, or a lack of ability which has been discussed prior to the performance review.

Traditionally, definitions have regressed downwards from a highly positive, eg 'exceptional' description to a negative, eg 'unsatisfactory' definition as in the following typical example:

A   Outstanding performance in all respects.

B   Superior performance, significantly above normal job requirements.

C   Good all round performance which meets the normal requirements of the job.

D   Performance not fully up to requirements. Clear weaknesses requiring improvement have been identified.

E   Unacceptable; constant guidance is required and performance of many aspects of the job is well below a reasonable standard.

Another increasingly popular approach is to have a rating scale which refers to achievement levels and provides positive reinforcement. This is in line with a culture of continuous improvement. The example given below emphasizes the positive and improvable nature of individual performance.

Very effective	Achieves all the objectives of the job. Exceeds required standards and consistently performs in a thoroughly proficient manner beyond normal expectations.
Effective	Achieves required objectives and standards of performance and meets the normal expectations of the role.
Developing	Achievements are stronger in some aspects of the job than others. Most objectives are met but there is room for performance improvements in a number of areas.
Improvable	Achievements are generally below expectations. There is considerable room for improvement in several definable areas.

Positive definitions aim to avoid the use of terminology for middle-ranking but entirely acceptable performers such as 'satisfactory' or 'competent' which seem to be damning people with faint praise.

This scale deliberately avoids including an 'unacceptable' rating or its equivalent on the grounds that if someone's performance is totally unacceptable and unimprovable this should have been identified during the continuous process of performance management and corrective action initiated at the time. This is not something that can be delayed for several months until the next review when a negative formal rating is given, which may be too demotivating or too late. If action at the time fails to remedy the problem the employee may be dealt with under a capability procedure and the normal performance review suspended until the problem is overcome. However, the capability procedure should still provide for performance assessments to establish the extent to which the requirements set out in the informal or formal warnings have been met. Note also that in order to dispel any unfortunate associations with other systems such as school reports, this 'positive' scale does not include alphabetic or numerical ratings.

Some organizations have included 'learner/achiever' or 'unproven/too soon to tell' categories for new entrants to a grade for whom it is too early to give a realistic assessment.

Number of rating levels

There is a choice of the number of levels – there can be three, four, five or even six levels as described below. The e-reward (2014) survey found that the

FIGURE 9.2   A three-category rating scheme

Fulfilling expectations

In order to fulfil the expectations agreed for your role, you and your manager will agree at your review how you have:

- worked with others and developed yourself;
- followed through processes and made improvements;
- met the needs of internal/external customers;
- achieved key financial and business results.

The expectations are stretching and demanding and if you achieve them you will have done well and made a full and balanced contribution which has delivered the requirements of the business.

The majority of staff achieve what we expect of them and are currently assessed at this level – we expect this to continue in the future.

Exceeding expectations

People who exceed the expectations agreed for their role will be exceptional for two reasons:

- expectations of all of us are generally stretching and rise over time, so to have exceeded them denotes an approach which has added value beyond these normal high standards;
- performance is assessed not only in the job but also compared to colleagues doing similar jobs, so a clearly differentiated contribution will have been made.

People who exceed expectations can therefore expect higher pay awards and faster salary progression.

Not fulfilling expectations

We hope that there will not be many people who do not fulfil expectations. Such people will be counselled and supported to improve their performance but if, in the end, their contribution has not met the requirements of the business, they can expect to receive a smaller pay rise or no pay rise at all.

---

most popular number of levels was five (61 per cent of respondents). Four levels were used by 18 per cent, three by 9 per cent and six by 2 per cent.

Advocates of three grades contend that people are not capable of making any finer distinctions between performance levels. They know the really good and poor performers when they see them and have no difficulty in placing the majority where they belong, ie in the middle category. Figure 9.2 provides an example of a three category scheme used by a large financial services company in which the definitions of levels are more comprehensive than usual.

Those who prefer more than three grades (by far the majority of e-reward survey respondents) take the opposite but equally subjective view that raters *do* want to make finer distinctions and feel uncomfortable at dividing people into superior (average or above average) sheep, and inferior (below average) goats. They prefer intermediate categories in a five point scale or a wider range of choice in a four or six point scale.

The advocates of a larger number of points on the scale also claim that this assists in making the finer distinctions required in a performance-related pay system. But this argument is only sustainable if it is certain that managers are capable of making such fine distinctions (and there is no evidence that they can) and that these can be equitably reflected in meaningful pay increase differentials.

The most popular five level scales typically provide for two superior performance levels, a fully satisfactory level and two shades of less than capable performance. The rationale is that raters prefer this degree of fineness in performance definition and can easily recognize the middle grade and distinguish those who fall into higher or lower categories. It is also in accord with the typical way in which the normal curve of distribution is expressed where the middle category includes 60 per cent of the population, the next higher or lower categories each comprise 15 per cent of the population and the remaining 10 per cent is distributed equally between the highest and lowest category. This normal curve was originally applied to the distribution of intelligence in the form of IQs (intelligence quotients). It was believed that general ability is also distributed in the same pattern. However, this is a highly questionable assumption, which has not been substantiated by research. When confronted with a five level scale raters can be tempted to over-concentrate on the middle rating and avoid discriminating sufficiently between superior and inferior performers. Alternatively, five level scales can lead to 'rating drift' – a tendency to push ratings into higher categories. This can only be avoided by carefully wording the level descriptions to ensure that the middle category is used appropriately and by training managers in rating methodology.

Four level scales are sometimes used, often with positive definitions as in the example given earlier. They provide for finer distinctions than a three level scale while helping to avoid the problems inherent in five level scales of either central tendency or rating drift.

The rationale for a six level scale is that it gives a wider range and, like the four level scale, eliminates the tendency in five level scales either to pick mainly the central rating or to give in to the temptation to drift upwards from it. Another perceived benefit of having six levels is that the core of competent performers who are given a third level are aware that there are three levels below them. This is assumed to have a greater motivational value than being placed in the third of five grades with only two lower categories. But this number of levels presumes that managers are capable of consistently making the fine distinctions necessary and there is no evidence that this is the case.

The format to use is a matter of choice and judgement. Many organizations have five levels and some are settling for three levels, but there is no evidence that any single approach is clearly much superior to another, although the greater the number of levels the more is being asked of managers in the shape of discriminatory judgement. It does, however, seem to be preferable for level definitions to be positive rather than negative and for them to provide as much guidance as possible on the choice of ratings. It is equally important to ensure that level definitions are compatible with the culture of the organization and that close attention is given to ensuring that managers use them as consistently as possible.

Arguments for and against overall rating

Rating is used by the majority of organizations with performance management or appraisal systems, especially if they have merit pay, and there are arguments for doing so. But there are also persuasive arguments against rating. The pros and cons are discussed below.

Arguments for rating

The arguments for rating are that:

- It satisfies a natural wish that people have to know where they stand. But this is only desirable if the manager's opinion is honest, justified and fair, and the numbers or letters convey what is really felt and are meaningful.

- It provides a convenient means of summing up judgements so that high or low performances can easily be identified (as long as the judgements are consistent and fair).

- It motivates people by giving people something to strive for in the shape of higher ratings (as long as they know what they have to do to get a better assessment).

- It is not possible to have merit pay without an overall rating (assuming merit pay is wanted or needed and that there are indeed no alternatives, which there are, see Chapter 16).

- It can provide a basis for identifying high flyers for a talent management programme or for generally predicting potential. But past performance is only a predictor of future performance when there is a connecting link, ie there are elements of the present job which are also important in a higher level job.

Arguments against

Ratings are largely subjective and it is difficult to achieve consistency between the ratings given by different managers (ways of achieving consistent judgements are discussed below). Because the notion of 'performance' is often unclear, subjectivity can increase. Even if objectivity is achieved, to sum up the total performance of a person with a single rating is a gross oversimplification of what may be a complex set of factors influencing that performance – to do this suggests that the rating will be a superficial and arbitrary judgement. To label people as 'average' or 'below average', or whatever equivalent terms are used, is both demeaning and demotivating. The whole performance review meeting may be dominated by the fact that it will end with a rating, thus severely limiting the forward-looking and developmental focus of the meeting which is all-important. This is particularly the case if the rating governs performance or contribution pay increases.

Furnham (2004) raised a number of questions about the rating process, including the issue of what should be observed and recorded, the availability of reliable performance standards and the evaluative and judgemental nature of the process.

There are also many well-known rating errors. Grote (1996) lists nine:

1 *Contrast effect.* The tendency of a rater to evaluate people in comparison with other individuals rather than against the standards for the job.

2 *First impression error.* The tendency of a manager to make an initial positive or negative judgement of an employee and allow that first impression to colour or distort later information.

3 *Halo or horns effect.* Inappropriate generalizations from one aspect of an individual's performance to all areas of that person's performance.

4 *Similar-to-me effect.* The tendency of individuals to rate people who resemble themselves more highly than they rate others.

5 *Central tendency.* The inclination to rate people in the middle of the scale even when their performance clearly warrants a substantially higher or lower rating.

6 *Negative and positive skew*. The opposite of central tendency: the rating of all individuals as higher or lower than their performance actually warrants.

7 *Attribution bias*. The tendency to attribute performance failings to factors under the control of the individual and performance successes to external causes.

8 *Recency effect*. The tendency of minor events that have happened recently to have more influence on the rating than major events of many months ago.

9 *Stereotyping*. The tendency to generalize across groups and ignore individual differences.

Powerful attacks on rating were made by Coens and Jenkins (2002) and Lee (2005).

Attacks on rating

Coens and Jenkins

Ratings are not a good idea because of the unintended consequences – the insidious, destructive and counterproductive effects of giving people ratings about their work performance. Whether accurate or not, people are psychologically affected by ratings. And except for people rated at the highest end of the scale, the impact is usually negative ... Our ability to fairly measure the performance level of an individual is severely hampered by the unknowable effects of systems and random variations.

Lee

● The rating process is actually a by-product of the attempt to measure performance outcomes. An excessive emphasis on measurement can be misguided. The desired end that is lost in measuring performance is not measurement at all, but rather description.

● Poor ratings can stigmatize performance and cause unnecessary resistance to the acceptance of feedback.

● The goal is to have the employee assist us in describing, interpreting and redirecting performance feedback, not reacting to the ratings. Feedback can accomplish the same positive goal as a rating without the negative side effects.

● If the goal is performance improvement, then feedback – not labelling past efforts – is the preferred tool.

- Although ratings can be positive they can also be punitive and focus attention on the negative rather than the possible. The only message the employee gets from a poor rating is; 'Stop doing what you have been punished for doing'. This kind of rating may not even be an adequate description, since many ratings are a summary of a number of activities collected over time. It does not focus attention on what to do to get better.

- Ratings are feedback but feedback of the worst kind.

If an organization believes that it cannot do without ratings there are things that can be done to improve their accuracy and consistency.

Achieving accuracy in overall ratings

Murphy and Cleveland (1995) suggested that rating accuracy is improved when:

- good and poor performance are clearly defined;
- the principle of distinguishing among workers in terms of their levels of performance is widely accepted;
- there is a high degree of trust in the system;
- low ratings do not automatically result in the loss of valued rewards;
- valued rewards are clearly linked to accuracy in performance appraisal.

Achieving consistency in ratings

The following methods are available for increasing consistency.

Training

Training can take place in the form of 'consistency' workshops for managers who discuss how ratings can be objectively justified and test rating decisions on simulated performance review data. This can build a level of common understanding about rating levels. This is sometimes called 'frame of reference training' (Bernadin *et al*, 2000). The purpose of this training is to teach managers how to match a rating to performance by ensuring that the definitions of rating levels are understood and provide guidance and practice on how to use them.

Peer reviews (calibration)

Groups of managers meet to review the pattern of each other's ratings and challenge unusual decisions or distributions. This process of calibration or moderation is time-consuming but is possibly the best way to achieve a reasonable degree of consistency, especially when the group members share some knowledge of the performances of each other's staff as internal customers.

Monitoring

The distribution of ratings is monitored by a central department, usually HR, which challenges any unusual patterns and identifies and questions what appear to be unwarrantable differences between departments' ratings.

Consistency at a price can also be achieved by forced distribution as described below.

Forced distribution

Forced distribution means that raters have to conform to a laid down distribution of ratings at different levels. The pattern of forced distribution may correspond to the normal bell-shaped curve which has been observed to apply to IQ scores, although there is no evidence that performance in an organization is distributed normally – there are so many other factors at work such as recruitment and development practices. Employees subjected to forced distribution have to be allocated to sections of the curve in accordance with performance assessments. For example, as illustrated in Figure 9.3, the highest level performers would be placed in category A – the first 15 per cent of the

FIGURE 9.3   Forced distribution of employees

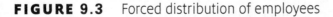

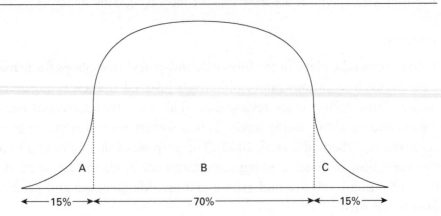

curve. The middle 70 per cent would be placed in category B in the centre of the curve and the bottom 15 per cent would be placed in category C.

Other distributions can be adopted, for example, 15 per cent A, 75 per cent B and 10 per cent C, on the assumption that a company's recruitment and development activities produce more top players than also rans. Three categories are the most common although a five level A to E system is used in some organizations. This is a less popular choice because it requires more refinement of judgement than is likely to be possible and creates an underclass of Ds who have been forced into that group whether or not they are below par.

Forced distribution achieves consistency of a sort but managers and staff rightly resent being forced into this sort of straitjacket. Only 8 per cent of the respondents to the e-reward 2014 survey of performance management used it. There was some disagreement about its value. In some cases, respondents felt that they were a positive tool to use because they made sure that line managers could not give a blanket 'satisfactory' score to everyone and had to differentiate between different individual's performance levels. But some held the opposite view. One said: 'Do not force performance distribution as it is not productive and does not embrace a pay for performance culture with success'.

Armstrong and Ward (2005) noted from their case study research that using indicative ranges, quotas or forced distribution systems pushes managers to make 'relative' assessments of their staff – often as part of a moderation process with other managers – that can often resemble crude 'horse-trading'. They are making rating decisions to ensure that the score profile in their team or department broadly fits the indicative ranges. The consequence of this can be that an individual may score a box 2 when assessed against their objectives, but be given a box 3 rating because there are already 'too many' box 2 performers in the team. This can be confusing for everyone and demotivating for those staff who are 'moderated' down to a lower rating. They can work earnestly towards their objectives all year in the expectation that if they meet or exceed them, then they will be assessed and rewarded appropriately. However, imposing a forced distribution mechanism means that two people in different departments who are equally effective in meeting their objectives can receive different ratings and performance pay.

A survey of 200 HR professionals by the Novations Group (2006) found that they reported a range of negative outcomes, including reduced productivity and collaboration and damage to morale and employee engagement.

Conclusions on overall rating

There are arguments both for and against overall rating. But the majority of organizations favour it for three main reasons: (1) it informs merit pay decisions, (2) it identifies high flyers for talent management purposes or poor performers for remedial action or dismissal and (3) it tells employees where they stand. Some either ignore the cons or are unaware of them. But many are concerned with the real problems of inaccuracy and inconsistency although there are ways of tackling these as discussed above. The alternative to a crude overall assessment is to adopt an analytical approach as described below. This can cover both results and behaviours (competencies) and ensure that any overall rating is better informed by reference to balanced information covering a range of performance dimensions.

Analytical rating

Analytical rating deals separately with key role requirements in terms of results or levels of competency. It therefore enables performance to be analysed in greater detail, covering each important aspect of a role rather than dealing with it as a whole. This avoids the oversimplification of an overall rating and enables more attention to be paid to specific developmental or performance improvement needs. However, analytical rating can be the basis for reaching an overall conclusion on performance expressed in a summary rating. Analytical rating can be conducted by means of an analytical framework or graphic rating scales.

Analytical framework

In an analytical framework each area is assessed and rated on a scale which may be restricted to only three levels to simplify choice. An analytical rating framework for a database administrator derived from the role profile in Chapter 1 (Figure 1.3) is illustrated in Figure 9.4. This lists the key result areas to which would be added specific goals or standards agreed at the performance planning stage.

If an overall rating needs to be made this could be based on a judgement by reference to the ratings under each heading. Alternatively, points could be attached to each assessment, eg A = 3, B = 2 and C = 1. The overall rating

FIGURE 9.4   Example of an analytical rating framework

	Definition	Goals	Assessment of performance in relation to goals	Rating*
Key result areas and goals	1 Identify database requirements for all projects that require data management in order to meet the needs of internal customers.			
	2 Develop project plans collaboratively with colleagues to deliver against their database needs.			
	3 Implement project plans in accordance with defined criteria, within the predefined budget and within the agreed time scale.			
	4 Support underlying database infrastructure to ensure that the level of service delivery required is achieved.			
	5 Ensure security of the database infrastructure through adherence to established protocols and develop additional security protocols where needed.			
Competency requirements	1 Aim to get things done well and set and meet challenging goals, create own measures of excellence and constantly seek ways of improving performance.			
	2 Analyse information from range of sources and develop effective solutions/recommendations.			
	3 Communicate clearly and persuasively, orally or in writing, dealing with technical issues in a manner which can be readily understood by internal clients.			
	4 Work participatively on projects with technical and non-technical colleagues.			
	5 Develop positive relationships with colleagues as the supplier of an internal service.			
	6 Fully aware of business needs in developing and operating the database.			

* A = exceeds expectations   B = meets expectations   C = does not meet expectations

could then be based on the total number of points, eg A = more than 25 points, B = 10–24 points and C = less than 10 points. This enables employees to be ranked if a forced ranking procedure is used but it is a mechanistic method which appears to offer greater accuracy than the judgements involved can support.

Graphic rating scales

Graphic rating scales provide guidance on ratings by anchoring the rating scale with statements describing the results or sort of behaviour which indicate that a particular rating level is justified. The intention is that these 'anchors' should ease the choice of levels and obtain consistency in the judgements made by different assessors. Graphic rating scales have become more sophisticated since they were introduced in the 1920s in that they now provide detailed descriptions of the rating levels, often based on research, rather than the crude references in the original versions to personality traits. An analytical approach is used in which scales cover different aspects of behaviour and results. The types of graphic rating scales are:

- behavioural rating scales based on the critical incident technique, the two main types of scales being behaviourally anchored rating scales (BARS) and behavioural observation scales (BOS);
- results-based rating scales;
- competency-based rating scales.

The critical incident technique

The development of behavioural rating scales was influenced by the critical-incident technique developed by Flanagan (1954). His research led to the conclusion that to avoid trait assessment (merit rating) and over-concentration on output (management by objectives) appraisers should focus on critical behaviour incidents which were real, unambiguous and illustrated clearly how well individuals were performing their tasks.

Flanagan advocated that managers should keep a record of these incidents and use them as evidence of actual behaviour during review meetings, thus increasing objectivity. He defended this proposal against the suggestion that he was asking managers to keep 'black books' on the grounds that it was positive as well as negative examples that should be recorded and that it would be better to make a note at the time rather than rely on memory, which is selective and may only recall recent events.

The critical incident technique did not gain much acceptance in its original form, perhaps because the 'black book' accusations stuck, but also because it seemed to be time-consuming. In addition, the problem was raised of converting the incident reports into an overall rating.

But the concept of critical incidents has had considerable influence on methods of developing competency frameworks, where it is used to elicit data about effective or less effective behaviour. The technique is used to assess what constitutes good or poor performance by analysing events which have been observed to have a noticeably successful or unsuccessful outcome, thus providing more factual, 'real' information than by simply listing tasks and guessing performance requirements. Used in this way the critical incident technique will produce schedules of 'differentiating competencies' which can form the basis for assessing and, if desired, rating competency levels. Differentiating competencies define the behavioural characteristics which high performers display as distinct from those characterizing less effective people, ie the performance dimensions of roles. The critical incident method is also used to develop behaviourally anchored rating scales as described below.

Above all, even if the Flanagan concept of critical incidents has not survived as a specific assessment technique, it does provide the basis for evidence-based performance management – analysis and assessment processes which rely on factual evidence rather than opinion.

Behaviourally anchored rating scales

Behaviourally anchored rating scales (BARS) were originally conceived by Smith and Kendall (1963). They consist of specific behavioural descriptions defining points against each scale (ie 'behavioural anchors') which represent a dimension, factor or work function considered important for performance. The statements range from a description of the worst-quality performance to one that describes the best, with all the other statements at appropriate intervals between. The aim is to guide managers on which level to select.

The following is an example of a BARS for teamworking:

A   Continually contributes new ideas and suggestions. Takes a leading role in group meetings but is tolerant and supportive of colleagues and respects other people's points of view. Keeps everyone informed about own activities and is well aware of what other team members are doing in support of team objectives.

B   Takes a full part in group meetings and contributes useful ideas frequently. Listens to colleagues and keeps them reasonably well informed about own activities while keeping abreast of what they are doing.

C   Delivers opinions and suggestions at group meetings from time to time, but is not a major contributor to new thinking or planning activities. Generally receptive to other people's ideas and willing to change own plans to fit in. Does not always keep others properly informed or take sufficient pains to know what they are doing.

D   Tendency to comply passively with other people's suggestions. May withdraw at group meetings but sometimes shows personal antagonism to others. Not very interested in what others are doing or in keeping them informed.

E   Tendency to go own way without taking much account of the need to make a contribution to team activities. Sometimes uncooperative and unwilling to share information.

F   Generally uncooperative. Goes own way, completely ignoring the wishes of other team members and taking no interest in the achievement of team objectives.

It is believed that the behavioural descriptions in such scales discourage the tendency to rate on the basis of generalized assumptions about personality traits (which were probably highly subjective) by focusing attention on specific work behaviours. But there is still room for making subjective judgements based on different interpretations of the definitions of levels of behaviour and how they relate to the employee's behaviour.

Like other scales, behaviourally anchored rating scales can be manipulated because they are transparent to raters who know how their responses to a behavioural item will affect the final appraisal. BARS take time and trouble to develop and are not in common use except in a modified form as the

dimensions in a differentiating competency framework. It is the latter application which has spread into some performance management processes.

Behavioural observation scales

Behavioural observation scales (BOS) as developed by Latham and Wexley
(1977) attempt to avoid the BARS problem of focusing on specific behaviours
by using more generalized behavioural statements. They consist of summated
scales based on statements about desirable or undesirable work behaviour.
These are complete behavioural statements, eg 'Conducts performance reviews
on time', 'Conducts the performance review as a dialogue with the employee'.
The headings are devised through the factor analysis of critical incidents.
Factor analysis is the statistical analysis of the interactions between the effects
of random (independent) variables. The assessor records the frequency with
which an employee is observed engaged in a specified behaviour on a five point
Likert scale. An example of a behavioural item for appraising a sales representative is: 'Knows the price of competitive products' and this is assessed on
the following scale:

	Never	Seldom	Sometimes	Generally	Always
Rating	1	2	3	4	5
*Frequency (% of time)**	0	1–20%	21–40%	41–99%	100%

*Managers record the frequency with which they have observed the employee behaving in this way.

According to Latham *et al* (2007) behavioural observation scales are regarded
as the most practical rating method by users. It was claimed that they produce fewer rating errors than other methods as long as raters have been
trained in their use. Their superiority to other scales arises from the fact that
they are based on Wherry and Bartlett's (1982) theory of rating (summarized
earlier in this chapter). This included the recommendation that recorded
critical incidents should be used to help improve the validity of assessments.

   However, Kane and Bernardin (1982) detected what they called a fatal flaw
in this system. They pointed out that:

   This scale is used to rate the observed occurrence rates of selected behaviors
   identified as being illustrative of desirable and undesirable ways of carrying out
   job functions. Each rating interval is assumed to connote a constant degree of
   performance satisfactoriness, regardless of the behavior it is used to characterize

(allowing, of course, for its transformation to its scale complement in the case of undesirable behaviors). The problem that this scale design raises is that a given occurrence rate interval does not, in fact, connote a constant level of performance satisfactoriness for all job behaviors.

Results-based scales

Results-based scales simply get raters to assess the extent to which perform-ance goals have been achieved for each key result area and overall as illustrated in Figure 9.5.

FIGURE 9.5   Results-based rating scale

Key result area	Often fails to meet agreed performance goals 1	Generally meets agreed performance goals 2	Often exceeds agreed performance goals 3
Overall			

Results-based rating scales are often used in conjunction with the competency-based scales described below.

Competency-based scales

Competency-based scales are graphic rating scales which use descriptions of different levels of competency as anchors for rating purposes. They typically refer to the elements of an organization's competency framework especially when they include 'critical incident' descriptions of effective and ineffective behaviour. A three-point scale for one element is illustrated in Figure 9.6.

FIGURE 9.6   A three-point scale for a behavioural competency

Develop positive relationships with colleagues as the supplier of an internal service		
1	2	3
• Fails to build up or maintain good relationships with internal customers • Often difficult to deal with • Unresponsive to others' contributions, feelings and concerns	• Makes time for people • Offers relevant advice • Generally responds within a reasonable time scale to requests for assistance	• Maintains effective working relationships at all levels in the organization • Takes the initiative in developing database systems which anticipate the needs of internal customers • Responds immediately to requests for help or advice

Competency-based scales work best when they are derived from a well-researched competency framework which is understood by the managers and employees concerned. It is essential that they are trained in their use.

Competency-based rating can also be used to assess the levels reached by employees for the specific competencies defined for their role. An example was given earlier in Figure 9.4 which also covers the assessment of results.

Conclusions on analytical rating

Analytical rating at least means that a more searching assessment can be made and recorded. But it does not avoid the problems of overall rating. Judgement on ratings has still to be exercised even though guidance is available on the allocation of levels. This guidance, as the examples given earlier show, tends to be generalized and selective and has to be interpreted.

It is best to develop guidelines in conjunction with managers and test them before they are finalized. Managers will need to be trained in their use. This should include frame of reference training to gain understanding of level definitions and how performance in terms of results or behaviour should be linked to them. Methods of combining judgements on each performance dimension into a summary evaluation should be covered and calibration exercises as described earlier will be helpful.

Visual methods of assessment

An alternative approach to rating is to use a visual method of assessment. This takes the form of an agreement between the manager and the individual on where the latter should be placed on a matrix or grid as illustrated in Figure 9.7, which was developed for a charity. A 'snapshot' is thus provided of the individual's overall contribution which is presented visually and so can provide a better basis for analysis and discussion than a mechanistic rating. The assessment of contribution refers both to outputs and to behaviours.

FIGURE 9.7   A performance matrix

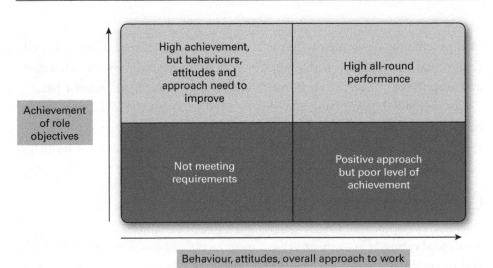

The review guidelines accompanying the matrix are as follows:

- You and your manager need to agree an overall assessment. This will be recorded in the summary page at the beginning of the review document. The aim is to get a balanced assessment of your contribution through the year. The assessment will take account of how you have performed against the responsibilities of your role as described in the role profile; objectives achieved and competency development over the course of the year. The assessment will become relevant for pay increases in the future.

- The grid on the annual performance review summary is meant to provide a visual snapshot of your overall contribution. This replaces a more conventional rating scale approach. It reflects the fact that your contribution is determined not just by results, but also by your overall approach towards your work and how you behave towards colleagues and customers.

- The evidence recorded in the performance review will be used to support where your manager places a mark on the grid.

- Their assessment against the vertical axis will be based on an assessment of your performance against your objectives, performance standards described in your role profile, and any other work achievements recorded in the review. Together these represent 'outputs'.

- The assessment against the horizontal axis will be based on an overall assessment of your performance against the competency level definitions for the role.

- Note that someone who is new in the role may be placed in one of the lower quadrants but this should be treated as an indication of development needs and not as a reflection on the individual's performance.

A similar 'matrix' approach has been adopted in a financial services company. It is used for management appraisals to illustrate their performance against peers. It is not an 'appraisal rating' – the purpose of the matrix is to help individuals focus on what they do well and also any areas for improvement. Two dimensions – business performance and behaviour (management style) – are reviewed on the matrix as illustrated in Figure 9.8 to ensure a rounder discussion of overall contribution against the full role demands rather than a short-term focus on current results.

This is achieved by visual means – the individual is placed at the relevant position in the matrix by reference to the two dimensions. For example a strong people manager who is low on the deliverables would be placed somewhere in the top left hand quadrant but the aim will be movement to a position in the top right hand quadrant.

A performance matrix used by a division of Unilever is shown in Figure 9.9. This measures the 'how' of performance on the vertical axis and the 'what' on the horizontal axis. The matrix model also contains guidelines on the possible actions that can be taken for each assessment quadrant.

FIGURE 9.8   Performance matrix in a financial services company

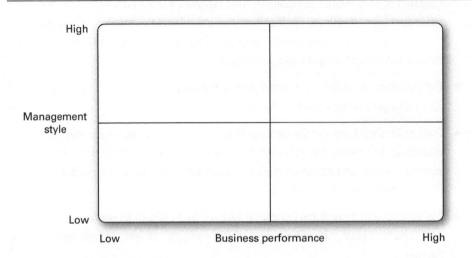

FIGURE 9.9   Assessment and action matrix – Unilever

	Inconsistent in meeting agreed individual business targets	Consistently meets agreed individual business targets
Consistently meeting expectations	**Possible actions:** • reward • set milestones • provide feedback • training • coach to improve delivery	**Possible actions:** • recognize and reward • challenge/stretch • expose • coach
Inconsistent in meeting expectations	**Possible actions:** • set milestones • provide feedback • coach/monitor/track • decision to continue or end employment	**Possible actions:** • recognize and reward • provide feedback • provide mentoring or coaching • acknowledge contribution

HOW

WHAT

Those organizations that have used visual assessments are enthusiastic about the extent to which it takes the heat out of rating and provides a sound basis for discussing and implementing development needs.

Conclusion

Performance assessment is a necessary and important performance management activity but it is one of the most difficult ones to get right. Attempts to use mechanistic methodologies involving overall rankings or ratings can prove of doubtful value. Analytical performance management methods are much better. But there is much to be said for the visual assessment approach.

References

Aguinis, H (2005) *Performance Management*, Upper Saddle River NJ, Pearson Education

Arkin, A (2007) Force for good? *People Management*, 8 February, pp 26–29

Armstrong, K and Ward, A (2005) *What Makes for Effective Performance Management?* London, The Work Foundation

Bernadin, H K, Kane, J S, Ross, S, Spina, J D and Johnson, D L (1995) Performance appraisal design, development and implementation, in G R Ferris, S D Rosen, and D J Barnum (eds), *Handbook of Human Resource Management*, Cambridge MA, Blackwell

Coens, T and Jenkins, M (2002) *Abolishing Performance Appraisals: Why they backfire and what to do instead*, San Francisco CA, Berrett-Koehler

DeNisi, A S and Pritchard, R D (2006) Performance appraisal, performance management and improving individual performance: a motivational framework, *Management and Organization Review*, 2 (2), pp 253–77

e-reward (2004) *Survey of Contingent Pay*, Stockport, e-reward

e-reward (2014) *Survey of Performance Management*, Stockport, e-reward

Flanagan, J C (1954) The critical incident technique, *Psychological Bulletin*, 51, pp 327–58

Fletcher, C (2001) Performance appraisal and management: the developing research agenda, *Journal of Occupational and Organizational Psychology*, 74 (4), pp 473–87

Furnham, A (2004) Performance management systems, *European Business Journal*, 16 (2), pp 83–94

Grote, D (1996) *The Complete Guide to Performance Appraisal*, New York, AMACOM

Jawahar, I M and Williams, C R (1997) Where all children are above average: the performance appraisal purpose effect, *Personnel Psychology*, 50, pp 905–25

Kane, J S and Bernardin, H J (1982) Behavioral observation scales and the evaluation of performance appraisal effectiveness, *Personnel Psychology*, 35 (3), pp 635–41

Latham, G P and Wexley, K N (1977) Behavioural observation scales, *Personnel Psychology*, **30**, pp 255–68

Latham, G, Sulsky, L M and Macdonald, H (2007) Performance management, in P Boxall, J Purcell and P Wright (eds), *Oxford Handbook of Human Resource Management*, Oxford, Oxford University Press

Lee, C D (2005) Rethinking the goals of your performance management system, *Employment Relations Today*, **32** (3), pp 53–60

Machine Design (2007) Forced ranking of employees bad for business, (editorial), September, pp 2–3

McGregor, D (1957) An uneasy look at performance appraisal, *Harvard Business Review*, May–June, pp 89–94

Meisler, A (2003) Dead man's curve, *Workforce Management*, June, pp 44–49

Murphy, K R and Cleveland, J (1995) *Understanding Performance Appraisal*, London, Sage

Novations (2006) *Uncovering the Growing Disenchantment with Forced Ranking Performance Management Systems*, www.novations.com

O'Malley, M (2003) Forced ranking, *WorldatWork Journal*, First Quarter, pp 31–39

Pfeffer, J and Sutton, R I (2006) *Hard facts, Dangerous Half-Truths and Total Nonsense*, Cambridge MA, Harvard Business School Press

Pulakos, E D, Mueller-Hanson, R A and O'Leary, R S (2008) Performance management in the US, in A Varma, P S Budhwar and A DeNisi (eds), *Performance Management Systems: A global perspective*, Abingdon, Routledge

Roberts, E R (1994) Maximizing performance appraisal system acceptance: perspectives from municipal government personnel administrators, *Public Personnel Management*, **23** (4), pp 525–48

Rowe, K (1964) An appraisal of appraisals, *Journal of Management Studies*, **1** (1), pp 1–25

Saffie-Robertson, M C and Brutus, S (2021) The impact of interdependence on performance evaluations: the mediating role of discomfort with performance appraisal, *The International Journal of Human Resource Management*, **25** (3), pp 459–73

Scullen, S E, Bergey, P K and Aiman-Smith, L (2005) Forced distribution ratings and the improvement of workforce potential: a baseline simulation, *Personnel Psychology*, **58** (1), pp 1–31

Silverman, M, Kerrin, M and Carter, A (2005) *360-degree Feedback: Beyond the spin*, Brighton, Institute for Employment Studies

Smith, P C and Kendall, L M (1963) Retranslation of expectations: an approach to the construction of unambiguous answers for rating scales, *Journal of Applied Psychology*, **47**, pp 853–85

Strebler, M T, Bevan, S and Robertson, D (2001) *Performance Review: Balancing objectives and content*, Brighton, Institute for Employment Studies

Wherry, R J and Bartlett, C J (1982) The control of bias in ratings: a theory of rating, *Personnel Psychology*, **35** (3), pp 21–51

Coaching

10

Coaching is a personal (usually one-to-one) on-the-job approach to helping people to develop their skills and levels of competence. The need for coaching may arise from formal or informal performance reviews but opportunities for coaching will emerge during normal day-to-day activities. Every time a manager delegates a new task to someone a coaching opportunity is created to help the individual learn any new skills or techniques needed to get the job done. Every time a manager provides feedback to an individual after a task has been completed there is an opportunity to help that individual do better next time. Coaching as part of the normal process of management consists of:

- Making people aware of how well they are performing by, for example, asking them questions to establish the extent to which they have thought through what they are doing.

- Controlled delegation – ensuring that individuals not only know what is expected of them but also understand what they need to know and be able to do to complete the task satisfactorily. This gives managers an opportunity to provide guidance at the outset – guidance at a later stage may be seen as interference.

- Using whatever situations which may arise as opportunities to promote learning.

- Encouraging people to look at higher-level problems and how they would tackle them.

As Lee (2005) explained: 'The coaching model of performance management redefines the relationship between the supervisor and the subordinate. The two work together to help the subordinate perform at his or her very best.' Coaching involves short-term interventions designed to remedy problems that interfere with the employee's performance but it is also concerned with longer-term development and continuous learning.

The process of coaching

As described by the CIPD (2007) coaching is essentially a non-directive form of development. Evered and Selman (1989) defined the following essential characteristics that define good coaching: developing a partnership, commitment to produce a result, responsiveness to people, practice and preparation, a sensitivity to individuals, and a willingness to go beyond what has already been achieved.

Woodruffe (2008) suggested that coaching should aim to:

- amplify an individual's own knowledge and thought processes;
- improve the individual's self-awareness and facilitate the winning of detailed insight into how the individual may be perceived by others;
- create a supportive, helpful, yet demanding, environment in which the individual's crucial thinking skills, ideas and behaviours are challenged and developed.

Approach to coaching

Coaching can provide motivation, structure and effective feedback if managers have the required skills and commitment. When coaching, managers look for the best in people and try to build on their strengths, rather than dwelling on their weaknesses. The aim is to help people to help themselves. Coaching encourages self-directed learning using any resources such as e-learning that are available. It is not a matter of spoon-feeding people.

Coaching may be informal but it needs to be planned. It is not simply checking from time to time on what people are doing and then advising them on how to do it better. Nor is it occasionally telling people where they have gone wrong and throwing in a lecture for good measure. As far as possible, coaching should take place within the framework of a general plan of the areas and direction in which individuals will benefit from further development. Coaching plans should be incorporated into the personal development plans set out in a performance agreement.

Techniques of coaching

Good coaching is about encouraging people to think through issues, getting them to see things differently, enabling them to work out solutions for themselves which they can 'own', and empowering them to do things differently. Hallbom and Warrenton-Smith (2005) recommend the following coaching techniques:

- ask high-impact questions – 'how' and 'what' open-ended questions that spur action rather than 'why' questions that require explanations;
- help people to develop their own answers and action plans;
- identify what people are doing right and then make the most of it rather than just trying to fix problems – coaching is success driven;
- build rapport and trust – make it safe for employees to express their concerns and ideas; get employees to work out answers for themselves – people often resist being *told* what to do, or how to do it.

Coaching skills

A good coach is one who questions and listens. Coaching will be most effective when the coach understands that his or her role is to help people to learn and individuals are motivated to learn. They should be aware that their present level of knowledge or skill or their behaviour needs to be improved if they are going to perform their work to their own and to others' satisfaction. Individuals should be given guidance on what they should be learning and feedback on how they are doing, and, because learning is an active not a passive process, they should be actively involved with their coach who should be constructive, building on strengths and experience.

To do all this good coaches have listening, analytical and interviewing skills and the ability to use questioning techniques, give and receive performance feedback, and create a supportive environment conducive to coaching. The following criteria for evaluating the performance of a coach were listed by Gray (2010):

- establishes rapport;
- creates trust and respect;
- demonstrates effective communication skills;
- promotes self-awareness and self-knowledge;
- uses active listening and questioning techniques;
- assists goal development and setting;

- motivates;
- encourages alternative perspectives;
- assists in making sense of a situation;
- identifies significant patterns of thinking and behaving;
- provides an appropriate mix of challenge and support;
- facilitates depth of understanding;
- shows compassion;
- acts ethically;
- inspires curiosity;
- acts as a role model;
- values diversity and difference;
- promotes action and reflection.

These are demanding requirements and managers need encouragement, guidance, training and, indeed, coaching to meet them.

Developing a coaching culture

Following CIPD research, Clutterbuck and Megginson (2005) described a coaching culture as one where 'coaching is the predominant style of managing and working together and where commitment to improving the organization is embedded in a parallel commitment to improving the people'. A culture of coaching is linked to the basic performance management processes of providing feedback and reinforcement as Lindbom (2007) explained.

A culture of coaching is one in which the regular review of performance and just-in-time feedback is expected. Employees depend on reinforcement when they have done things correctly and understand that a constructive critique of their work when it needs improvement helps them to be more effective. For managers, this culture sets the standard for recognition for jobs well done. The culture of coaching also sets the expectation for feedback – positive or for improvement – that is specific, behavioural and results-based. This type of culture is self-reinforcing as it leads to improved performance, which encourages employees to seek more feedback and managers to see the value of coaching as the key requirement of their job.

In a coaching culture managers believe that people can succeed, that they can contribute to their success and that they can identify what people need to be able to do to improve their performance. They recognize that coaching can provide motivation, structure and effective learning and see performance management as an enabling, empowering process which focuses on learning requirements. Hamlin *et al* (2006) commented that: 'Truly effective managers and managerial leaders are those who embed effective coaching into the heart of their management practice'.

Developing a coaching culture in which managers have the skills and commitment to coach informally as well as on more formal occasions is difficult. It takes time and is a matter of guidance, training, encouragement and the example provided by senior managers and colleagues. As Lindbom (2007) emphasize: 'Coaching must become part of the organization's identity by including it in core competencies and behaviour expectations'. HR or learning and development specialists have an important role. They can act as mentors (or establish a team of mentors) to provide guidance and encouragement.

References

Chartered Institute of Learning and Development (2007) *Coaching Fact Sheet*, London, CIPD

Clutterbuck, D and Megginson, D (2005) *Making Coaching Work*, London, CIPD

Evered, R D and Selman, J C (1989) Coaching and the art of management, *Organizational Dynamics*, **18** (2), 16–32

Gray, D A (2010) Building quality into executive coaching, in J Gold, R Thorpe and A Mumford (eds), *Gower Handbook of Leadership and Management Development*, Farnham, Gower, pp 367–85

Hallbom, T and Warrenton-Smith, A (2005) *Journal of Innovative Management*, Summer, pp 39–48

Hamlin, R G, Ellinger, A D and Beattie, R S (2006) Coaching at the heart of managerial effectiveness: a cross-cultural study of managerial behaviours, *Human Resource Development International*, **9** (3), pp 305–31

Lee, C D (2005) Rethinking the goals of your performance management system, *Employment Relations Today*, **32** (3), pp 53–60

Lindbom, D (2007) A culture of coaching: the challenge of managing performance for long-term results, *Organization Development Journal*, **25** (1), pp 101–06

Woodruffe, C (2008) Could do better? *Must* do better! *British Journal of Administrative Management*, January, pp 14–16

Managing underperformers

11

Performance management is a positive process which involves building on strengths. But it is also about helping people to improve. This may not be a problem – the improvements required might be marginal and easily achieved. Sometimes, however, underperformance is more serious and has to be managed. This chapter starts with an analysis of the problem and then describes ways of dealing with underperformers.

The problem of underperformance

A survey covering 139 organizations with a combined total of 300,000 staff conducted by IRS (Wolff, 2008) found that four-fifths had experienced underperformance to some extent while one in 10 had experienced it to a considerable extent. Only 8 per cent of respondents felt that their efforts to deal with poor performance had been successful and two-thirds of them did not consider that managers at their organization were capable of managing it.

Managers, as Schaffer (1991) pointed out, sometimes use a variety of psychological mechanisms for avoiding the unpleasant truth that performance gaps exist. These mechanisms include:

- *Evasion through rationalization:* Managers may escape having to demand better performance by convincing themselves that they have done all they can to establish expectations.

- *Reliance on procedures:* Management may rely on a variety of procedures, programmes and systems to produce better results. Top managers say, in effect, 'Let there be performance-related pay, or performance management or whatever' and sit back to wait for these panaceas to do the trick, which, of course, they will not unless they are part of a sustained effort led from the top, and are based on a vision of what needs to be done to improve performance.

- *Attacks that skirt the target:* Managers may set tough goals and insist that they are achieved, but still fail to produce a sense of accountability in subordinates.

Dealing with underperformers

Managing underperformers should be a positive process which is based on feedback throughout the year and looks forward to what can be done by individuals to overcome performance problems and, importantly, how managers can provide support and help. Note should be taken of the comment by Charles Handy (1989) that this should be about 'applauding success and forgiving failure'. He suggests that mistakes should be used as an opportunity for learning – 'something only possible if the mistake is *truly* forgiven because otherwise the lesson is heard as a reprimand and not as an offer of help'.

When dealing with poor performers the following comments by Howard Risher (2003) should be remembered:

Poor performance is best seen as a problem in which the employer and management are both accountable. In fact, one can argue that it is unlikely to emerge if people are effectively managed. This is another way of putting the old Army saying: 'There are no bad soldiers, only bad officers'.

Poor performance may be wholly or partly the fault of the system. When looking at underperformance it is necessary to consider systemic as well as individual problems.

General approaches to managing underperformance

In general, respondents to the IRS survey (Woolf, 2008) suggested that the key to solving poor performance is communication, coupled with clarity about expectations and objectives, early intervention and ensuring managers have a clear view of the underlying problem before applying a solution. It is important to ensure that underperforming employees understand and acknowledge there is a problem when it can be attributed to them and accept some responsibility for achieving a solution. Depending on the cause, provision of support through training or coaching and regular contact with the line manager is also important. But by far the most effective measure is to have competent and confident managers who are prepared to tackle the problem. Most respondents to the survey advocated an agreed improvement plan as the first step followed by regular but informal progress reviews.

Specific approaches to managing underperformance

The specific approaches adopted by respondents to the IRS 2008 survey were:

- the manager and employee jointly agree a performance improvement plan with time scales – 81 per cent;
- the manager and the employee agree to more regular, informal performance reviews – 68 per cent;
- a joint agreement on the provision of specific coaching or training – 61 per cent;
- the manager agrees to provide more coaching or guidance – 52 per cent;
- a joint re-evaluation of performance expectations – 52 per cent.

These are all valid ways of managing underperformance but they will be most effective if they are incorporated in a staged procedure as described below which can provide a framework for managers and a basis for guidance and training.

The five basic steps

1 Identify and agree the problem

Analyse the feedback and, as far as possible, obtain agreement from the individual on what the shortfall has been. Feedback may be provided by managers but it can in a sense be built into the job. This takes place when individuals are aware of their targets and standards, know what perform-ance measures will be used and either receive feedback/control information automatically or have easy access to it. They will then be in a position to measure and assess their own performance and, if they are well-motivated and well-trained, take their own corrective actions. In other words, a self-regulating feedback mechanism exists. This is a situation which managers should endeavour to create on the grounds that prevention is better than cure.

2 Establish the reason(s) for the shortfall

When seeking the reasons for any shortfalls the manager should not crudely try to attach blame. The aim should be for the manager and the individual jointly to identify the facts that have contributed to the problem. It is on the basis of this factual analysis that decisions can be made on what to do about it by the individual, the manager or the two of them working together.

It is necessary first to identify any causes which are due to weaknesses in the system or outside the control of either the manager or the individual. Any factors which *are* within the control of the individual and/or the manager can then be considered. What needs to be determined is the extent to which the reason for the problem is because of a fault in the system itself or the way in which the system has been managed. If it is established that the individual is at least partly responsible for the poor performance it can then be agreed whether this is because he or she:

- did not receive adequate support or guidance from his/her manager;
- did not fully understand what he/she was expected to do;
- could not do it – ability;
- did not know how to do it – skill;
- would not do it – attitude.

3 Decide and agree on the action required

Action may be taken by the individual, the manager or both parties. This could include:

- taking steps to improve skills or change behaviour – the individual;
- changing attitudes – this is up to individuals as long as they accept that their attitudes need to be changed; the challenge for managers is

that people will not change their attitudes simply because they are told to do so – they can only be helped to understand that certain changes to their behaviour could be beneficial not only to the organization but also to themselves;

- providing more support or guidance – the manager;
- clarifying expectations – joint;
- developing abilities and skills – joint, in the sense that individuals may be expected to take steps to develop themselves but managers may provide help in the form of coaching, additional experience or training.

Whatever action is agreed both parties must understand how they will know that it has succeeded. Feedback arrangements can be made but individuals should be encouraged to monitor their own performance and take further action as required.

4 *Resource the action*

Provide the coaching, training, guidance, experience or facilities required to enable agreed actions to happen.

5 *Monitor and provide feedback*

Both managers and individuals monitor performance, ensure that feedback is provided or obtained and analysed, and agree on any further actions that may be necessary.

Use of a capability procedure

Every attempt should be made to deal with performance problems as they arise or at least consider them dispassionately at a review meeting. However, further action to deal with underperformers if all else fails may be necessary. But when confronted with such situations many organizations have recognized that to go straight into a disciplinary procedure with its associations with misconduct is not the best way to handle them. They believe it is better to have a special capability procedure for performance issues, leaving the disciplinary procedure as the method used to deal with cases of misconduct. A capability procedure is typically staged as follows:

1 If a manager believes that an employee's performance is not up to standard an informal discussion is held with the employee to establish the reason and to agree the actions required to improve performance by the employee and/or the manager.

2 Should the employee show insufficient improvement over a defined period a formal interview will be arranged with the employee (together with a representative if so desired). The aims of this interview will be to (a) explain the shortfall between the employee's performance and the required standard, (b) identify the cause(s) of the unsatisfactory performance and determine what – if any – remedial treatment (eg training, retraining, support, etc) can be given, (c) set a reasonable period for the employee to reach the standard and (d) agree on a monitoring system during that period and tell the employee what will happen if that standard is not met.

3 At the end of the review period a further formal interview will be held, at which time if the required improvement has been made (a) the employee will be told of this and encouraged to maintain the improvement, (b) if some improvement has been made but the standard has not yet been met, the review period will be extended, (c) if there has been no discernible improvement and performance is still well below an acceptable standard consideration will be given to whether there are alternative vacancies which the employee would be competent to fill; if there are, the employee will be given the option of accepting such a vacancy or being considered for dismissal, and (d) in the absence of suitable alternative work, an employee who is clearly below an acceptable standard is liable to be dismissed.

4 Employees may appeal against their dismissal.

Although capability action can be used as a means of overcoming performance problems it should be treated as a separate procedure which is not regarded as part of the normal processes of performance management. These processes should help to identify performance problems which they will deal with on the spot, if at all possible. Only if this fails are these problems transferred to the capability system for resolution.

This separation of performance management processes and capability procedures is important because of the serious harm that would be done to the positive performance improvement and developmental aspects of performance management if employees felt that the process was simply being used to collect evidence for use in taking disciplinary action. Performance reviews can become threatening affairs if they are perceived as placing sticks in the hands of management with which they can beat employees.

If the problem has to be transferred to the capability procedure it is highly desirable to state what the problem is in full, with any supporting evidence which is available. Reference can be made to the fact that the problem was identified earlier as part of the continuing process of performance management but the content of any performance review form produced following a review meeting should not be used as evidence. The capability warning must be complete in itself.

In practice this may not cause much difficulty as long as the manager follows the guidelines for managing performance throughout the year as described in Chapter 1. These suggest that immediate action is taken to deal with performance problems – they should not be saved up to be discussed at a formal review meeting some time after the event. Raising problems immediately means that they are dealt with as a normal management process, and the capability procedure should only be resorted to when this process fails in spite of every effort to make it succeed.

References

Handy, C (1989) *The Age of Unreason*, London, Business Books

Risher, H (2005) Getting serious about performance management, *Compensation & Benefits Review*, November/December, pp 18–26

Schaffer, R H (1991) Demand better results and get them, *Harvard Business Review*, March–April, pp 212–19

Wolff, C (2008) Managing employee performance, *IRS Employment Review*, 890, 4 February, pp 1–12

PART THREE
Applications of performance management

Managing organizational performance

The management of organizational performance is the continuing responsibility of top management who plan, organize, monitor and control activities and provide leadership to achieve strategic objectives and satisfy the needs and requirements of stakeholders. Individual and team performance management systems as discussed elsewhere in this book play an important part. But they function within the context of what is done to manage organizational performance and to develop effective work systems.

Managing organizational performance is a complex business which is examined in this chapter under the following headings:

- The process of managing organizational performance
- The strategic approach to managing organizational performance
- Business performance management systems
- Increasing organizational capability
- Performance management and human capital management
- Developing a high-performance culture
- Measuring performance

The process of managing organizational performance

As Gheorghe and Hack (2007) observed: 'Actively managing performance is simply running a business – running the entire business as one entity. It's a continuous cycle of planning, executing, measuring results and planning the next actions. In the context of a larger strategic initiative, that means continuous improvement'. They noted that:

> The fundamental problem managers face as they make day-to-day decisions is an inability to link their actions to key performance measures. What managers need is more enterprise intelligence, actionable information that enables them to know where their problems are, in real time, know who their key performers are without combing through a stack of reports, know where their company is at risk, before the numbers turn bad, and, most of all, know which process could improve performance.

The management of organizational performance takes place on a number of dimensions. It is a strategic approach which has to take account of the needs of multiple stakeholders and makes use of business performance management systems.

The dimensions of managing organizational performance

Sink and Tuttle (1990) stated that managing organizational performance includes five dimensions:

1 Creating visions for the future.

2 Planning – determining the present organizational state, and developing strategies to improve that state.

3 Designing, developing and implementing improvement interventions.

4 Designing, redesigning, developing, and implementing measurement and evaluation systems.

5 Putting cultural support systems in place to reward and reinforce progress.

The overall approach to managing organizational performance

The management of organizational performance as described in the rest of this chapter is based on processes of strategic performance management supported by the use of a business performance management system. In general it is concerned with developing organizational capability which means creating a high-performance culture, human capital management and talent management.

In particular it makes use of various approaches to measuring and monitoring performance.

The strategic approach to managing organizational performance

A strategic approach to managing organizational performance takes a broad and long-term view of where the business is going and manages performance in ways which ensure that this strategic thrust is maintained. The objective is to provide a sense of direction in an often turbulent environment so that the business needs of the organization and the individual and collective needs of its employees can be met by the development and implementation of integrated systems for managing and developing performance.

Organizational performance management systems are strategic in the sense that they are aligned to the business strategy of the organization and support the achievement of its strategic goals. They focus on developing work systems and the working environment as well as developing individuals. To create the systems and make them function effectively it is necessary to ensure that the strategy is understood, including, as Kaplan and Norton (2000) put it: 'The crucial but perplexing processes by which intangible assets will be converted into tangible outcomes'. The notion of mapping strategy was originated by them as a development of their concept of the balanced scorecard (see later in this chapter). Strategy maps show the cause-and-effect links through which specific improvements create desired outcomes. They describe the elements of the organization's systems and their interrelationships and therefore provide a route map for systems improvement leading to performance improvement. In addition, they give employees a clear line of sight into how their jobs are linked to the overall goals of the organization and provide a visual representation of a company's critical goals and the relationships between them that drive organizational performance. Bourne *et al* (2003) call them 'success maps' which act as diagrams which show the logic of how the goals of the organization interact to deliver overall performance. An example of a strategy map is given in Figure 12.1.

This map shows an overall objective to improve profitability as measured by return on capital employed. In the next line the map indicates that the main contributors to increased profitability are increases to the gross margin

FIGURE 12.1 A strategy map

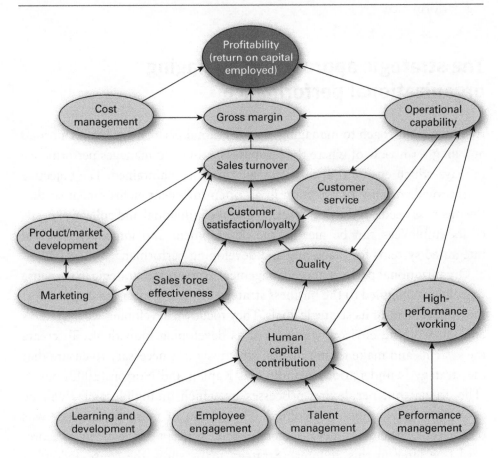

(the difference between the value of sales and the cost of sales), improvements to operational capability and better cost management. At the next level down the objective is to increase sales turnover in order to increase the gross margin. How this is to be achieved is set out in the next group of goals and their interconnections comprising increases in customer satisfaction and sales force effectiveness, innovations in product/market development and marketing, and improvements in customer service and quality levels. The key objective of improving operational capability is underpinned by developments in high-performance working and the contribution of the organization's human capital. The latter is supported by human resource management goals in the fields of performance management, talent management, employee engagement and learning and development.

The overall objective of increasing profitability in this example addresses the concerns of only one section of the stakeholders of an organization, ie the investors. This need would probably be given precedence by many quoted companies. But there are other goals which relate to their other stakeholders, for example those related to corporate social responsibility. These could be catered for in separate strategy maps. Better still, they could be linked to their commercial goals. Public and voluntary sector organizations will certainly have goals which relate to all their stakeholders as well as their overall purpose. A stakeholder approach to strategic performance management is required.

Performance management strategy is based on the resource-based view that it is the strategic development of the organization's rare, hard to imitate and hard to substitute human resources which produces its unique character and creates competitive advantage. The strategic goal will be to 'create firms which are more intelligent and flexible than their competitors' (Boxall, 1996) by developing more talented staff and by extending their skills base, and this is exactly what performance management aims to do.

Armstrong and Ward (2005) summed up the strategic role of performance management:

> There is also opportunity for performance management to help drive through organizational change. Instead of being a tactical initiative, perhaps performance management has a more strategic role to play. The challenge is for performance management to retain a strategic role rather than tending towards tactical activities, such as the process. Performance management can provide a new way of looking at performance and help to embed new behaviours and facilitate the move to a culture that is both more open and more focused on the achievement of new outputs.

The strategic approach adopted by Johnson & Johnson was described by Wortzel-Hoffman and Boltizar (2007) as follows:

> As we embarked on developing an integrated performance and development process into the organization, we knew that driving change and an enhanced process requires a cultural shift within an organization. The best performance management becomes a continuous process and is not a one time event; it takes time and effort and a dedication to developing people. We also knew that from a business standpoint it was critical to build and develop the talent pipeline of the organization to meet the aggressive business goals and dynamically changing marketplace.

Implementing strategic organizational performance management

Strategic organizational performance management starts with a definition of the areas of activity and achievement which are most important to the organization. These are its critical success factors. They can include:

- Financial (profitability, shareholder value, cost control etc)
- Market share
- Sales
- Productivity
- Quality
- Customer service
- Innovation
- People management
- Corporate social responsibility.

Strategic goals can be set in each of these areas to which individual goals can be aligned as described in Chapter 5. Alignment is a key aspect of performance management.

The stakeholder approach to strategic organizational performance management

Atkinson *et al* (1997) argued that a company exists to serve the goals of its multiple stakeholders – employees, customers, suppliers, regulators and the community at large as well as shareholders. Companies must provide for explicit or implicit contracts with its stakeholders. Performance management systems should guide the design and implementation of processes which satisfy the requirements of each stakeholder group and monitor and evaluate the extent to which the organization is meeting these needs.

The performance prism

A multiple stakeholder framework for performance management – the performance prism – was formulated by Neely *et al* (2002). This is based on the proposition that organizations exist to satisfy their stakeholders and their wants and needs should be considered first. Neely *et al* contended that companies in particular must assume a broader role than simply delivering value to their shareholders. To be successful over time, even for and on behalf of shareholders, businesses must address multiple stakeholders. If companies do not give each of their stakeholders the right level of focus, both their corporate reputation and their market capitalization – and therefore shareholder value – are likely to suffer in one way or another. The performance prism can facilitate or structure the analysis of multiple stakeholders in preparation for applying performance measurement criteria.

They explained the term 'performance prism' as follows:

> A prism refracts light. It illustrates the hidden complexity of something as apparently simple as white light. So it is with the performance prism. It illustrates the true complexity of performance measurement and management. It is a thinking aid which seeks to integrate five related perspectives and provide a structure that allows executives to think through the answers to five fundamental questions:
>
> **1** *Stakeholder Satisfaction:* Who are our stakeholders and what do they want and need?
>
> **2** *Stakeholder Contribution:* What do we want and need from our stakeholders?
>
> **3** *Strategies:* What strategies do we need to put in place to satisfy these wants and needs?
>
> **4** *Processes:* What processes do we need to put in place to satisfy these wants and needs?
>
> **5** *Capabilities:* What capabilities – people, practices, technology and infrastructure – do we need to put in place to allow us to operate our processes more effectively and efficiently?

Moullin (2002) described how in a charity the performance prism was used to develop a 'success map', which showed the main needs of the various stakeholders. Performance measurements were then developed for each group of them followed by an integrative strategy.

Business performance management systems

A business performance management system can be used to support the achievement of the performance management strategy. It is an information technology (IT) based approach to organizational performance management described by Frolick and Ariyachandra (2006) as a series of business processes and applications designed to optimize both the development and the execution of business strategy. There are two primary tasks. First, to facilitate the creation of strategic goals and second, to support the subsequent management of the performance required to reach those goals. Strategic goals are developed by stipulating specific goals and key performance indicators that are meaningful to the organization. The goals and indicators are then associated with operational metrics (ie measurements) for planning, monitoring and control purposes which are linked to the business strategy. The system is concerned with the entire enterprise in contrast to other IT applications which focus on specific operational areas such as customer relations.

The performance management framework consists of four core activities as shown in Figure 12.2. The first two steps represent the formulation of business strategy while the last two steps define how to modify and execute strategy. This closed loop process captures business strategy and then translates it into strategically aligned business operations.

A business performance management system as provided by suppliers such as Oracle is based on a common database which allows every department of a business to store and retrieve information in real-time. The information has

FIGURE 12.2   The business performance planning cycle

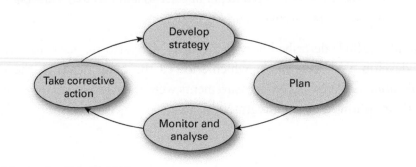

SOURCE: Ariyachandra and Frolick, 2008

to be reliable, accessible, and easily shared. A modular approach means that businesses can select the software modules they need from the vendor and add new modules of their own.

Transactional systems such as enterprise resource planning (a company-wide information system designed to coordinate all the resources, information, and activities needed to complete business processes such as order fulfilment or billing), customer relationship management (CRM), supply chain management (SCM), and human capital management (HCM) help to run day-to-day business operations. Business performance management systems integrate these systems and enable executives to manage the business strategically by providing information across all functions. This is aligned to strategic imperatives by answering three basic questions: (1) Where have we been? (2) Where are we now? (3) Where are we going? and providing the basis for answering the fourth key question: (4) How do we get there?

Pritchard (2008) pointed out that any enterprise-wide business performance management improvement initiative must include managers and employees from across the organization. All functions have to operate in unison. And if the company doesn't integrate financial and non-financial data, there is only so much that a business performance management tool can do to help decision-makers understand the results.

Organizational capability

Organizational capability is the capacity of an organization to function effectively. It is about the ability of an organization to guarantee high levels of performance, achieve its purpose (sustained competitive advantage in a commercial business), deliver results and, importantly, meet the needs of its stakeholders. The development of organizational capability is concerned with the organization as a system and is in line with the belief expressed by Coens and Jenkins (2002) that to 'focus on the overall "system" of the organization yields better results than trying to get individual employees to improve their performance'.

The aim is to increase organizational effectiveness by obtaining better performance from people, getting them to work well together, improving organizational processes such as the formulation and implementation of strategy and the achievement of high quality levels of customer service, and facilitating the management of change.

This has to take place in a context in which organizations are increasingly embracing a new management culture based on inclusion, involvement and participation, rather than on the traditional command, control and compliance paradigm which Flaherty (1999) claimed 'cannot bring about the conditions and competence necessary to successfully meet the challenges of endless innovation; relentless downsizing, re-engineering, and multicultural working holistically'. This new management paradigm requires the development of a high-performance work environment through management practices that value and support achievement, growth and learning. It also calls for facilitative behaviours that focus on employee empowerment, learning and development. In other words, it needs performance management.

Organizational capability and organizational development

As described by Beer (1980), organizational development is 'a system wide process of data collection, diagnosis, action planning, intervention and evaluation'. Traditionally, organization development or OD was based on behavioural science concepts, but the focus has shifted to a number of other approaches such as human capital management, talent management, change management, high-performance work systems, total quality management and, importantly performance management. Cummins and Worley (2005) noted that the practice of OD has gone 'far beyond its humanistic origins by incorporating concepts from organization strategy that complement the early emphasis on social processes'. Organizational capability could be regarded as an outcome of organizational development but with the focus more on performance management.

Performance management and human capital management

Human capital management (HCM) is concerned with obtaining, analysing and reporting on data which informs the direction of people management strategies. Performance management data is an important source of information on human capital and its contribution to business. Lawler and McDermott (2003) observed that:

It is very difficult to effectively manage human capital without a system that measures performance and performance capability... An effective performance management system should be a key building block of every organization's human capital management system.

Given the growing recognition of human capital as a source of organizational value (ie the resource-based view) and the pressure therefore on organizations to collect, analyse and report on their human capital, performance management data is likely to become a key source of information both on the value of human capital and on the management activity needed to manage and deploy this asset.

Performance management data can be used to:

- demonstrate an organization's ability to raise competence levels;
- assess how long it takes for a new employee to reach optimum performance;
- provide feedback on development programmes including induction, coaching and mentoring in terms of increased performance or capacity to take on new roles;
- demonstrate the success of internal recruitment programmes;
- indicate how successful an organization is at achieving its goals both at the individual, team and department level;
- track skills levels and movement in any skills gap in the organization;
- match actual behaviour against desired behaviour;
- assess commitment to values and mission;
- assess understanding of strategy and contribution.

Developing a high-performance culture

Organizations achieve sustained high performance through the systems of work they adopt but these systems are managed and operated by people. Ultimately, therefore, high-performance working is about improving performance through people. This can be done by the development and implementation of a high-performance culture through high-performance work systems in which performance management plays an important part.

High-performance cultures

High-performance cultures are ones in which the achievement of high levels of performance is a way of life. The characteristics of such cultures are:

- Management defines what it requires in the shape of performance improvements, sets goals for success and monitors performance to ensure that the goals are achieved.

- Alternative work practices are adopted such as job redesign, autonomous work teams, improvement groups, team briefing and flexible working.

- People know what's expected of them – they understand their goals and accountabilities.

- People feel that their job is worth doing, and there is a strong fit between the job and their capabilities.

- People are empowered to maximize their contribution.

- There is strong leadership from the top which engenders a shared belief in the importance of continuing improvement.

- There is a focus on promoting positive attitudes that result in an engaged, committed and motivated workforce.

- Performance management processes are aligned to business goals to ensure that people are engaged in achieving agreed goals and standards.

- Capacities of people are developed through learning at all levels to support performance improvement and are provided with opportunities to make full use of their skills and abilities.

- A pool of talent ensures a continuous supply of high performers in key roles.

- People are valued and rewarded according to their contribution.

- People are involved in developing high performance practices.

- There is a climate of trust and teamwork, aimed at delivering a distinctive service to the customer.

- A clear line of sight exists between the strategic aims of the organization and those of its departments and its staff at all levels.

High-performance work systems

High-performance cultures can be developed through a high-performance work system (HPWS) which is described by Becker and Huselid (1998) as: 'An internally consistent and coherent HRM system that is focused on solving operational problems and implementing the firm's competitive strategy'. They suggested that such a system 'is the key to the acquisition, motivation and development of the underlying intellectual assets that can be a source of sustained competitive advantage'. This is because it has the following characteristics:

- It links the firm's selection and promotion decisions to validated competency models.

- It is the basis for developing strategies that provide timely and effective support for the skills demanded to implant the firm's strategies.

- It enacts compensation and performance management policies that attract, retain and motivate high-performance employees.

High-performance work systems embody ways of thinking about performance in organizations and how it can be improved. They are concerned with developing and implementing bundles of complementary practices which as an integrated whole will make a much more powerful impact on performance than if they were dealt with as separate entities.

The basic features of a HPWS were described by Shih *et al* (2005) as follows:

- *Job infrastructure* – workplace arrangements that equip workers with the proper abilities to do their jobs, provide them with the means to do their jobs, and give them the motivation to do their jobs. These practices must be combined to produce their proper effects.

- *Training programmes to enhance employee skills* – investment in increasing employee skills, knowledge and ability.

- *Information sharing and worker involvement mechanisms* – to understand the available alternatives and make correct decisions.

- *Compensation and promotion opportunities that provide motivation* – to encourage skilled employees to engage in effective discretionary decision-making in a variety of environmental contingencies.

The contribution of performance management

Performance management contributes to the development of a high-performance culture by delivering the message in an organization that high performance is important. It defines high performance at an organizational level and at an individual level and links the two by describing how individuals can contribute to their organization's results. It explains how performance should be measured and the steps that should be taken to monitor results in comparison with expectations. The means of getting high performance are provided by motivating people, defining the performance expectations implicit in the psychological contract, creating high levels of engagement and enhancing skills and competencies through feedback, coaching and personal development planning.

Measuring performance

Managing organizational performance means measuring and monitoring performance by the use of measures or metrics. The significance of measurement and the principles governing its use are discussed below. As also covered in this section, there is a choice of measures and these can be expressed and categorized as key performance indicators (KPIs), scorecards, or the balanced scorecard. They can be communicated by means of dashboards.

The significance of measurement

As was emphasized by the Association for Management Information in Financial Services (AMIF, 2005):

> Objectives, which may vary from organization to organization, are met by the choices management makes in deploying its resources. Management's ability to make informed decisions is tied to the quality of management information available to them... In order to determine 'good' performance versus 'bad' performance it is necessary to have a well-defined base against which to compare actual results. This includes defining in advance the expectation as to acceptable performance.

The approach to measurement

The four principles governing the use of performance measures as defined by Quinn (2003):

1 *Measure the right things* – the system must measure activities that directly contribute to an organization's performance.

2 *Clearly communicate what will be measured* – measures that are ill defined, and/or not communicated will not be used or understood.

3 *Consistently apply the measures* – measures should be applied consistently to all units of the organization; failure to do so will result in loss of support for the system.

4 *Act on the measures* – the measurement data must be used in a constructive way. Not using the data or misapplying the data will have the same results – a lack of support for the measurement system.

Neely *et al* (2002) counselled that it is necessary to question constantly what is measured by answering two fundamental questions: Do we need it? Why do we need it? They comment that:

> We need to evaluate constantly whether or not the measures we have are the right ones for the organization. And if not, we need to find a way to get rid of them so that we do not waste time and effort capturing data that no one is using. In short, we need to practice 'metricide' (ie do not let any metric or measure persist beyond its natural and useful life).

At BP Lubricants as reported by Elliott and Coley-Smith (2005) the principles followed in developing their performance measurement system were:

- To focus the business on areas of strategic importance.
- To make sure employees have the right information, at the right time to make the right decisions in support of strategy.
- To clearly understand the value-to-cost relationship of communication activities.
- To develop a measurement mindset that focuses people on improving performance.

But a word of caution is necessary about the concept of managing by metrics. Figures can conceal more than they reveal and it is possible for people to hide behind them. Data can be misleading. It is not enough just to tick boxes. Metrics may be a start but they cannot be relied on by themselves. If there is a problem the story behind the figures needs to be investigated, especially when the failure is systemic.

Types of measures

Traditionally, organizational performance measurement systems were uni-dimensional – focused entirely on financial measures related to shareholder value such as return on capital employed, economic value added, earnings per share and price/earnings ratio and added value. But such traditional accounting-based performance measurement systems are insufficient in modern organizations where it is recognized that relationships with em-ployees, customers, suppliers and other stakeholders are crucial aspects of how the organization is performing. Financial measures cannot evaluate important factors such as innovation, employee engagement, employee relations and levels of customer and employee satisfaction. These factors are sometimes called leading indicators (Gjerde and Hughes, 2007) because they inform management of the progress made on initiatives undertaken to improve performance. Measures of financial performance are lagging indicators because they reflect past results. Achieving an objective related to a lead measure indicates that performance is on track, and achieving an objective related to a lag measure shows that the goal has been accomplished. To identify lead measures it is necessary to establish what are the key factors that drive performance – the key performance indicators (KPIs) which form the basis of the performance monitoring and measurement system.

Jack Welch, former CEO of the General Electric Company, as quoted by Krames (2004) said that the three most important things you need to measure in a business are customer satisfaction, employee satisfaction and cash flow. Sink and Tuttle (1990) listed seven measurement categories of organ-izational performance: (1) effectiveness, (2) efficiency, (3) quality, (4) quality of working life, (5) innovation, (6) cost and prices, and (7) productivity.

The European Foundation for Quality Management EFQM model has the following elements:

- *Leadership* – how the behaviour and actions of the executive team and all other leaders inspire, support and promote a culture of total quality management.

- *Policy and strategy* – how the organization formulates, deploys and reviews its policy and strategy and turns it into plans and actions.

- *People management* – how the organization realizes the full potential of its people.

- *Resources* – how the organization manages resources effectively and efficiently.

- *Processes* – how the organization identifies, manages, reviews and improves its processes.

- *Customer satisfaction* – what the organization is achieving in relation to the satisfaction of its external customers.

- *People satisfaction* – what the organization is achieving in relation to the satisfaction of its people.

- *Impact on society* – what the organization is achieving in satisfying the needs and the expectations of the local, national and international community at large.

- *Business results* – what the organization is achieving in relation to its planned business goals and in satisfying the needs and expectations of everyone with a financial interest or stake in the organization.

Key performance indicators

Key performance indicators (KPIs) are the results or outcomes which are identified as being crucial to the achievement of high performance and provide the basis for setting goals and measuring performance. As noted in Chapter 5 they are important when measuring individual performance and they are just as important at the organizational level. They must take account of the requirements of all stakeholders and should add social responsibility to the list of business goals by including discretionary environmental initiatives, diversity and employee well-being in the set of KPIs.

An organizational KPI is a special kind of metric. It measures something that is strategically important to the organization such as sales per square metre, added value per employee, rate of stock turnover, cost per unit of output, time to market, and levels of employee engagement. In other words, as Schiff (2008) put it: 'A KPI is a metric that matters. You can have many metrics, but an organization needs only a handful of KPIs. Everything can't be considered "key," or nothing will stand out from the pack and get the attention it deserves'. The range of KPIs in different organizations is typically between six and twelve.

KPIs provide the basis for defining the crucial goals for which individuals are accountable. The measurement system has to ensure that performance in relation to the KPIs is recorded and analysed and that this information is passed on to accountable managers for action. Thus they facilitate the alignment of organizational and business goals.

Scorecards

Scorecards record performance related to a set of KPIs. In effect, they are report cards on the organization's performance. For example, they can show sales per square metre in a store, comparing actuals with targets and analysing trends. Dagan (2007) emphasized that: 'You should also not get carried away with trying to jam too many KPIs into your scorecard displays. Although the optimal number depends on your organization, a rule of thumb is that six to ten KPIs are sufficient in most cases'. It should be possible to drill down into supporting tabular and graphical data to investigate any issues raised by the scorecard.

The balanced scorecard

Traditionally, scorecards tended to concentrate on financial measures. Kaplan and Norton (1992, 1996) devised the balanced scorecard as a means of ensuring that businesses used both financial and operational measures thus achieving a more balanced view of their performance. They explained that the balanced scorecard approach 'puts strategy and vision, not control at the centre'. As described in Chapter 5 (Figure 5.3) it requires managers to look at the business from the four related perspectives of customers, innovation and learning, internal performance requirements and finance. Some organizations have replaced the innovation and learning perspective with a broader people or human capital element.

Schneiderman (1999) recommended that balanced scorecards work best when good metrics are available. They should be clearly defined and easy to understand, accessible when needed to those who can best use them and linked to an underlying data system which enables the root causes of poor scorecard results to be identified and dealt with.

Dashboards

A dashboard is a graphical display, designed to convey key performance measures on an organization's intranet system to a wide audience so that they can be assimilated and acted upon easily and swiftly. Dover (2004) commented that: 'Dashboards are predominantly a data-delivery vehicle. Dashboards use dials, "traffic light" displays and graphs to make perform-ance information available as and when required.' An example of a basic dashboard with just three dials is illustrated in Figure 12.3.

FIGURE 12.3   Example of a dashboard

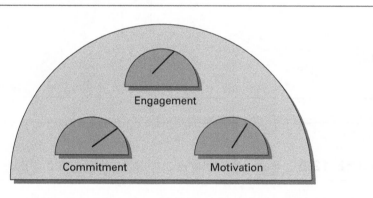

As described by Dagan (2007) dashboards provide a rapid and convenient way for people to assess how they are doing by reference to the business metrics critical to their place in the organization. They can thus initiate prompt corrective action as needed. Dashboards can be constructed using real-time or near real-time feeds from a data warehouse frontline system. Dashboard displays can be enhanced with charts, graphs, or even tabular data. However, it is important not to make the entry screen too busy because this might divert attention away from the important metrics. An alternative is to provide facilities for obtaining supporting information. For example, if a traffic light system shows a KPI that is red or yellow, then a click of the mouse should enable the user to drill down to pinpoint some of the under-lying causes. Drill down could be available to several layers with each layer providing even more details. Examples of a more elaborate dashboard which incorporates a traffic light system and one based on entirely on traffic lights are given in Figures 12.4 and 12.5 respectively.

FIGURE 12.4   Example of a dashboard with (1) dials, (2) traffic lights, (3 and 4) graphs

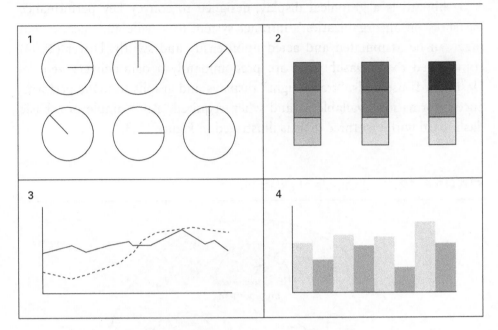

FIGURE 12.5   Human capital reporting 'traffic light' dashboard

Area	Key drivers of committed employees					Outcomes	
	Pay	Length of service	Coaching	Resource management	Values	Retention	Customer commitment
1	⬤	⬤	⬤	⬤	⬤	⬤	⬤
2	⬤	⬤	⬤	⬤	⬤	⬤	⬤
3	⬤	⬤	⬤	⬤	⬤	⬤	⬤
4	⬤	⬤	⬤	⬤	⬤	⬤	⬤

○ Green   ● Amber   ● Red

Developing measures

Each of the approaches to performance management based on measurement described above – scorecards, balanced scorecards and dashboards – depend on the quality of the measures used. The following steps should be taken when developing them:

1 Involve as many as possible of those concerned in the development programme.

2 Identify the key factors that drive performance.

3 Define the key performance indicators (KPIs).

4 Define what metrics are required, ie what should be measured and why, in order to provide information on performance related to each KPI.

5 Decide how to measure – how information related to the measures and performance with regard to each KPI should be collected and presented.

6 Set up a system for communicating information on performance through such media as scorecards or dashboards.

References

AMIF (2005) Basic tenets of performance management in financial institutions, *Journal of Performance Management*, **18** (3), pp 17–21

Armstrong, K and Ward, A (2005) *What Makes for Effective Performance Management?* London, The Work Foundation

Atkinson, A A, Waterhouse, J H and Wells, R B (1997) A stakeholder approach to strategic performance measurement, *Sloan Management Review*, **38** (3), pp 25–37

Becker, B E and Huselid, M A (1998) High performance work systems and firm performance: a synthesis of research and managerial implications, *Research on Personnel and Human Resource Management*, **16**, pp 53–101

Beer, M (1980) *Organization Change and Development: A systems view*, Santa Monica CA, Goodyear

Bourne, M, Franco, M and Wilkes, J (2003) Corporate performance management, *Measuring Business Excellence*, **7** (3), pp 15–21

Boxall, P F (1996) The strategic HRM debate and the resource-based view of the firm, *Human Resource Management Journal*, **6** (3), pp 59–75

Coens, T and Jenkins, M (2002) *Abolishing Performance Appraisals: Why they backfire and what to do instead*, San Francisco CA, Berrett-Koehler

Cummins, T G and Worley, C G (2005) *Organization Development and Change*, Mason OH, South Western

Dagan, B (2007) Dashboards and scorecards aid in performance management and monitoring, *Natural Gas & Electricity*, September, pp 23–27

Dover, C (2004) Dashboards can change your culture, *Strategic Finance*, October, pp 42–48

European Foundation for Quality Management http://www.efqm.org/. Accessed 24 February 2014

Elliott, S and Coley-Smith, H (2005) Building a new performance management model at BP, *SCM*, August/September, pp 4–8

Frolick, M and Ariyachandra, T R (2006) Business performance management: one truth, *Information Systems Management*, **23** (1), pp 41–48

Gheorghe, C and Hack, J (2007) Unified performance management: how one company can tame its many processes, *Business Performance Management*, November, pp 17–19

Gjerde, K A and Hughes, S B (2007) Tracking performance: when less is more, *Management Accounting Quarterly*, **9** (1), pp 1–12

Kaplan, R S and Norton, D P (1992) The balanced scorecard – measures that drive performance, *Harvard Business Review*, January–February, pp 71–79

Kaplan, R S and Norton, D P (1996) Using the balanced scorecard as a strategic management system, *Harvard Business Review*, January–February, pp 75–85

Kaplan, R S and Norton, D P (2000) Having trouble with your strategy? Then map it, *Harvard Business Review*, September–October, pp 167–76

Krames, J A (2004) *The Welch Way*, New York, McGraw-Hill

Lawler, E E and McDermott, M (2003) Current performance management practices, *WordatWork Journal*, Second Quarter, pp 49–60

Moullin, M (2002) *Delivering Excellence in Health and Social Care*, Buckingham, Open University Press

Neely, A, Adams, C and Kennerley, M (2002) *The Performance Prism: The Scorecard for measuring and managing business success*, Harlow, Pearson Education

Pritchard, A (2008) The new BPM: enterprise performance management, *Business Performance Management*, March, pp 28–30

Quinn, F J (2003) Measurement – the right way, *Logistics Management*, **42** (3), p 9

Schiff, C (2008) Three things you should know about dashboards, *DM Review*, June, p 29

Schneiderman, A M (1999) Why balanced score cards fail, *Journal of Strategic Performance Measurement*, January, pp 6–10

Shih, H-A, Chiang, Y-H and Hsu, C-C (2005) Can high performance work systems really lead to better performance? *Academy of Management Conference Paper*, pp 1–6

Sink, D S and Tuttle, T C (1990) The performance management question in the organization of the future, *Industrial Management*, **32** (1), pp 4–12

Wortzel-Hoffman, N and Boltizar, S (2007) Performance and development planning: a culture shift perspective, *Organization Development Journal*, **25** (2), pp 195–200

Managing team performance

13

It is remarkable how little has been researched or written about performance management for teams. This is in spite of the emphasis on good team work and high performance teams which, as described by Katzenbach and Smith (1993): 'Invest much time and effort explaining, shaping and agreeing on a purpose that belongs to them, both collectively and individually. They are characterised by a deep sense of commitment to their growth and success.'

One of the frequently voiced criticisms of individual performance management is that it inhibits good teamwork. But the possibility of extending it to teams does not seem to have occurred to many commentators.

Teams and performance

As Purcell *et al* (1998) observed, teams are the 'elusive bridge between the aims of the individual employee and the objectives of the organisation ... teams can provide the medium for linking employee performance targets to the factors critical to the success of the business'. How well this is done depends on the following factors that affect team performance:

- the clarity of the team's goals in terms of expectations and priorities;
- how work is allocated to the team;
- how the team is working (its processes) in terms of cohesion, ability to handle internal conflict and pressure, relationships with other teams;
- the extent to which the team is capable of managing itself – setting goals and priorities, monitoring performance;
- the quality of leadership – even self-managed teams need a sense of direction which they cannot necessarily generate by themselves;

- the level of skill possessed by individual team members (including multi-skilling);
- the systems and resources support available to the team.

Overall, as suggested by Jones (1995): 'Teams need to have a shared purpose. They also need to have the necessary mix of skills and abilities and to be mutually accountable for the outcome.' Bunderson and Sutcliffe (2003) made the point that team goal orientation captures the 'shared understanding of the extent to which a team emphasizes learning or performance goals, and, consequently, helps to facilitate group decision-making, collaborative problem solving, and intragroup coordination that maintain the group's emphasis on learning or performance goals'. Research by Yaping et al (2013) revealed evidence 'that a team learning goal and team performance approach goal are positively related to team creativity and individual creativity'.

Team competencies

The following is a selection of some of the key competencies for team members as developed by Hay/McBer (Gross, 1995):

- *Interpersonal understanding* – accurate interpretation of others' concerns, motives and feelings and recognition of their strengths and weaknesses.
- *Influence* – using appropriate interpersonal styles and logical arguments to convince others to accept ideas or pleas.
- *Customer service orientation* – demonstrating concern for meeting the needs of internal and external customers.
- *Adaptability* – adapting easily to change.
- *Teamwork and co-operation* – developing collaborative work which generates acceptable solutions.
- *Oral communication* – expressing ideas in group situations.
- *Achievement orientation* – setting and meeting challenging objectives.
- *Organizational commitment* – performing work with broader organizational goals in mind.

Performance measures for teams

Performance measures for teams will be related to the purpose of the team and its particular objectives and standards of performance. The following are some examples of how performance measures are established and used by various organizations:

- *Automobile Association Finance Division* – in the processing department, where high volume and routine tasks have to be performed, the measures are productivity and quality.
- *The Benefits Agency* – measures are agreed between managers and team members based on task definition, performance standards and time scales.
- *Dartford Borough Council* – measures are related to targets which are set for tasks that are suitable for all or most of the team to undertake together and are distinct from the tasks set for individual team members.
- *IBM* – 'bid teams' (project teams responsible for developing solutions for customers) have their performance measured by reference to their success in winning contracts.
- *Lloyds Bank* – the performance of branch teams below junior management level is related to two challenges: the 'sales challenge', which is linked to branch sales against target, and the 'service challenge' which is based on data obtained from customer questionnaires and mystery shopping.
- *Rank Xerox* – the performance measures or 'metrics' for sales teams are based on customer satisfaction, sales revenue and market share.

These measures are mainly concerned with output, activity levels (eg speed of servicing), customer service and satisfaction, and financial results.

Type of measures

A distinction was made by Harrington-Mackin (1994) between output/result measures of team performance and input/process measures.

The output/results comprise:

- the achievement of team goals;
- customer satisfaction;
- quantity of work;
- quality of work;
- process knowledge;
- maintenance of technical systems.

The input/process measures comprise:

- support of team process;
- participation;
- collaboration and collective effort;
- participative decision-making;
- interpersonal relations;
- acceptance of change;
- adaptability and flexibility.

Team performance management processes

Team performance management activities follow the same sequence as for individual performance management:

- agree goals;
- formulate plans to achieve goals;
- implement plans;
- monitor progress;
- review and assess achievement;
- redefine goals and plans in the light of the review.

The aim should be to give teams with their team leaders the maximum amount of responsibility to carry out all activities. The focus should be on self-management and self-direction.

The processes of setting performance goals and process objectives and conducting team and individual reviews are described below.

Setting performance goals

Performance goals for teams are set in much the same way as individual goals (see Chapter 5). They will be based on an analysis of the purpose of the team and its accountabilities for achieving results. Targets and standards of performance should be discussed and agreed by the team as a whole. These may specify what individual members are expected to contribute. Project teams will agree project plans which define what has to be done, who does it, the standards expected and the time scale.

Setting process objectives

Process objectives are also best defined by the team getting together and agreeing how they should conduct themselves as a team. The list of team competencies and performance measures referred to earlier in this chapter can be used, including:

- interpersonal relationships;
- the quality of participation and collaborative effort and decision-making;
- the team's relationships with internal and external customers;
- the capacity of the team to plan and control its activities;
- the ability of the team and its members to adapt to new demands and situations;
- the flexibility with which the team operates;
- the effectiveness with which individual skills are used;
- the quality of communications within the team and between the team and other teams or individuals.

Team performance reviews

Team performance review meetings analyse and assess feedback and control information on their joint achievements against objectives and project plans. The agenda for such meetings could be as follows:

General feedback review:

- progress of the team as a whole;
- problems encountered by the team which have caused difficulties or hampered progress;
- helps and hindrances to the operation of the team.

Work reviews:

- how well the team has functioned;
- review of the individual contribution made by each team member – ie peer review (see below);
- discussion of any new problems encountered by individual team members.

Group problem solving:

- analysis of reasons for any shortfalls or other problems;
- agreement of what needs to be done to solve them and prevent their re-occurrence.

Update goals:

- review of new requirements, opportunities or threats;
- amendment and updating of objectives and project plans.

Reviewing the performance of individual team members

Individual team members can influence team performance in two ways: (1) the actual job they are doing and the skills, competencies and behaviour they apply to the work and (2) the job they perform as team members and how they therefore influence team performance.

Processes for managing team performance should not neglect the needs of team members. As Mohrman and Mohrman (1995) pointed out: 'Performance among individuals, teams and organisations need to fit, but individual needs must be met at the same time.' They ask how individual needs can be met while still encouraging the sharing required at the group level. Their answer is:

First, teams have to be managed in a way that enables individuals to feel they can influence group performance. They must provide opportunities for involvement and for team self-management. Second, the team must be managed so that the individual's needs to have excellent performance recognized are met.

Individuals should receive feedback on their contribution to the team and recognition by their team leader and fellow team members for their accomplishments. Special attention should be given to their personal development, not only as members of their existing team, but also for any future roles they may assume in other teams, as individual contributors, or as team leaders.

Individuals should agree their goals as team members with their team leader but these can also be discussed at team meetings. Personal goals and personal development plans can also be formulated for agreement with the team leader. In performance reviews, team leaders and individuals can concentrate on the latter's contribution to the team, the level of performance in terms of teamwork competencies, and progress in implementing personal development plans.

Peer review processes can also be used in which team members assess each other under headings such as:

- overall contribution to team performance;
- contribution to planning, monitoring and team review activities;
- maintaining relationships with other team members and internal/external customers;
- communicating;
- working flexibly (taking on different roles in the team as necessary);
- co-operation with other team members.

Peer reviews can form part of a 360-degree feedback process as described in Chapter 7.

References

Bunderson, J S and Sutcliffe, K M (2003) Management team learning orientation and business unit performance, *Journal of Applied Psychology*, 88, pp 552–60
Gross, S E (1995) *Compensation for Teams*, New York, Hay
Harrington-Mackin, D (1994) *The Team Building Tool Kit*, New York, AMACOM

Jones, T W (1995) Performance management in a changing context, *Human Resource Management*, 34 (3), pp 425–42

Katzenbach, J and Smith, D (1993) *The Magic of Teams*, Boston, MA, Harvard Business School Press

Mohrman, A M and Mohrman, S A (1995) Performance management is 'running the business', *Compensation & Benefits Review*, July–August, pp 69–75

Purcell, J, Hutchinson, S and Kinnie, N (1998) *The Lean Organisation*, London, IPD

Yaping, G, Tae-Yeol, K, Deog-Ro, L and Jing, Z (2013) A multilevel model of team goal orientation, information exchange, and creativity, *Academy of Management Journal*, 56 (3), pp 827–51

Performance management and employee engagement

14

It was suggested by Mone and London (2010) that: 'Performance management, effectively applied, will help you to create and sustain high levels of engagement, which leads to higher levels of performance'. Gruman and Saks (2011) observed that: 'Modern developments often make it difficult for supervisors to "manage" subordinates' performance. In such an environment it may be more effective for supervisors to focus less on managing performance than on managing the context in which performance occurs, and on fostering the development of employee engagement as a driver of enhanced performance.' Risher (2012) referred to the solid evidence provided by the Gallup Organization's research that 'effective performance management contributes to higher levels of engagement – and better performance'.

In this chapter the contribution of performance management to levels of employee engagement is examined by answering five questions: (1) What is employee engagement? (2) Why is it important? (3) What are the enablers of engagement? (4) What part is played by performance management in supporting these enablers? and (5) How can an organization ensure that performance management plays its part?

What is employee engagement?

The first reference to employee engagement was made by Kahn (1990) who defined it as a psychological state experienced by employees in relation to their work, together with associated behaviours. Macey *et al* (2009) stated that engagement was 'an individual's purpose and focused energy, evident to others in the display of personal initiative, adaptability, effort and persistence directed towards organizational goals'.

Why is engagement important?

Purcell (2013) contended that: 'Employee engagement is worth pursuing, not as an end in itself, but as a means of improving working lives and company performance'. Guest (2009) explained that the benefits of engagement were as follows:

> Employee engagement will be manifested in positive attitudes (for example job satisfaction, organizational commitment and identification with the organization) and behaviour (low labour turnover and absence and high citizenship behaviour) on the part of employees; and evidence of perceptions of trust, fairness and a positive exchange within a psychological contract where two-way promises and commitments are fulfilled.

Alfes *et al* (2010) observed that engaged employees perform better, are more innovative than others, are more likely to want to stay with their employers, enjoy greater levels of personal well-being and perceive their workload to be more sustainable than others. Wiley (2008) reported that research conducted by The Kenexa High Performance Institute in 158 organizations from a wide range of industries showed that both earnings per share and three-year total shareholder return were directly linked to employee engagement. Research by Towers Watson (2012) found that companies with high and sustainable engagement levels had an average one-year operating margin that was close to three times higher than those with lower levels. As quoted by Rayton *et al* (2012), Marks and Spencer's research showed that over a four-year period stores with improving engagement had, on average, delivered £62 million more sales to the business every year than stores with declining engagement. Sainsbury's have found clear link between higher levels of engagement and sales performance, with the level of colleague engagement contributing up to 15 per cent of a store's year-on-year growth.

What are the enablers of engagement?

It was explained by Daniels (2011) that the main factors affecting engagement are job autonomy, support and coaching, feedback, opportunities to learn and develop, task variety and responsibility. Engage for Success (2014) stated that the four key enablers of engagement are:

1 Visible, empowering leadership providing a strong strategic narrative about the organization, where it's come from and where it's going.

2 Engaging managers who focus their people and give them scope, treat their people as individuals and coach and stretch their people.

3 Employee voice throughout the organizations, for reinforcing and challenging views, between functions and externally, employees are seen as central to the solution.

4 Organizational integrity – the values on the wall are reflected in day-to-day behaviours. There is no 'say–do' gap.

But it was claimed by Macey *et al* (2009) that the most important enabler of engagement is the work environment and the jobs people do. They noted that: 'Engagement requires a work environment that does not just demand more but promotes information sharing, provides learning opportunities and fosters a balance in people's lives, thereby creating the bases for sustained energy and personal initiative.' They also commented that 'When people have the opportunity to do work in a way that: (a) effectively uses their skills; (b) fits their values and (c) provides them the freedom to exercise choice, they will be fully motivated to engage in their work.' They observed that 'Engaged employees feel that their jobs are an important part of who they are' and that 'the feeling of engagement cannot occur without a specific purpose or objective'.

What part is played by performance management?

Performance management can provide general support for all the Engage for Success enablers by ensuring that employees are aware of the goals and values of the organization and are given a voice in discussing their own goals in relation to those of the business. Moreover managers can use performance management to increase understanding of what the espoused values are and apply the processes involved to demonstrate that these are values in use. But above all, performance management supports the second of the four enablers by encouraging managers to focus on their people and give them scope, treat them as individuals and coach and stretch them. As MacLeod and Clarke (2009) point out, managers who foster engagement '...offer clarity for what is expected from individual members of staff, which involves some stretch, and much appreciation and feedback/coaching and training'.

Performance management also has a part to play in achieving the conditions for engagement specified by Macey *et al* (2009), namely that 'Engaged employees feel that their jobs are an important part of who they are' and that 'the feeling of engagement cannot occur without a specific purpose or objective'. Mone and London (2010) commented that performance management enhances engagement by giving greater meaning to the work that employees do. They explained that engagement can be driven by setting performance goals and establishing development plans that support the career success of employees. The ways in which performance provides specific support are set out below.

Role development

Role development is the continuous process through which roles are defined or modified as work proceeds and evolves. The part people play in carrying out their roles can develop over time as people grow into them and with them, responding to opportunities and changing demands, acquiring new skills and developing competencies.

Levels of engagement will increase if the individual's role is designed or developed in accordance with the principles set out by Hackman and Oldham (1974) in their job characteristics model. They identified five core job characteristics:

1 *Skill variety*: the degree to which a job requires an employee to perform activities that challenge his or her skills and abilities.

2 *Task identity*: the degree to which the job requires completion of an identifiable piece of work.

3 *Task significance*: the degree to which the job outcome has a substantial impact on others.

4 *Autonomy*: the degree to which the job gives an employee freedom and discretion in scheduling work and determining how it is performed.

5 *Feedback*: the degree to which an employee gets information about the effectiveness of his or her efforts – with particular emphasis on feedback directly related to the work itself rather than from a third party (for example, a manager).

Hackman and Oldham explained that if the design of a job satisfied the core job characteristics the employee would perceive that the work was worthwhile, would feel responsible for the work and would know if the work had been completed satisfactorily. The outcome of this would be high-quality work performance and high job satisfaction as a result of intrinsic motivation. In current terms, this means higher levels of engagement.

Role development is a continuous process but the discussion between the manager and the individual on the latter's role at the start of the performance management cycle enables more formal agreement to be reached on where role requirements need to be clarified or amended. This may include defining new key result areas or redefining existing ones. In doing this attention can be given to the principles of the job characteristics model especially those concerned with skill variety, task identity, task significance and autonomy and how their application may enhance engagement.

Providing a sense of purpose

Engagement is most likely to be enhanced when people have a clear sense of purpose in carrying out tasks which they believe to be worthwhile. Perhaps one of the most important performance management activities is that of setting goals as described in Chapter 5. These are most likely to promote engagement when they are relevant, precise, measurable, trackable, challenging, achievable and, importantly, agreed. Goals can be specified as performance targets or performance standards and provide the basis for monitoring progress and for providing feedback.

The Watson Wyatt 2008–2009 survey stated that 'our data shows that engaged employees have frequent work related discussions with their immediate manager in comparison to their colleagues with medium to low engagement levels. Forty-three per cent of high engaged employees receive feedback at least once a week compared to only 18 per cent of employees with low engagement'.

Feedback

Feedback to people on how they are doing is one of the key performance management processes. It is provided by managers informally during the year or formally at a performance review meeting. Research by Kuvaas (2011) found that performance management is more likely to result in good performance when employees receive high levels of feedback regularly.

Positive feedback is a method of reinforcement which can increase levels of engagement by convincing people that they are doing well and that therefore the job they are doing is worthwhile.

Recognition

Performance management provides opportunities for recognizing achievements through feedback. Macey and Schneider (2008) argued that when leaders recognize good performance this will have a positive effect on employee engagement by engendering a sense of attachment to the job. It can demonstrate that employees are valued by their manager and the organization. Recognition is a powerful form of reward which encourages the behaviour which characterizes engaged employees, for example, exercising discretionary effort.

Learning and development

Engagement is enhanced if employees are provided with learning opportunities to develop their skills and further their careers. If performance management is seen as a means of identifying and meeting learning and development needs, as it should be, then it will contribute to increasing levels of work or job engagement. Performance management also provides the basis for coaching by line managers and others to increase skills or overcome deficiencies.

Psychological contracts

As noted by Gruman and Saks (2011) employees tend to have implicit and/or explicit expectations on what they want from an organization. Such expectations can be the basis of psychological contracts which involve reciprocal and interdependent obligations and therefore relationships between employees and employers. In accordance with social exchange theory these relationships evolve over time into trusting, loyal and mutual commitments as long as the parties abide by certain 'rules of exchange'. These rules involve reciprocal behaviour so that the actions of one party lead to a response or actions by the other party. Thus, as stated by Gruman and Saks:

> According to social exchange theory, employees will be more engaged themselves when their psychological contract has been fulfilled [and] performance management processes are the key factors in developing psychological contracts.

How can an organization ensure that performance management plays its part?

As described above, the contribution performance management can make to enhancing engagement is potentially considerable. Clearly, however, that contribution will only be made if performance management works well. And that is a very big if. The issues as spelt out in Chapter 4 are formidable. The biggest one is the all too common situation of line managers not having the inclination to carry out their performance management duties properly if at all or, even if they are ready to try, do not possess the range of demanding skills required.

To deal with this problem it is first necessary to design or modify the performance management system and ensure that the role of managers and the skills they need are quite clear. The more managers can be involved in the design or redesign process the better. In defining the processes used and the skills required particular attention needs to be paid to those skills which are instrumental in increasing engagement levels, namely role definition and development, goal setting, providing informal feedback throughout the year as well as formal feedback in review meetings, recognizing achievements, identifying learning needs, agreeing learning and development plans and coaching. They need to receive extensive training in these skills which would include coaching and mentoring as well as formal courses.

It is also necessary to remember that performance management is a two-way process. The individuals involved are not just at the receiving end of what their managers do. Individuals are there to make their own contribution. They can play an important part jointly with their managers in making performance management successful. Individuals should be involved in the design of the system and provided with training. In itself, this will provide an additional means through which they can become more engaged in their work.

References

Alfes, K, Truss, C, Soane, E C, Rees, C and Gatenby, M (2010) *Creating an Engaged Workforce*, London, CIPD

Daniels, K (2011) *Employee Engagement Fact Sheet*, London, CIPD

Engage for Success (2014) *The Four Enablers of Engagement*, engageforsuccess.org (accessed 2 February 2014)

Gruman, J A and Saks, A M (2011) Performance management and employee engagement, *Human Resource Management Review*, **21** (2), pp 123–36

Guest, D (2009) *Review of Employee Engagement: Notes for a discussion* (unpublished), prepared specifically for the MacLeod and Clarke 2009 review of employee engagement

Hackman, J R and Oldham, G R (1974) Motivation through the design of work: test of a theory, *Organizational Behaviour and Human Performance*, **16** (2), pp 250–79

Kahn, W A (1990) Psychological conditions of personal engagement and disengagement at work, *Academy of Management Journal*, **33** (4), pp 692–724

Kuvaas, B (2011) The interactive role of performance appraisal reactions and regular feedback, *Journal of Managerial Psychology*, **26** (2), pp 123–37

Macey, W H and Schneider, B (2008) The meaning of employee engagement, *Industrial and Organizational Psychology: Perspectives on Science and Practice*, **1**, pp 3–30

Macey, W H, Schneider, B, Barbera, K M and Young, S A (2009) *Employee Engagement*, Malden MA, Wiley-Blackwell

MacLeod, D and Clarke, N (2009) *Engaging for Success: Enhancing performance through employee engagement*, London, Department for Business Innovation and Skills

Mone, E M and London, M (2010) *Employee Engagement Through Performance Management: A practical guide for managers*, New York, Routledge

Purcell, J (2013) Employee voice and engagement, in C Truss, R Deldridge, K Alfes, A Shantz and E Soane (eds), *Employee Engagement in Theory and Practice*, London, Routledge, pp 236–49

Rayton, B, Dodge, T and D'Analeze, G (2012) *Nailing the Evidence*, London, Engage for Success

Risher, H (2012) Employers need to focus on improving performance management, *Compensation & Benefits Review*, **44** (4), pp 188–90

Towers Watson (2012) *Global Workforce Study*, London, Towers Watson

Watson Wyatt (2008–2009) *Continuous Engagement: The Key to Unlocking the Value of Your People*, London, Watson Wyatt

Wiley, J (2008) *Engaging the Employee*, Wayne PA, Kenexa High Performance Research Institute

Performance management and talent management

15

Talent management relies on performance management to provide a basis for identifying and rewarding (in the broadest sense) talented people. Performance management ensures that employees develop their talent by learning from experience through constructive feedback, by coaching and by the formulation and implementation of personal development plans. Michaels *et al* (2001), who initiated the talent management movement, identified one of the five imperatives that companies need to act on if they are going to win this war as 'using job experience, coaching and mentoring to cultivate the potential in managers' – all aspects of performance management.

Talented people possess special gifts, abilities and aptitudes which enable them to perform effectively. Talent management is the process of identifying, developing, recruiting, retaining and deploying these people. The term may refer simply to management succession planning and management development activities, although this notion does not really add anything to these familiar processes except a new, although admittedly quite evocative, name. It is better to regard talent management as a more comprehensive and integrated bundle of activities the aim of which is to secure the flow of talent in an organization, bearing in mind that talent is a major corporate resource.

Performance management is about the development of talent and is therefore an integral part of talent management. In this chapter the process of talent management and its links to performance management are explored and the ways in which these links function are described.

The process of talent management

The process of talent management is based on the proposition that 'those with the best people win'. Since McKinsey and Company popularized the term in the 1990s it has become recognized as a major resourcing activity, although its elements are familiar. The fundamental concept of talent management – that it is necessary to engage in talent planning to build a talent pool by means of a talent pipeline – is a key concern of human resource management.

Talent management was defined by Tansley and Tietze (2013) as follows: 'Talent management contains strategies and protocols for the systematic attraction, identification, development, retention and deployment of individuals with high potential who are of particular value to an organization'. However, this definition refers to 'individuals with high potential' and although this may be the usual approach, some people believe that talent management covers everybody on the grounds that all people have talent and talent management activities should not be restricted to the favoured few.

Talent management starts with the business strategy and what it signifies in terms of the future demand for talented people. Ultimately, the aim is to develop and maintain a pool of talented people through the talent pipeline, which consists of the processes of resourcing, career planning and talent development that maintain the flow of talent needed by the organization.

Talent management and performance management are linked in three ways. First, performance management can be used to identify talent as far as this is possible; second, it provides a basis for developing talent; and third it helps to increase the engagement levels of talented people as explained in Chapter 14. A model of how performance management is the basis for talent management at CEMEX is shown in Figure 15.1.

Identifying talent

Information for talent audits can be generated by a performance management system which helps to identify those with abilities and, therefore, it is presumed, potential. This could be a standard system as described in Chapter 1 or, in addition, 360-degree feedback could be used to provide a detailed assessment of talent and development needs from different perspectives

FIGURE 15.1   Performance management as the foundation of talent management at CEMEX

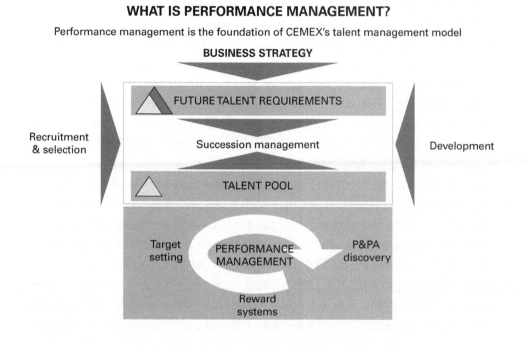

WHAT IS PERFORMANCE MANAGEMENT?

Performance management is the foundation of CEMEX's talent management model

BUSINESS STRATEGY

FUTURE TALENT REQUIREMENTS

Recruitment & selection

Succession management

Development

TALENT POOL

Target setting

PERFORMANCE MANAGEMENT

P&PA discovery

Reward systems

(see Chapter 7). McDonnell and Collings (2011) observed that: 'Obtaining accurate and timely information is vital to successfully identifying high potentials – hence the importance of having some form of objective formalized measures'. A performance management system may also include specific assessments of potential.

Identifying ability

The purpose of the performance assessment part of a performance review is to establish the level of ability someone achieves, preferably in terms of the competencies displayed in achieving results. This helps with the establishment of talent pools – the resources of talent available to an organization. It may be assumed that those given high ratings should be considered for inclusion in an 'A' list as possessing high potential. If a forced distribution of performance ratings is used, as described in Chapter 9, the 10 or 15 per cent of people given the top rating could be placed on the list.

Identifying potential

Relying on assessments of ability to indicate potential is in accordance with the claim made by Fombrun *et al* (1984) that managers should perform well in the present to succeed in the future. Performance management assessments can provide reasonable indications of ability levels, if carried out properly, ie when reviews focus on comparing evidence of the results achieved and the behaviour displayed in achieving those results with expectations in the form of performance goals and competency requirements. However, *pace* Fombrun *et al*, past performance is only a predictor of future performance when there is a connecting link, ie there are elements of the present job which are also important in a higher level job.

But it can be argued that a more specific assessment of potential is required and traditionally this was associated with management succession planning with which talent management in its early days was practically synonymous. Management succession planning attempted to ensure that managers who left the organization, died, or were promoted or transferred could be replaced by people with the abilities and experience needed to perform the vacant job well in the shortest possible time. It was often a formal process involving the preparation of schedules covering each manager and listing performance and potential ratings, indicating the position(s) to which they might be promoted and when, and naming possible successors. At different stages in their careers, managers may be categorized as being ready to do the next job now, or being ready for a specified higher-grade position in, say, two years' time, or as a high-flyer on the 'A list' who has senior management potential. Such assessments could generate development plans such as leadership and development programmes, special assignments and job rotation.

Performance appraisal forms often had potential boxes for managers to tick as in the example in Figure 15.2.

However, assessing potential is difficult. Managers base their judgement on what they observe about current performance. This will not necessarily indicate that the individual will be capable of carrying greater responsibility in the future when the demands and competencies required may be quite different. In an attempt to deal with this problem some organizations have required potential assessments to be made by managers at a one higher level than the immediate manager in consultation with the latter. It is assumed that the higher level manager will be more detached and know more

FIGURE 15.2   Potential assessment

	Indicate your view of potential by means of a tick against the appropriate heading	
A	Considerable potential for promotion to at least two grades above present level.	
B	Definite potential for promotion to one or two grades above present level.	
C	Some potential for promotion to one grade above present level.	
D	Unlikely to be promoted above present level.	
	Indicate the position(s) to which the job holder could be promoted and when.	

about the requirements for more senior roles. Another way of attempting to deal with this problem is to give managers guidance in a competency framework on what they should look for in the shape of definitions of competency requirements at different levels. An example is given in Chapter 9 (Figure 9.6).

However, it is difficult to provide convincing data on potential or promotability and the scope for formal succession planning is limited in today's more flexible and rapidly changing organizations where elaborate succession plans may well be out of date as soon as they are made.

As McDonnell and Collings (2011) emphasized:

> Succession planning has evolved from the traditional short-term focus on replacing senior managers if they happened to leave without prior warning. There is now a more long-term aim of developing a cadre of key talent who are able to take on higher level roles, potentially roles that may not currently exist... The utilization of talent pools consisting of employees with key generic type competencies and skills allows the organization far greater scope when positions become available. Management will be able to select the most suitable candidate from a pool of candidates and train the person into the specific requirements of that particular role.

This is what Cappelli (2008) called a 'talent on demand' policy. This means that the organization ensures that there are plenty of talented people around in talent pools to fill vacancies as they arise, bearing in mind that the most talented or ambitious individuals may not want to wait very long. Talent on demand arrangements depend on a performance management system which provides for the degree of competency people display to be assessed to establish whether they are eligible for entry into a talent pool. Talent pools may be established at different levels, for example, in Standard Chartered, as junior, mid-level and senior pools. The qualifications for entry to any such pools may be defined in terms of levels of competency set out for each heading in a competency framework.

Performance management approaches such as those described above coupled with information on present performance can provide some indication of potential. But it will never be perfect. Assessments of potential are forecasts based on evidence which is not always reliable. They have to be made but there is likely to be a wide margin of error. Performance management will provide some guidance but not definitive information.

Developing talent

The development of talent is the most important part performance management can play in talent management. How it does this is considered fully in Chapter 16. However, to summarize, the contribution made by performance management to learning and development follows the stages in the cycle as described below.

At the planning stage the performance management agreement includes a role profile which defines expectations in the form of competency, knowledge and skills. Developmental plans and targets are set at this stage which may be set out in a personal development plan which spells out what an individual, the manager and the organization intends to do about talent development. This may include coaching and broadening experience, self-development, e-learning as well as formal training.

As a continuous process the learning and development aspects of performance management continue throughout the year as the personal development plan is implemented and coaching and formal training takes place.

At the review and assessment stages of the performance management cycle the results achieved over the year are evaluated and new or revised personal development plans agreed.

References

Cappelli, P (2008) *Talent on Demand: Managing talent in an uncertain age*, Boston MA, Harvard Business School Press

Fombrun, C J, Tichy, N M and Devanna, M A (1984) *Strategic Human Resource Management*, New York, Wiley

McDonnell, A and Collings, D G (2011) Identification and evaluation of talent in MNEs, in H Scullion and D G Collings (eds), *Global Talent Management*, London, Routledge, pp 56–73

Michaels, E G, Handfield-Jones, H and Axelrod, B (2001) *The War for Talent*, Boston MA, Harvard Business School Press

Tansley, C and Tietze, S (2013) Rites of passage through talent management stages: an identity work perspective, *International Journal of Human Resource Management*, 24 (9), pp 1799–1815

Performance management and learning

16

Performance management has an important learning and development role. Learning takes place at every point in the cycle: planning, managing performance throughout the year and monitoring and reviewing outcomes. It could therefore be regarded as a natural process but the likelihood of its happening is increased if (1) there is a framework for learning which is provided by personal development plans as part of the overall planning and implementation activities and (2) the opportunity to coach is seized upon whenever possible. This chapter starts with a discussion of how people learn through performance management and this leads to an analysis of the learning opportunities. It concludes with a description of personal development planning. Coaching was dealt with in Chapter 10.

Helping people to learn through performance management

It was pointed out by Reynolds (2004) that: 'Improvement and learning are causally related; obtain the will to improve and the process of learning will follow'. He also commented that 'The experience of work always will provide the richest learning laboratory'. This is where performance management comes in; first by specifically helping people to appreciate the need for developing their performance and where and how it should take place, and secondly by ensuring that they learn from experience. Performance management can also help to identify specific learning needs that can be satisfied by formal courses on or off the job or by e-learning. But the most important contribution of performance management is the help it provides to the development of a climate for learning – a 'growth culture'. This offers scope for guiding people through their work challenges, ensuring that they have the time and resources required to learn, and, crucially, giving them the feedback and support they need to learn.

Learning opportunities

Performance management provides learning opportunities during its three main stages: performance agreement and planning, managing performance throughout the year and performance review.

The performance agreement as a framework for learning

The learning opportunities offered by performance management are based on the initial activities in the performance agreement and planning part of the cycle. This includes a joint analysis of the individual's role so that a new or updated role profile can be produced which sets out what results are to be achieved and what competencies are needed to deliver those results. Discussions take place on ways in which the individual's role could be developed so that it becomes more challenging from the viewpoint not only of new tasks to be accomplished but also the need to acquire or extend knowledge and skills in order to carry out those tasks. The aim is to provide what Reynolds (2004) calls 'supported autonomy'; freedom for employees to manage their work within certain boundaries (policies and expected behaviours) but with support available as required. Career opportunities and the learning required to realize them are also discussed. Areas where performance needs to be improved are identified and the learning required to achieve these improvements is agreed. The outcome is a personal development plan as described later in this chapter.

Learning throughout the year

Learning is inseparable from activity, and like performance management it is a continuous process. Every task carried out by someone presents a learning opportunity and it is the duty of managers to help people become aware of this and to support the day-to-day learning that takes place. They should enable people to understand how to tackle a new task and what additional knowledge or skills they will need. Guidance can be provided by asking questions on what individuals need to know and be able to do to undertake a task, leaving them as far as possible to think for themselves but helping them when necessary.

Feedback throughout the year rather than during an annual performance review is also an important means of helping people to learn. They can be asked to analyse their performance – the results they achieved in undertaking a task and the ways in which those results were achieved. Where they recognize a need for improvement they can discuss with their manager any additional coaching, training or experience they require.

Performance reviews as learning events

Performance reviews, whether conducted formally or informally, can be regarded as learning events. Learning opportunities are provided before, during and after formal meetings. Prior to a review individuals can be encouraged to think about what they feel they want to learn, new skills they would like to acquire and the direction in which they want to develop. During the review individuals can present to the reviewer their views about what they have learned and what they need to learn. A dialogue can take place in which learning needs can be analysed and a diagnosis agreed on priority areas. Individuals should be encouraged to take responsibility for their own learning and for implementing the outcomes of the learning process. The outcome of the review could be a personal development plan as described below. Following the review learners and their managers can monitor progress against agreed targets.

Personal development planning

Personal development planning aims to promote learning and to provide people with the knowledge and portfolio of transferable skills which will help to progress their careers. A personal development plan sets out what people need to learn to develop their capabilities, improve their performance and further their career. Individuals are responsible for formulating and implementing the plan which provides a self-organized learning framework, indicating what they have to do with support from their managers and the organization. It serves as a point of reference for monitoring and reviewing the implementation of the plan.

The planning process

Personal development plans are based on an understanding of what people do, what they have done, what knowledge and skills they have and what knowledge and skills they need. The aims are to be specific about what is to be achieved and how it is to be achieved, to ensure that the learning needs and actions are relevant, to indicate the time scale, to identify responsibility and, within reason, to ensure that the learning activities will stretch those concerned.

Plans are always related to work and the capacity to carry it out effectively. They are *not* just about identifying training needs and suitable courses to satisfy them. Training courses may form part of the development plan, but a minor part; other learning activities such as those listed below are more important:

- coaching;
- adopting a role model (mentor);
- observing and analysing what others do (good practice);
- extending the role (job enrichment);
- project work – special assignments;
- involvement in other work areas;
- involvement in communities of practice (learning from others carrying out similar work);
- action learning;
- e-learning;
- guided reading.

Action planning

The action plan sets out what needs to be done and how it will be done under headings such as:

- learning needs;
- outcomes expected (learning objectives);

- learning activities to meet the needs;
- responsibility for learning – what individuals will do and what support they will require from their manager, the HR department or other people;
- timing – when the learning activity is expected to start and be completed.

The plans can be recorded on simple forms with four columns covering: (1) development objectives and outcome expected, (2) action to be taken and when, (3) support required, and (4) evidence required to show that the planned learning activity has been undertaken successfully.

Introducing personal development planning

The introduction of personal development planning should not be undertaken lightly. It is not just a matter of adding a new page to the performance review form and telling people to fill it up. Neither is it sufficient just to issue guidance notes and expect people to get on with it.

Managers, team leaders and individuals all need to learn about personal development planning. They should be involved in deciding how the planning process will work and what their roles will be. The benefits to them should be understood and accepted. It has to be recognized that everyone will need time and support to adjust to a culture in which they have to take much more responsibility for their own learning. Importantly, all concerned should be given guidance on how to identify learning needs, on the means of satisfying those needs, and how they should make use of the facilities and opportunities which can be made available to them.

Reference

Reynolds, J (2004) *Helping People Learn*, London, CIPD

Performance management and reward

17

Performance management can play a major role in a total reward system in which each reward element is linked together and treated as an integrated and coherent whole. These elements comprise base pay, merit or performance-related pay, employee benefits and non-financial rewards – intrinsic rewards from the work itself.

It is sometimes assumed that the main purpose of performance management is to generate ratings to inform contribution or performance-related pay decisions. But there is more to performance management than that. It can provide for a whole range of rewards in order to encourage job engagement and promote commitment. These rewards can take the form of recognition through feedback, opportunities to achieve, the scope to develop skills, and guidance on career paths. All these are non-financial rewards which can make a longer-lasting impact than financial rewards.

Performance management is, or should be, about developing people and rewarding them in the broadest sense. Approaches to using performance management to provide non-financial rewards are discussed below. The rest of the chapter deals with performance management and pay.

Performance management and non-financial rewards

Non-financial rewards are provided by performance management through recognition, the provision of opportunities to succeed, skills development, and career planning.

Performance management and recognition

Performance management involves recognizing people's achievements and strengths. They can be informed through feedback about how well they are performing by reference to achievements and behaviours. They can be thanked, formally and informally, for what they have done. They can be helped to understand how they can do even better by taking action to make the best use of the opportunities the feedback has revealed.

Performance management and the provision of opportunities to achieve

Performance management processes are founded on joint agreements between managers and their staff on what the roles of the latter are and how they can be developed (enriched). It is therefore an essential part of job or role design and development activities.

Performance management and skills development

Performance management can provide a basis for motivating people by clarifying goals and defining what has to be done to achieve them. It provides an agreed framework for coaching and support to enhance and focus learning.

Performance management and career planning

Performance management reviews provide opportunities to discuss the direction to which the careers of individuals are going and what they can do – with the help of the organization as part of its talent management programme – to ensure that they follow the best career path for themselves and the organization.

Performance management and pay

Performance management is not inevitably associated with pay, although this is often assumed to be the case, especially in the United States. A survey by Armstrong and Baron (2004) found that only 42 per cent of respondents with performance management had merit or performance pay.

However, organizations with merit pay must have a means of deciding on increases and this has to be based on some form of assessment. The most typical approach is the generation of ratings following performance reviews to inform merit pay decisions.

But quite a few organizations do not use ratings at all (23 per cent of the respondents to the e-reward 2014 survey). Instead they adopt what might be called 'holistic' assessment. This involves assessing the level of contribution and therefore possible awards in the shape of base pay increases or bonuses. Consideration is given both to what individuals have contributed to the success of their team and to the level of competence they have achieved and deployed. Pay policy will indicate that team members who are fully contributing at the expected level will be paid at or around what is often called 'the reference point' for the grade (a reference point represents the rate of pay appropriate for someone who is fully competent in the role and is aligned to market rates in accordance with the organization's market pay policies). If, in the judgement of the line manager, individuals are achieving this level of contribution but are paid below their peers at the reference point, the pay of such individuals would be brought up to the level of their peers or towards that level if it is felt that the increase should be phased. Individuals may be paid above the reference point if they are making a particularly strong contribution or if their market worth is higher.

The policy guideline would be that the average pay of those in the grade should broadly be in line with the reference point unless there are special market rate considerations which justify a higher rate. Those at or above the reference point who are contributing well could be eligible for a cash bonus. A 'pay pot' would be made available for distribution with guidelines on how it should be used.

This approach depends largely on the judgement of line managers, although they would be guided and helped in the exercise of that judgement by HR. Its acceptability to staff as a fair process depends on precise communications generally on how it operates and equally precise communications individually on why decisions have been made. The assessment of contribution should be a joint one as part of performance management and the link between that assessment and the pay decision should be clear.

Methods used to decide on pay increases

Ratings were used to inform performance pay increases by 80 per cent of the respondents to the e-reward 2014 performance management survey. They used the following methods to decide on pay increases:

- Through a pay matrix, relating performance awards etc to ratings by use of a scale – 40 per cent.

- Through forced distribution, performance awards distributed among employees by defining the percentage who should be rated at each level (a 'quota' system) – 8 per cent.

- Through guidelines, guidance on average awards, with restrictions on minimum and maximum amounts that can be awarded – 41 per cent.

- Other – 11 per cent.

The remaining 20 per cent of respondents who did not use ratings tended to be from smaller organizations or the public sector. They decided on pay increases in the following ways:

- By a holistic reference to performance and pay in relation to peers, market worth and, possibly, potential – 32 per cent.

- By reference to assessments of the market worth of the individual – 3 per cent.

- By reference to the outcomes of a performance review where it has been expressed generally that performance merits, for example, a high, average or below average increase – 10 per cent.

- By reference to the ranked performance of peers – 7 per cent.

- Other – 48 per cent.

The 'other' methods often involved hybrids of the other categories such as guidelines without maxima and minima or guidance with a higher degree of discretion.

An example of how pay decisions are made in a finance sector company is given below:

We look at a number of things when making a decision on an individual's pay. One will be the size of the role as determined by job evaluation and we also consider market data and location to determine the average salary that you would expect to pay for that role. We then look at how the individual has performed over the last twelve months: Have they contributed what was expected of them? Have they contributed above and beyond their peers? Have they underperformed in respect of what was required of them? These are not ratings, they are just guidelines given to managers as to whether the individual should be given an average, above average or below average increase. We have a devolved budget and managers have to make decisions as to what percentage they should give to different people. We suggest that if, for example, a manager has six people carrying out the same roles then, from an equal pay point of view, if they are delivering at the same level and are all competent, they should be getting similar salaries. Individuals paid below the market rate who are performing effectively may get a bigger pay rise to bring them nearer the market rate for the role.

Reconciling performance management and pay

Focusing on performance management as a means of deciding on pay awards may conflict with the developmental purposes of performance management. This is more likely to be the case if ratings are used – the performance review meeting will concentrate on the ratings that emerge from it and how much money will be forthcoming. Issues concerning development and the non-financial reward approaches discussed earlier will be subordinated to this preoccupation with pay. Many organizations attempt to get over this problem by holding development and pay review meetings on separate dates, often several months apart (decoupling). Some such as the finance company described earlier do without formulaic approaches (ratings) altogether, although it is impossible to dissociate contingent pay completely from some form of assessment even if this is limited to making decisions on which employees should have above average, average or below average increases or no increase at all.

The problem of reconciling the developmental aspects of performance management or appraisal and pay has been with us for decades. Armstrong commented as long ago as 1976 that:

It is undesirable to have a direct link between the performance review and the reward review. The former must aim primarily at improving performance and, possibly, assessing potential. If this is confused with a salary review, everyone becomes over-concerned about the impact of the assessment on the increment...
It is better to separate the two.

Many people since then have accepted this view in principle but have found it difficult to apply in practice. As Kessler and Purcell (1993) argued:

> How distinct these processes (performance review and performance-related pay) can ever be or, in managerial terms, should ever be, is perhaps debatable. It is unrealistic to assume that a manager can separate these two processes easily and it could be argued that the evaluations in a broad sense should be congruent.

And Armstrong and Murlis (1998) commented that:

> Some organisations separate entirely performance pay ratings from the performance management review. But there will, of course, inevitably be a read-across from the performance management review to the pay-for-performance review.

The issue is that if you want to pay for performance you have to measure performance. And if you want, as you should do, the process of measurement to be fair, equitable, consistent and transparent, then you cannot make pay decisions, on whatever evidence, behind closed doors. You must convey to people how the assessment has been made and how it has been converted into a pay increase. This is a matter of procedural justice which demands that where there is a system for assessing performance and competence, (1) the assessment should be based on 'good information and informed opinion', (2) the person affected should be able to contribute to the process of obtaining evidence to support the assessment, (3) the person should know how and why the assessment has been made, and (4) the person should be able to appeal against the assessment.

References

Armstrong, M (1976) *A Handbook of Personnel Management Practice*, 1st edition, London, Kogan Page

Armstrong, M and Baron, A (2004) *Managing Performance: Performance Management in Action*, London, CIPD

Armstrong, M and Murlis, H (1998) *Reward Management*, 4th edition, London, Kogan Page

e-reward (2005) *Survey of Performance Management Practice*, Stockport, e-reward

Kessler, I and Purcell, J (1993) *The Templeton Performance-Related Pay Project: Summary of Key Findings*, Oxford, Templeton College

International performance management

18

The two inter-related applications of international performance management are covered in this chapter: first, its use by multinational firms in their foreign subsidiaries and second, how expatriate employees are dealt with. The system adopted in either case may be essentially similar to a typical national, one-country approach, ranging from a fairly crude performance appraisal tick-box methodology to one which has the sophisticated features of a fully developed process.

Performance management in the subsidiaries of multinationals

As Dowling *et al* (2008) observed: 'By its very nature, a multinational is a single entity that faces a global environment which means that it simultaneously confronts differing national environments'. When considering how to operate performance management the dilemma facing multinational enterprises is the extent to which there should be one standardized system throughout the organization rather than local systems which fit the circumstances of the country concerned. This is the issue of convergence or divergence as discussed below.

Convergence and divergence

All multinational corporations have the problem of achieving a balance between international consistency and local autonomy. They must therefore decide on the extent of convergence (centralization) or divergence (localization). Briscoe *et al* (2012) remarked that: 'International HRM strategy has to deal with the issue of whether to standardize HRM policies and practices from headquarters, or to localize them to meet local conditions, or do both (eg combination of core policies established by HQ with localized practices to accommodate local culture and practices)'.

If the choice is to adopt convergence to some degree or in selected areas it is necessary to remember Tayeb's (2005) proposition that it is generally easier to transfer strategies and policies than practices. Rather than trying to impose central practices, in certain cases it may be preferable simply to set out broad policy guidelines expressing and underpinning the values that the parent company would like to be applied throughout the organization. Pudelko and Harzing (2007) argued that those who favoured convergence assumed that 'in management, *best practices* can be defined that are universally valid and applicable, irrespective of national culture or institutional context'. But they also observed that: 'We should not expect every subsidiary to be brought into the best practices scheme in the same way'.

Festing and Eidems (2011) reported that: 'In the course of increasing globalization, more and more MNEs [multinational enterprises] are being forced to compete globally and simultaneously adapt their business strategies to changing local demands'. They also suggested that 'firms tend not to standardize a whole HRM system but rather focus on single practices'. Performance management is often one of those practices.

Research conducted by Reilly and Williams (2012) indicated that the following were the upsides and downsides of what they called a 'one-country' approach by HR, ie convergence:

The upsides are:

- Promotes common values
- Delivers consistent treatment to staff
- Exports good business practice to all parts of the organization
- Greater control over dispersed operations
- Cost control.

The downsides are:

- Harmonization can stifle innovation
- Centre loses touch with sharp end of the business

- Ill-conceived policies subverted at a local level
- HR is focus for frustration as agent of the corporate centre.

Approaches to international performance management

The amount of convergence or divergence in international performance management systems can vary in five ways:

1 *Total convergence (standardization)* – using the parent company's scheme throughout the international organization.

2 *Partial convergence* – foreign subsidiaries use a version of the parent company's system modified to take account of local factors such as culture and work systems. Alternatively, they ensure that their own systems conform to policy guidelines issued by headquarters, possibly including certain requirements such as the design of the forms or methods of rating.

3 *Total divergence (localization)* – foreign subsidiaries use their own systems.

4 *Partial divergence* – foreign subsidiaries can use their own systems as long as they are in line with certain basic principles, for example, that performance management should be a continuous process of joint planning, agreement, dialogue and feedback (examples of guiding principles are given in Chapter 22).

5 *Dual system* – using local, possibly partly converged schemes, for subsidiary company employees and reserving the headquarters scheme for expatriates.

Considerations affecting the approach

A system that has worked well at headquarters will not necessarily transfer well to a foreign subsidiary. A study by Gerringer *et al* (2002) covering ten countries found that a centralized performance management system generally failed to fulfil its purpose.

The issues discussed below need to be taken into account when deciding on the type of performance management system to be used, the extent to which standardized performance management systems are desirable and, in so far as they are standardized, how they should be managed. There are no easy solutions. Each case has to be decided in accordance with individual circumstances. But it is helpful to be aware of the potential pitfalls so that action can be taken in advance to avoid them, as far as possible.

The particular issues affecting the use of performance management in foreign subsidiaries are cultural differences, environmental differences, the increased difficulty in influencing and controlling line managers and the problem of achieving consistent rating results.

Cultural differences

Cultural differences may affect the ability of a multinational firm to implement a standardized international system. For example Shen (2005) noted that: 'In some Asian countries such as China and Japan, feedback is not normally given in order to "save face" and group meetings are often held in performance management processes to achieve group harmony. This aspect of Asian culture is very different from Western culture where individualism is emphasized.'

Environmental differences

The maturity of subsidiaries in terms of their productivity, ability to penetrate markets, availability of skilled employees and work practices will vary and it may be difficult for some subsidiaries to meet the standards of performance expected by the parent company. Environmental differences such as levels of political stability and standards of living will also affect the results achieved by subsidiaries. Garland *et al* (1990) give an example:

> One does not fire a Mexican manager because worker productivity is half the American average. In Mexico, this would mean that this manager is working at a level three or four as high as the average Mexican plant... The way we measure worker productivity is exactly the same, but the numbers come out differently because of the environmental difference.

Account should be taken of these differences but it is easy for a remote headquarters to be unaware of how local factors affect performance levels.

Line managers

Even in a one-country domestic setting, performance management can easily fail because the line managers on whom the system depends lack the skill or the inclination to do it properly. In an international organization control over how line managers implement performance management will be even more difficult owing to the diversity of operations, the geographical separation between headquarters and foreign subsidiaries and, possibly, the unwillingness of local managers to take much notice of commands from a remote centre.

Rating problems

The achievement of reliable and consistent appraisal ratings in a domestic setting is difficult; in an international operation it is virtually impossible. Care should therefore be taken in designing and interpreting rating systems. If it is felt that they are essential it may be best to leave them to the local subsidiary and not try to introduce a suspect universal system.

What happens in practice

The 2014 e-reward survey of performance management established that 71 per cent of the respondents' companies required subsidiaries to operate the standard corporate performance management system. Where this was not the policy, respondents adopted one of the following approaches:

- subsidiaries left to decide for themselves – 12 per cent;
- subsidiaries required to use performance management but allowed to have their own system – 11 per cent;
- subsidiaries required to use performance management but allowed to have their own system subject to following corporate guidelines – 6 per cent.

Briscoe *et al* (2012) observed that multinational Western country-of-origin companies were likely to use a standardized approach to performance management in their subsidiaries. This was warranted 'for the sake of global integration, uniformity, organizational culture cohesiveness, fairness, mobility of global employees, and as a control mechanism'. And it can be argued that replicating domestic practices simplifies the process of collecting and interpreting data.

Gregersen *et al* (1993) found in their research sample of US multinational firms that 76 per cent of them used the same standardized appraisal forms internationally. But they also found that subsidiary firms often tended not to follow corporate practices and when they did use standardized procedures this reduced the effectiveness of the appraisals.

The trend towards convergence was confirmed by the Global HR Research Alliance study as reported by Stiles (2007) which concluded that:

> In performance management we found little or no difference across the world. We witnessed a concerted effort on the part of group HR departments to maintain global standards supported by global competencies (at foundation, managerial, technical and leadership level), common evaluation processes and common approaches to rewards. It was difficult, therefore, to find many distinctive local practices.

International performance management in action

The international performance management process used by Standard Chartered Bank is illustrated in Figure 18.1.

FIGURE 18.1   International performance management system – Standard Chartered Bank

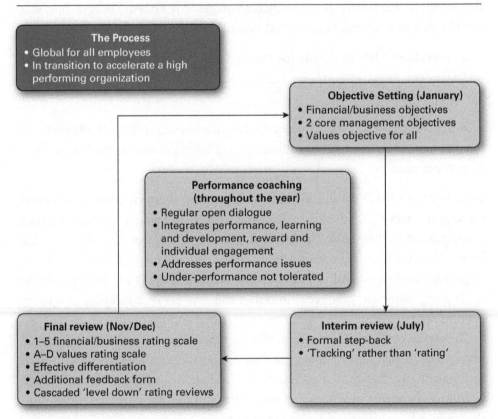

The Process
- Global for all employees
- In transition to accelerate a high performing organization

Objective Setting (January)
- Financial/business objectives
- 2 core management objectives
- Values objective for all

Performance coaching (throughout the year)
- Regular open dialogue
- Integrates performance, learning and development, reward and individual engagement
- Addresses performance issues
- Under-performance not tolerated

Final review (Nov/Dec)
- 1–5 financial/business rating scale
- A–D values rating scale
- Effective differentiation
- Additional feedback form
- Cascaded 'level down' rating reviews

Interim review (July)
- Formal step-back
- 'Tracking' rather than 'rating'

SOURCE: Armstrong and Baron (2005)

As reported by Coleman and Chambers (2005), Serono SA, the Swiss bio-technology company with offices around the world, needed a performance management system that was not only consistent but also flexible enough to adjust to the laws governing employment in each of its far-flung operations.

Each Serono operating unit has its own objectives which are aligned to overarching corporate goals. Units in each country tailor their performance management systems for compliance with local laws, customs and budgets. An information technology system was developed to automate perform-ance management for Serono's global operations. The analytical tools built into this system enable HR at the centre to gain an overview of how the organization as a whole is evaluating its employees. For example, data on assessments presented as bell curves (graphs showing distributions in the form of a curve shaped like a bell), reveal the extent to which appraisal scores are out of line with what is regarded as a normal distribution.

Performance management for expatriates

An expatriate was defined by Lee and Donohue (2012) as 'any individual who relocates from his/her home base to an international location for business or work purposes and sets up temporary residence in the host country'.

The management of expatriates on international assignments is a major factor determining success or failure in a global business. Expatriates are expensive. They can be hard to manage because of the problems associated with adapting to and working in unfamiliar environments and cultures and concerns about their development and careers. Managing their perform-ance presents particular difficulties and the factors involved are discussed below.

Factors affecting expatriate performance

Issues such as culture shock and cross-cultural adjustment may adversely impact on the performance of expatriates. Pinto *et al* (2012) commented that: 'Socio-cultural adjustment and psychological well-being of expatriates and their families are preconditions for their success'.

One of the challenges of performance management for expatriates is that the type of skills developed and used in an international job are different from those developed and used in a domestic environment. These include managing a workforce with cultural differences, dealing with the different behavioural norms of clients, customers and government officials, and coping with a different legal system.

It may be feasible to set up a standardized set of performance factors at headquarters and get the host country evaluators to use these common headings while setting their own individual performance goals, bearing in mind corporate goals. Lee and Donohue (2012) developed and tested an expatriate performance scale consisting of six elements:

- Task performance
- Management and administration
- Teamwork and leadership
- Demonstrating effort
- Communication performance
- Maintaining self-discipline

Factors affecting performance management for expatriates

The effectiveness of performance management for expatriates is affected by the complexity of international business and the distance separating headquarters and subsidiaries. There may be problems with the choice of evaluator – should it be someone in the host country or the home country and, if the latter, will parent company evaluators know enough about the people they assess and the performance conditions those people face? A parent company evaluator's perception of good performance may differ from the reality of conditions in the subsidiary. There may be problems with long-distance communication. Contacts between the parent company evaluator and the expatriate being evaluated may be infrequent. A host country evaluator may lack the experience of a practised headquarters evaluator and management at head office may not trust local assessments. This problem may be less acute if the initial evaluation is to be carried out locally and reviewed at the centre or, better still, if the host country evaluator discusses the evaluation in advance with the home country evaluator.

If local evaluation is practised the following points made by Oddou and Mendenhall (2007) are relevant:

> Regardless of the effectiveness or availability of performance management tools, expatriate performance management success depends largely on the manager

and expatriate in question: how well they understand, internalize, and accept performance management, and how skilful they are in its implementation. To this end, appropriate performance management training should be given to all expatriates, including their superiors.

A performance management system for expatriates may basically resemble the standard headquarters system, but when operating it the considerations set out above need to be remembered. When setting performance goals and standards it is particularly necessary to remember the different conditions in which expatriates work, the performance issues they have to face and the special demands made upon them.

The arrangements may vary according to the level of the employees concerned. Research by Tahvanainen (2000) into performance management practices at Nokia Telecommunications found that although a global, standardized system was in place, there were differences in how expatriate performance was evaluated, particularly in terms of how performance goals were set, who set them and what type of goals they were. Senior host country managers were evaluated by more senior managers at headquarters against the performance goals specified in the incentive scheme. The evaluation of middle manager expatriates was typically done by their senior manager in the host country. If the expatriate also had a manager in the home country the host country manager usually discussed the expatriate's performance with that home country manager prior to conducting the evaluation.

References

Briscoe, D R, Schuler, R and Tarique, I (2012) *International Human Resource Management*, 4th edition, New York, Routledge

Coleman, T and Chambers, T (2005) Serono case study: global performance, evaluations and compensation, *Compensation & Benefits Review*, July/August, pp 61–65

Dowling, P J, Festing, M and Engle, A D (2008) *International Human Resource Management*, 5th edition, Andover, Cengage Learning EMEA

e-reward (2014) *Survey of Performance Management*, Stockport, e-reward

Festing, M and Eidems, J (2011) A process perspective on transnational HRM systems – a dynamic capability-based analysis, *Human Resource Management Review*, **21**, pp 162–73

Garland, J, Farmer, R N and Taylor, M (1990) *International Dimensions of Business Policy and Strategy*, Boston MA, PWS-Kent

Gerringer, J, Frayne, C and Milliman, J (2002) In search of 'best practices' in international human resource management: research design and methodology, *Asia Pacific Journal of Human Resources*, **40** (1), pp 9–37

Gregersen, H B, Hite, J M and Black, J S (1996) International performance appraisal in US multinational firms, *Journal of International Business Studies*, **27**, pp 711–13

Lee, L and Donohue, R (2012) The construction and validation of a measure of expatriate job performance, *International Journal of Human Resource Management*, **23** (6), pp 1197–1215

Oddou, G and Mendenhall, M (2007) Focusing on the international personnel performance appraisal process, *Human Resource Development Journal*, **8** (1), pp 41–62

Pinto, L H, Cabral-Cardoso, C and Werther, W B (2012) Compelled to go abroad: Motives and outcomes of international assignments, *International Journal of Human Resource Management*, **23** (11), pp 2295–2321

Pudelko, M and Harzing, A-W K (2007) Country of origin, localization, or dominance effect? An empirical investigation of HRM practices in foreign subsidiaries, *Human Resource Management*, **46** (4), pp 535–59

Reilly, P and Williams, T (2012) The challenges of global HR: one way to go? *People Management*, September, pp 28–31

Shen, J (2005) Effective international performance appraisals: easily said, hard to do, *Compensation and Benefits Review*, July/August, pp 70–79

Stiles, P (2007) A world of difference? *People Management*, 15 November, pp 36–41

Tahvanainen, M (2000) Expatriate performance management: the case of Nokia Telecommunications, *Human Resource Management*, **39** (2 and 3), pp 267–75

Tayeb, M H (2005) *International Human Resource Management: A Multinational Company Perspective*, Oxford, Oxford University Press

PART FOUR
Performance management in action

The impact of performance management

19

If performance management processes are intended to improve organizational performance how well do they perform? When asked, just over a half of the respondents to the e-reward 2014 survey of performance management said that the impact of performance management was 'fairly positive' while 8 per cent believed it to be 'very positive'. In contrast 8 per cent found performance management made a negative impact while 14 per cent believed there is no effect. It is interesting that a fifth of respondents said that they simply did not know. These results are equivocal, especially as they are probably based on opinion rather than evidence – only 31 per cent of the e-reward respondents carried out formal evaluations and these were mainly based on internal attitude surveys, not on research.

This chapter aims to provide an answer to the question of impact, so far as an answer can be provided, by looking at the evidence from research. As a background to this research, consideration is given first to how performance management is expected to improve performance and second to the problems of establishing the impact of performance management on corporate performance – the causality issue.

How performance management is expected to improve performance

Performance management is expected to improve organizational performance generally by creating a performance culture in which the achievement of high performance is a way of life. Specifically, the impact is supposed to be made by improving individual and, in the rare situations where this is catered for, team performance.

Individual performance development happens by indicating what good performance looks like, agreeing performance goals, identifying where performance needs to improve and deciding on the steps required to achieve that improvement through performance improvement plans, personal development plans and coaching. A more detailed description of what performance management *should* contribute was defined by Jones (1995) as follows:

- communicate a shared vision throughout the organization to help to establish and support appropriate leadership and management styles;
- define individual requirements and expectation of all employees in terms of the inputs and outputs expected from them thus reducing confusion and ambiguity;
- provide a framework and environment for teams to develop and succeed;
- provide the climate and systems which support reward and communicate how people and the organization can achieve improved performance;
- achieve improved performance;
- help people manage ambiguity.

It may be assumed that improvements in results will be guaranteed when managers and their team members work together throughout the year in using performance management processes such as goal setting, feedback, performance analysis and coaching. This could be regarded as an unrealistic aspiration – an optimistic belief – but it is the one that underpins the concept of performance management. The holy grail of performance management is to provide evidence that this belief is justified. But it isn't easy for the reasons given below.

Establishing the impact

Any explanation of the impact of HRM on organizational performance is likely to be based on three propositions: (1) that HR practices can make a direct impact on employee characteristics such as engagement, commitment, motivation and skill; (2) if employees have these characteristics it is probable that organizational performance in terms of productivity, quality and the delivery of high levels of customer service will improve; and (3) if such aspects of organizational performance improve, the financial results achieved by the organization will improve. This can be described as the HR value chain. The propositions highlight the existence of an intermediate factor between HRM and financial performance. This factor consists of the HRM outcomes in the shape of employee characteristics affected by HR practices. Therefore, HRM does not make a direct impact.

Establishing the impact between human resource management (HRM) practices, including performance management, and firm performance is also problematic because of causality issues. Determining the link between in-dependent and dependent variables (cause and effect) – is a major problem in research, especially in the HRM field. Correlation does not imply causation. It may be relatively easy to establish correlations in the shape of a demon-stration that X is associated with Y; it is much more difficult and sometimes impossible to prove that X causes Y.

Secondly, there is the phenomenon of reverse causation when a cause is pre-dated by an effect – A might have caused B but alternatively, B may have come first and be responsible for A. For example, it is possible to demon-strate that firms with effective learning and development programmes do better than those without. But it might equally be the case that it is high per-forming firms that introduce effective learning and development programmes. It can be hard to be certain.

In the light of these problems it is not surprising that there is little convinc-ing research evidence of a causal link between performance management and firm performance. As described below, there is indeed one research project which established that a causal relationship did exist between a performance management technique (goal setting) and individual performance (Latham and Locke, 1979) but this did not cover a complete performance manage-ment system. Research conducted by McDonald and Smith (1991) purported to demonstrate a causal relationship between performance management and firm performance but suffered from the problem of reversed causality. A few studies have found that high performing firms had performance management (but did not establish a link between firm performance and the presence of performance management). There is evidence from a number of surveys that HR people *believed* that there was a link without offering supporting evidence. But rigorous analysis of research conducted by Guest and Conway (1998) failed to prove a connection.

Evidence from research

Ten research projects which have examined the impact of performance management on overall firm performance or on aspects of individual performance are summarized below.

Bernadin et al *(1995)*

Bernardin *et al* found no changes in customer ratings or sales volume following 360-degree feedback.

Gallup

As reported by Risher (2005) Gallup has analysed its Q12 survey and found that employers with a formal performance review process have more engaged employees – 33 per cent versus 21 per cent – and fewer disengaged employees – 12 per cent versus 29 per cent.

Guest and Conway (1998)

The analysis by Guest and Conway covered the 388 organizations with performance management surveyed by Armstrong and Baron in 1998. The key criteria used for determining the effectiveness of performance management were the achievement of financial targets, development of skills, development of competence, improved customer care and improved quality. Against these criteria, over 90 per cent of respondents rated performance management as being moderately or highly effective.

But there were caveats. The analysis indicated that the views of respondents to the survey should all be viewed with extreme caution since they are often based on a very limited form of formal evaluation, or on an absence of any formal evaluation. This raises serious questions about the basis for the generally positive assessment of performance management.

Furthermore, detailed statistical analysis of the replies to the questionnaire failed to demonstrate consistent evidence of any link between the practice of performance management and outcomes such as the achievement of financial targets, achievement of quality and customer service goals and employee development goals. The conclusion reached was that this survey has produced no convincing evidence that performance management has an impact on overall organizational performance.

Institute of Personnel Management (1992)

It was reported by the IPM that their extensive research found no evidence that improved performance in the private sector is associated with the pursuit of formal performance management programmes. Poor financial performers were as likely to introduce performance management as good performers. There were no readily available and comparable measures of performance in the public sector to test this link even though performance management is more likely to be adopted in the public sector. However, one positive theme which was traced throughout the research was the extent to which performance management raised awareness of the pressures on the organization to perform.

Latham and Locke (1979)

As reported by Latham and Locke, 'In a 21-year programme of research, we have found that goal setting does not necessarily have to be part of a wider management system to motivate performance effectively. It can be used as a technique in its own right'.

Laboratory research established that 'individuals assigned hard goals persistently performed better than people assigned moderately difficult or easy goals'. 'Furthermore, individuals who had specific, challenging goals outperformed those who were given such vague goals as "do your best".'

Field research in a logging company involving 292 supervisors established that those who set specific production goals achieved the highest productivity. A further study of 892 supervisors produced the same result.

An analysis of ten field studies conducted by various researchers for a range of jobs showed that the percentage change in performance after goal setting ranged from 11 per cent to 27 per cent (median 16 per cent).

This research had considerable influence on the management-by-objectives movement. It is still regarded as a fundamental motivation theory and the Latham and Locke advice on goal setting as given in Chapter 5 is just as valid today.

McDonald and Smith (1991)

Research was conducted by McDonald and Smith covering 437 publicly quoted US companies. The findings were that the 205 respondents with performance management as opposed to the others without had:

- higher profits, better cash flows, stronger stock market performance and higher stock value;
- significant gains over three years in financial performance and productivity;
- higher sales growth per employee;
- lower real growth in number of employees.

The researchers commented that: 'In the successful companies the difference in managing employee performance seems to be that it is regarded as a mainstream business issue, not an isolated "personnel problem"'.

This looks like a classic case of reversed causality. Performance management systems may have generated successful companies but it is just as likely that the successful companies were the ones with the inclination and money to introduce sophisticated practices such as performance management.

Rodgers and Hunter (1991)

A meta-analysis by Rodgers and Hunter of 70 studies in goal setting, participation in decision-making and objective feedback (as included in typical management-by-objectives programmes) found that 68 of them showed productivity gains and only two showed productivity losses. This led to the conclusion that management by objectives programmes when properly implemented and when supported by top management had an almost universal positive effect on productivity.

Sibson and WorldatWork

As reported by Kochanski (2007) a survey by Sibson and WorldatWork found that high performing firms have strong leadership support for performance management. An analysis of total return to shareholders over a three year period (2003–2005) revealed that 64 per cent of the top performing companies had performance management systems that were rated as effective compared to only 36 per cent of the bottom performing companies. The companies that excelled at performance management (1) used their systems as the primary way to manage individual performance throughout the company, (2) have strong leadership support and (3) have more line champions. This may be another case of reversed causality.

Watson Wyatt

As cited by Pulakos *et al* (2008) a recent Watson Wyatt survey found that only 30 per cent of workers felt that their performance management system helped to improve performance. Less than 40 per cent said that the system established clear performance goals or generated honest feedback.

West et al (2002)

Michael West and his colleagues carried out a study of the relationship between human resource management practices and organizational performance in hospitals. They noted that: 'There is considerable evidence that the extensiveness and sophistication of appraisal are linked to changes in individual performance'. Their findings revealed strong positive associations between HR practices and the performance of hospitals as measured by patient mortality. The extent and sophistication of appraisal in the hospitals was particularly strongly related.

Conclusions

The results of these studies are mixed. But it is still possible to believe in the benefits of performance management to organizations. This belief rests on the assumption that people are more likely to respond positively and are more likely to work to improve their performance and develop their capabilities if they share in the processes of defining expectations and reviewing performance and competency against those expectations, and are involved in creating and implementing plans for developing their skills and competencies. If this happens generally (admittedly often a big if), and if the organization provides the managerial and systems support necessary, than the presumption that this will contribute to overall performance improvement is not unreasonable, even if it cannot be proved.

References

Armstrong, M and Baron, A (1998) *Performance Management: The New Realities*, London, CIPD

Bernardin, H J, Hagan, C and Kane, J (1995) The effects of a 360 degree appraisal system on managerial performance, *Proceedings at the 10th annual conference of the Society for Industrial and Organizational Psychology*, Orlando, FL

e-reward (2014) *Survey of Performance Management*, Stockport, e-reward

Guest, D E and Conway, N (1998) An analysis of the results of the IPD performance management survey, in M Armstrong and A Baron, *Performance Management: The New Realities*, London, CIPD

Institute of Personnel Management (1992) *Performance Management in the UK: An analysis of the issues*, London, IPM

Jones, T W (1995) Performance management in a changing context, *Human Resource Management*, 34 (3) pp 425–42

Kochanski, J (2007) Sibson reveals secrets of successful performance management, *Employee Benefit News*, September, pp 22–23

Latham, G P and Locke, E A (1979) Goal Setting – a motivational technique that works, *Organizational Dynamics*, Autumn, pp 442–47

McDonald, D and Smith, A (1991) A proven connection: performance management and business results, *Compensation & Benefits Review*, January–February, pp 59–64

Pulakos, E D, Mueller-Hanson, R A and O'Leary, R S (2008) Performance management in the US, in A Varma, P S Budhwar and A DeNisi (eds) *Performance Management Systems: A global perspective*, Abingdon, Routledge

Risher, H (2005) Getting serious about performance management, *Compensation & Benefits Review*, November–December, pp 18–26

Rodgers, R and Hunter, J E (1991) Impact of management by objectives on organizational performance, *Journal of Applied Psychology*, 76 (2), pp 322–36

West, M A, Borrill, C, Dawson, J, Scully, J, Carter, M, Anelay, S, Patterson, M and Waring, J (2002) The link between the management of employees and patient mortality in acute hospitals, *The International Journal of Human Resource Management*, 13 (8), pp 1299–1310

The state of performance management

20

The state of performance management in practice has been established by a number of surveys which provide evidence on the approaches adopted to performance management, opinions about performance management and insight into the issues that are being or need to be addressed. The surveys summarized in this chapter were conducted by:

- e-reward
- the CIPD
- Lawler, Benson and McDermott
- the Work Foundation
- WorldatWork

e-reward 2014

The e-reward 2014 survey of performance management obtained data about the performance management practices of 156 respondents. The information the survey provided on the features of performance management in the organizations covered is summarized in the introduction to this book. Other specific results of the survey are given in appropriate chapters. General conclusions on the outcomes of the survey are set out below.

Make it a continuous process

Respondents urged that performance management should not be a once a year activity, instead it should be part of the organization's culture to have both formal and informal discussions throughout the year.

Plan changes

Whether introducing a new system or making changes to an existing one, the clear message coming from the HR and reward professionals who responded to the survey, was to ensure that enough time was set aside to plan the project. Many said that it was easy to underestimate the time required to put something in place while others recommended the use of focus groups to ascertain employees' views and gain feedback on what motivates them prior to the initial design. Another suggestion was to pilot the system first, again gaining feedback from those involved in order to improve and enhance the system prior to finally putting it into place.

Keep it simple

Simplicity was a term that came up time and time again, whether it was the overall process, the number of performance measures and ratings or the online platform. Many of the survey respondents emphasized that the process has to be straightforward because they need line managers to engage in it – the more complex the process is, the less likely it is that this engagement will take place. Too much bureaucracy and 'form filling' can easily turn performance management into something considered an annual chore rather than a useful tool to motivate and engage both staff and their line managers. Similarly, complexity in terms of targets and ratings can mean that the line-of-sight between what is required of staff and good performance is in danger of becoming blurred.

Involve and communicate

Another key theme that emerged from the survey is the fundamental importance of communication and involvement. This particularly applied to line managers who are of central importance. Many of the survey respondents urged others to involve this group in all aspects of performance management, particularly at the design stage. Similarly, 'buy-in' from senior managers was considered essential to ensure that all aspects of the process received their public support.

Involvement obviously includes communication and this should include contact with staff as well as line and senior managers.

Make it an open process

Survey respondents emphasized that performance management should be an open process so that it is considered fair and transparent. If results are vague or shrouded in secrecy there is less chance employees will engage with the system which can lead to a negative rather than positive impact on motivation and performance.

Monitor, review and reinforce

Once in place the survey respondents recommended that systems need to be regularly monitored, reviewed and, if necessary, modified. At the same time, however, others warned of the dangers of making too many changes and running the risk of the system losing credibility and being perceived as another temporary arrangement before the next change.

Impact of performance management

The survey indicated that performance management is likely to make the most impact if:

1 There are well-defined links to business strategy.
2 Extensive training takes place of employees generally as well as line managers.
3 Close attention is paid to ensuring that line managers are engaged with performance management and have the skills required.
4 Performance management is formally evaluated at regular intervals.

CIPD 2009

The main findings of this survey of 507 individuals were as follows:

- There was a considerable degree of agreement that performance appraisal, objective-setting, regular feedback, regular reviews and assessment of development needs are the cornerstones of performance management.

- Respondents supported the inclusion in a performance management system of regular review meetings (90 per cent), objective-setting (85 per cent), regular feedback to individuals (83 per cent), performance appraisals (82 per cent) and assessment of development needs (75 per cent).

- The need to align performance management with a range of HR activities is recognized. The majority (69 per cent of respondents) advocated that it should be linked into at least four other HR processes and 58 per cent suggested that it should link to at least five. The activities with which performance management should be linked were named in order of popularity as learning and development, career development, coaching and mentoring, succession planning and talent management.

- There was a surprising amount of disagreement about what performance management is capable of achieving. The highest level of agreement was about the assertion that performance management enables individuals to understand what they ought to be doing. Thirty per cent of respondents agreed with this statement, but still a sizeable 13 per cent disagreed and 57 per cent neither agreed nor disagreed. Only 17 per cent agreed that performance management might have an impact on well-being and 26 per cent disagreed. Twenty-three per cent agreed that performance management helps line managers to manage people better and 25 per cent disagreed. An even more controversial result of the survey was that although 20 per cent agreed that performance management has a positive impact on individual performance, 21 per cent disagreed.

Lawler, Benson and McDermott 2012

Lawler, Benson and McDermott carried out a survey of 100 large US corporations. All of them reported that they had a performance management system. The main findings were as follows:

- Jointly agreed goals are more effective than handed down pre-set goals.

- The most effective goals were those driven by the business strategy. There is a correlation between the use of these goals and organizational performance.

- Only competency models that are based on business strategy are correlated with business performance.

- It is advantageous to hold a discussion on development separate from a discussion on performance effectiveness. This is because the difficulty of appraisal discussions makes it hard for individuals to concentrate on development matters (Note, this is a surprising conclusion. Development needs are best established by examining performance issues and separating the two might weaken the connection. It means adding an unnecessary extra formal session to the cycle which managers may at worst be unwilling to hold or at best resent. The aim should be to improve the quality of appraisal discussions so that development plans flow naturally from the discussion).

- The best designed system will fail if there is not the right leadership and management support practices in place.

- Measures of the effectiveness of the system are not frequently used.

- The use of web-based performance systems increased from 57 per cent in 2002 to 71 per cent in 2012. They have a great deal to offer with respect to speed, cost and the potential to integrate the results with the other pieces of the talent management process of the organization. But overall there was no evidence that such systems improve performance of the HR function or the organization.

- Fifty-eight per cent of the companies had one system for all employees. This was surprising because it is unlikely that one system will fit every job.

- The key to successful performance management is the ownership and leadership of senior management.

- Appraisal system designers seem to overlook the importance of providing the appraiser and the appraisee with training.

- There were few attempts to measure the effectiveness of performance management. All that is required is a regular audit of how well appraisals are carried out.

- Organizations need to create performance systems that are integrated with the other HR systems.

The Work Foundation 2005

This Work Foundation research carried out by Kathy Armstrong and Adrian Ward was based on six detailed case studies. It was concluded that the variety of approaches taken by the case study organizations shows that when it comes to performance management, one size does not fit all. Performance management can be used to achieve a range of aims. It is important for organizations consciously to adopt whatever aim suits the culture and its business strategy. It is also important not to expect performance management to be a panacea for all kinds of organizational ailments. Organizations need to be clear about the purpose of performance management. The challenge is for performance management to retain a strategic role rather than tending towards tactical activities, such as the process.

The common themes from the case studies were synthesized into a framework of seven elements that organizations must discuss and, more importantly, get right when looking to maximize the effectiveness of performance management in their organizations. These seven elements are:

1 *Process:* the means by which individual performance is directed, assessed and rewarded.

2 *People management capability:* the skills, attitude, behaviours and knowledge that line managers need in order to raise the performance standards of those around them.

3 *Motivation:* the extent to which the organization's approach to performance management unlocks discretionary effort among its employees.

4 *Measurement and reward:* the indicators or 'dials on the dashboard' that are used to assess individual performance and the organizational effectiveness of the whole performance management system, and how these are used to allocate rewards.

5 *Role of HR:* the extent to which HR leaders demonstrate subject matter expertise, draw on relevant theory and research evidence, and influence thought leaders in organizations to focus on the aspects of performance management that make the most difference to performance.

6 *Learning organizations:* the extent to which organizations are able to reflect objectively and learn from their own performance management experience, building on what works and refining where necessary.

7 *Role of culture and clarity of purpose:* the extent to which an approach to performance management resonates and is congruent with the broader culture of the organization in which it is being applied.

WorldatWork 2010

A survey in the United States by WorldatWork and Sibson Consulting in 2010 produced the following key findings:

- The top three goals of performance management were: differentiating distribution of rewards based on individual performance (66 per cent); establishing greater individual accountability (52 per cent); and supporting talent development (46 per cent).

- The top three performance management challenges that organizations reported were: managers lack courage to have difficult performance discussions (63 per cent); performance management is viewed as an 'HR process' rather than a 'business critical process' (47 per cent); and that they experienced poor goal setting.

- Evaluations from performance management were more likely to be linked to merit increases than to either short- or long-term incentives.

- Senior management in higher performing organizations were more likely to support the performance management process than those in lower performing organizations.

References

Armstrong, K and Ward, A (2005) *What Makes for Effective Performance Management?* London, The Work Foundation

Chartered Institute of Personnel and Development (2009) *Performance Management in Action*, London, CIPD

e-reward (2014) *Survey of Performance Management*, Stockport, e-reward

Lawler, E E, Benson, G S and McDermott, M (2012) What makes performance appraisals effective? *Compensation & Benefits Review*, 44 (4), pp 191–200

WorldatWork and Sibson Consulting (2010) *Study on the State of Performance Management*, Phoenix AR, WorldatWork

Performance management models

21

Models of performance management systems provide a useful means of summing up how performance management works which can be communicated to employees and provide the basis for education and training activities. The models come from the following organizations:

- AstraZeneca company
- Centrica
- DHL
- HalifaxBoS
- Pfizer Inc
- Raytheon
- Royal College of Nursing
- Standard Chartered Bank
- Victoria and Albert Museum
- Yorkshire Water.

The models illustrated include some that resemble the performance management model shown in Chapter 1. Others adopt a flow chart or diagrammatic approach. However all contain the essential elements of performance management, namely: planning, review and assessment.

FIGURE 21.1   Model of the performance management system in AstraZeneca

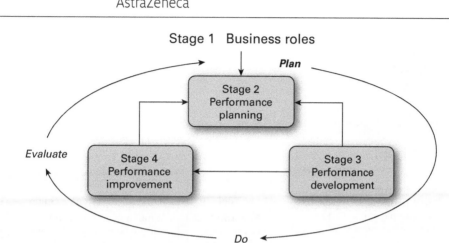

FIGURE 21.2   Model of the performance management system in Centrica

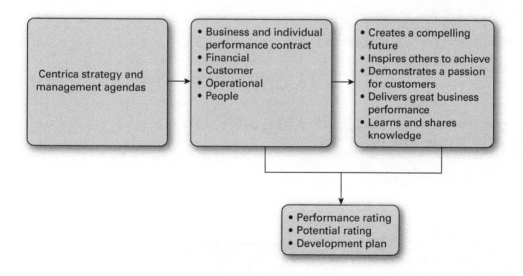

FIGURE 21.3   DHL's performance management cycle and the tools used to capture information and support the process

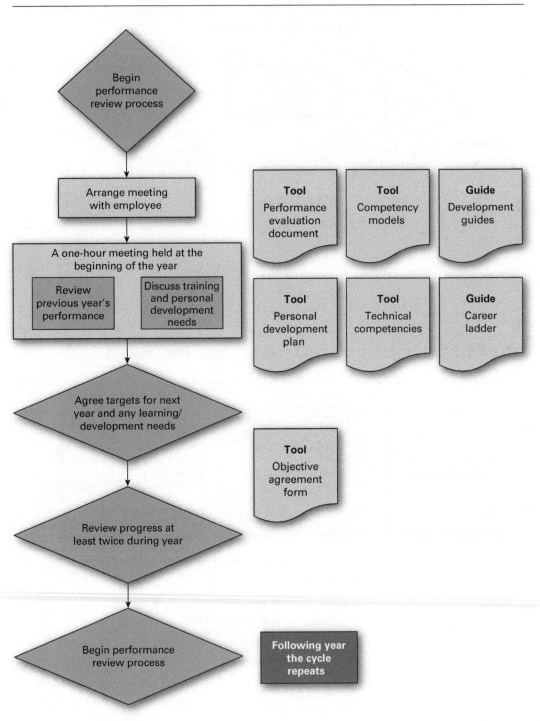

FIGURE 21.4 Model of the performance management system in HalifaxBoS

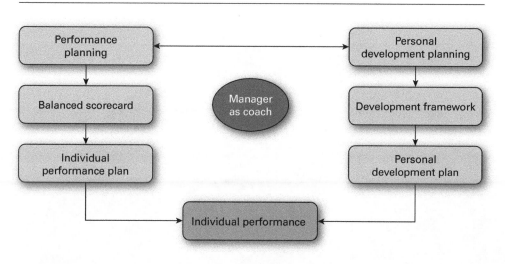

FIGURE 21.5 Model of the performance management system in Pfizer Inc

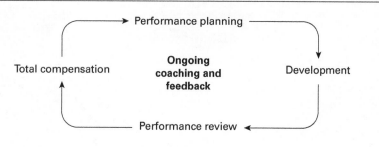

FIGURE 21.6 Model of the performance management system in Raytheon

FIGURE 21.7 Model of the performance management system in the Royal College of Nursing

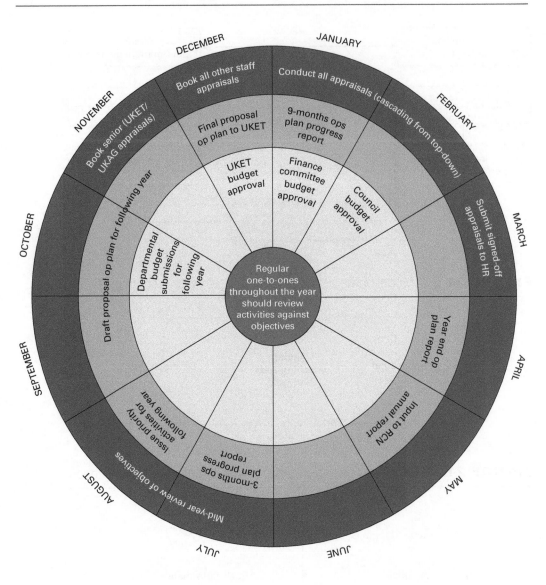

FIGURE 21.8   Managing for high performance model in
Standard Chartered Bank

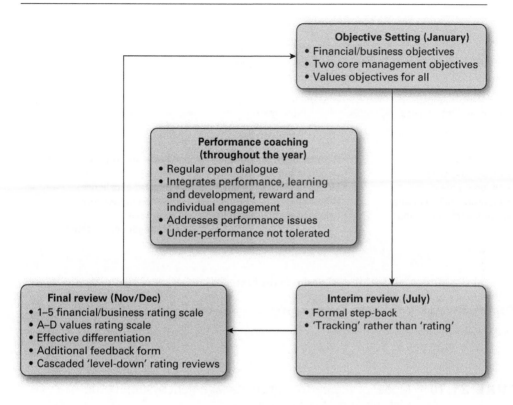

Objective Setting (January)
• Financial/business objectives
• Two core management objectives
• Values objectives for all

**Performance coaching
(throughout the year)**
• Regular open dialogue
• Integrates performance, learning
  and development, reward and
  individual engagement
• Addresses performance issues
• Under-performance not tolerated

Final review (Nov/Dec)
• 1–5 financial/business rating scale
• A–D values rating scale
• Effective differentiation
• Additional feedback form
• Cascaded 'level-down' rating reviews

Interim review (July)
• Formal step-back
• 'Tracking' rather than 'rating'

FIGURE 21.9   Managing for future high performance model in Standard Chartered Bank

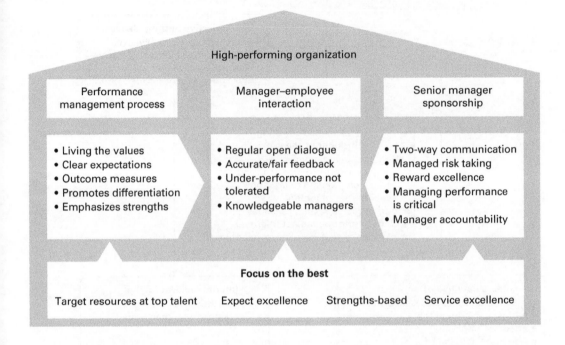

FIGURE 21.10   Model of the performance management system in the Victoria and Albert Museum

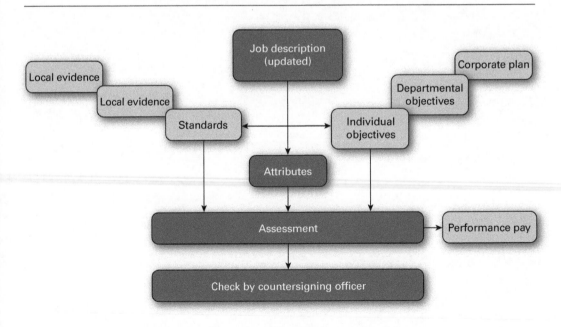

FIGURE 21.11 Model of the performance management system in Yorkshire Water

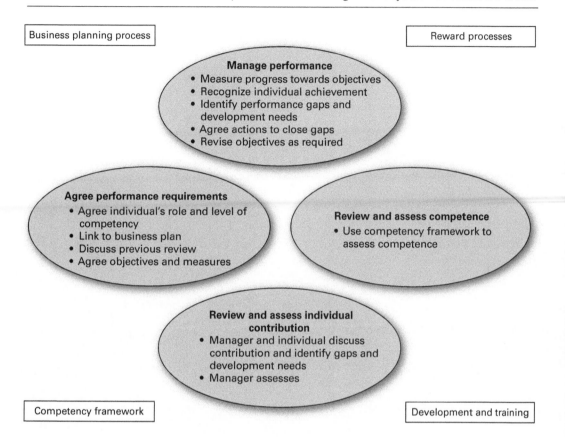

PART FIVE
The development and management of performance management

Developing performance management

22

It is not too difficult to conceptualize how performance management should function. It is much harder to ensure that it works in practice. It takes time, energy and determination to launch performance management successfully and to ensure that it continues to operate effectively. It is notable that most organizations which took part in the e-reward 2014 survey of performance management are at least considering ways in which they can alter and improve their performance management systems with over half of those surveyed saying that they have made changes to their arrangements in the last five years.

As described in this chapter it is necessary to start by understanding the development framework, the development stages and the contextual factors affecting performance management. The development process will take into account the material presented in Chapters 23 and 24 on the management of performance management including documentation and the role of line managers. Against this background, the next steps are to:

- conduct a diagnostic review;
- set objectives for performance management;
- decide on the approach to development;
- prepare and carry out the development and implementation programme involving people and paying particular attention to communication and training.

The toolkit in Appendix A covers the actions required in more detail.

FIGURE 22.1   The performance management development framework

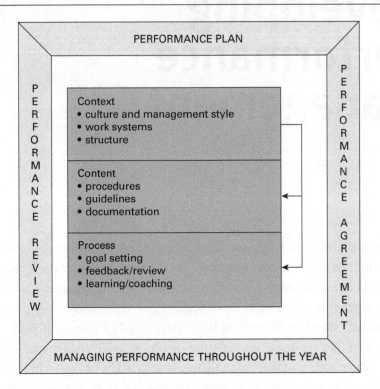

The development framework

Performance management can be regarded as a framework, as illustrated in Figure 22.1, within which a number of factors operate which will affect how it should be developed, introduced and evaluated.

The framework or essence of performance management is provided by the arrangements for agreeing performance requirements or expectations, preparing performance plans, managing performance throughout the year and analysing, assessing and reviewing performance.

Stages of development of performance management

The stages of development leading into operation and evaluation are shown in Figure 22.2.

FIGURE 22.2 Development, implementation, operation and evaluation of performance management

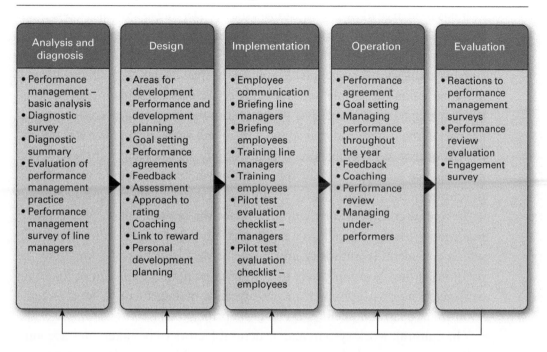

Contextual factors

The contextual or environmental factors of culture, management style, work systems and structure will strongly influence the content of performance management procedures, guidelines and documentation and the all-important processes which make it work (role analysis, goal setting, providing feedback, analysing and assessing performance and coaching).

Cultural considerations will affect performance management because it works best when it fits the existing values of the organization. Ideally, these should support high performance, quality, involvement, openness, freedom of communication and mutual trust. These may not have been put into practice in full, however vigorously they have been espoused. But top management must genuinely want to move in these directions and need to make it clear that everyone else should go along with them, using performance management as a lever for change. In performance management, there is too often a gap between the rhetoric and the reality. The process of developing and introducing performance management must concentrate on ensuring that worthy ambitions are translated into effective action by all concerned.

It has been argued by commentators such as Deming (1986) and Coens and Jenkins (2002) that it is the system of work that fundamentally determines the level of individual performance. It can be claimed equally strongly that systems are designed by people. Alternatively, they evolve through the actions and interactions of people without being consciously designed. They are certainly managed and operated by people. It can therefore be argued that people are part of the system and that some of them will work more effectively within it than others. It is important to take account of the system in developing performance management but this attention should be focused not only on the nature of the system but also on the impact it has on people and vice versa.

Structural considerations will also affect the way in which performance management is introduced. In a highly decentralized organization, or one in which considerable authority and power is devolved to some functions or divisions, it may be appropriate to encourage or permit each unit or function to develop its own approach to performance management as long as they conform to central guidelines on its basic principles.

The cultural, work system and structural factors to be taken into account will vary considerably between organizations, which is why there is no one best way to develop and introduce performance management.

Approach to developing performance management

The approach adopted to developing performance management has to recognize the reality of these contextual factors and the problems involved in meeting possibly demanding objectives and overcoming the practical and political difficulties that will get in the way of achieving sustained success. Following their research Strebler *et al* (2001) wrote about this as follows:

> Personnel management textbooks are full of touching accounts of how to design and implement performance appraisal and management schemes in organizations. The models they propose are based on a rational and linear logic which assumes that an organization's goals can be translated into individual goals which, in turn, can be delivered through feedback, training, development and reward. The reality of organizational life is somewhat different.

The following practical advice on the dos and don'ts of introducing performance management or making substantial changes to an existing scheme was given by the respondents to the e-reward 2014 survey.

Do:

- 'Work out why the organisation wants to have a performance management system. If the decision is to introduce or change the performance management system then make sure that the way it works reflects the organisation culture. Integrate the performance management system with other HR information systems.'

- 'Gain the support of senior people in the organisation. Do a lot of prep work including consultation with staff and managers to find out what kind of performance management system would work in this particular environment. Once agreed really invest in regular training and revision of how the process works.'

- 'Think about what you want from any performance management approach – why have it at all? Listen to feedback from your business owners/shareholders, senior management and staff/employee representatives, decide on the things that will make a difference to your business in the next five years and design your solution to meet that need. Remember, designing a system which picks out the best and worst can ignore the majority who become disenfranchised with performance management. Design it to engage the majority as this creates value.'

- 'Spend most time on consulting/communicating, particularly with the managers expected to do it, rather than on a clever "design".'

- 'Keep it simple and easy to understand. If changing an existing scheme, review what is wrong with current system before designing a new one. Time may be better spent embedding the existing one than changing it. Ensure system is backed up with regular performance discussions, not just a discussion once or twice a year.'

- 'Involve line managers in the design phase; asking what works and doesn't. Keep it simple. Explain the process to the whole work force. Let line managers own the process.'

- 'Get senior management to support you, otherwise it won't work. All the effort will be wasted. The biggest success factor is based on how it's rolled out.'

- 'Get senior management buy in to the process as any change needs to be driven from the top. Design your system through employee focus groups as they will tell you what they like and don't like about it. Use the feedback to improve the system. The employee focus group staff are more likely to champion the system as they have been instrumental in developing it which helps with engagement.'

- 'Consistency – one scheme for all, make it about good conversations, not just a process.'

- 'Be clear about what you are trying to achieve and how you will measure/evaluate whether you have achieved the aims. Have clear strategies and processes for dealing with poor performance and ensure managers are trained in how to deal with poor performance. Create a climate where implementing performance management systems are an absolutely necessary part of a manager's role and a real requirement of the job.'

- 'Assess what are the objectives/priorities for your organisation. Do some benchmarking and best practice but always link back to what will work for your organisation right now. Review the process. What was right a few years ago may now need changing.'

Don't:

- 'View performance management as an annual task such as appraisals; view it as a daily part of operations. Don't use appraisals as a means of dealing with performance issues, tackle them as soon as they become apparent through use of performance improvement plans for example, or if it is a conduct issue adopt a different line.'

- 'Use the process to emphasise the past. If you cannot pay much then do not use money as a key motivator.'

- 'Under-estimate the role of middle and line managers – they are the ones that will make or break your performance management process. Don't assume that because the goals and benefits of the scheme are clear to you, they will be understood, agreed and considered a priority by others. Forget that no matter what, the user interface of your performance management system in IT must be ridiculously easy to understand – even if the concepts behind them are not.'

- 'Try to do too much too soon – evaluate the culture of the business and ask if it's ready for the changes that you want to implement.'
- 'Think you will not have anomalies in trying to link pay and performance. Think line managers will have this on the top of their to do list unless there is either some pain or gain.'
- 'Think that a clever system is best.'
- 'Spend a lot of time designing forms and scoring systems.'
- 'Presume information is cascaded by managers.'
- 'Believe that performance management systems will please everyone – it's not possible.'
- 'Overcomplicate things by looking at 23 or 32 competencies.'
- 'Overcomplicate – it isn't necessary, don't do it for the sake of it, don't force people down an over-engineered process. If they set aligned objectives and have the skills to review these as well as the skills for challenging conversations – this is performance management!'
- 'Make the process too cumbersome with too many steps; if managers have too many evaluations to prepare, too many to validate, quality will be lost.'
- 'Make the appraisal such a big "event"; it should be part of a continuous process of coaching and feedback ... increasingly thinking that performance conversation should be de-linked to pay increase as it distorts the thinking.'
- 'Link the performance management directly to incentive pay. The focus switches from assessing employees – and getting the best out of them – to having an incentive pay figure in mind for an employee and using the performance management system to secure the incentive pay figure.'
- 'Let it become a box-ticking exercise, to be completed once or twice a year and then forgotten about. Don't let it be a negative experience for all involved, which might be overly bureaucratic and time-consuming, or punitive in nature.'

Developing performance management – preliminary steps

Before the development programme is planned and implemented there are a number of preliminary steps that need to be taken assuming that a new or radically amended scheme is under consideration. It is also assumed that someone within the organization will act as the sponsor of the development programme. She or he may be the head of HR or the head of a major HR function such as learning and development or talent management. The sponsor may in a sense be self-appointed – someone who believes strongly that something has to be done about performance management. The head of HR would need to persuade the chief executive that the preliminary work is necessary just as heads of HR functions would have to persuade the head of HR. Alternatively, the chief executive or a senior board member decides that action is necessary and appoints the sponsor who might well be the head of HR. The sponsor can then take the following steps, possibly with help from members of his or her team, one of whom may be designated as project manager.

1 Conduct an analysis and diagnosis of present arrangements.

2 Prepare a business case for performance management.

3 Consider system options.

4 Gain the full support of top management.

5 Consider how buy-in from line managers is to be achieved.

6 Prepare a project plan.

7 Plan for involvement.

8 Plan communications.

Analysis and diagnosis

The analysis will cover the features of the current arrangements and how well they are working. It may be conducted through interviews of a sample of managers and employees, by means of focus groups or by special surveys or by a combination of these. The diagnosis will establish what are the issues as the basis for the business case and the outline of how these issues may be addressed in a new or revised performance management system. Analytical and diagnostic checklists are included in the performance management toolkit (Appendix A).

The business case

The business case will seek to justify the development programme in terms of how the outcome will benefit the organization. It will explain the need to revise the present arrangements as revealed by the analysis and diagnosis. It will include preliminary suggestions on the objectives of a new system such as generally to develop a performance culture and specifically to improve individual and team performance and therefore organizational performance. These would be finalized at the start of the development programme.

Consider system options

Without prejudicing later consultation it is useful, and perhaps inevitable, at this stage to consider system options. A major consideration will be the design of the scheme. While the basic features of goal setting, feedback and review and assessment are likely to be present in any scheme the degree of complexity and the extent to which there is one monolithic approach will vary. It might be thought at this stage that the aim should be to keep it simple and to allow for variations in different contexts as long as the basic principles are followed. A second consideration will be whether the system should be web-based or paper-based (this is discussed in the next chapter). Finally, there may be questions about the coverage of the scheme. Should the same scheme apply to everybody or should there be different schemes for different categories of staff? It can be argued that the basic principles of the scheme should be the same for everyone. The jobs of all employees from the chief executive to the junior office worker have goals and competency requirements; the performance of all employees in reaching these goals needs to be reviewed and feedback provided. It would be invidious to distinguish between them. One exception may be the competency framework where a leadership element may be excluded for those without supervisory respon-sibilities. The 2014 e-reward survey found that 66 per cent of respondents had only one scheme. Most of the others had two schemes, one for senior management and the other for the rest of the staff.

Gain top management support

It is essential to gain the full support of top management at this stage. A compelling business case will help but this must be followed up with discussions on how the scheme might work and the role that top management can play in promoting it initially followed by encouragement at every stage of the implementation programme and beyond.

Consider how buy-in from line managers is to be achieved

It is vital to gain the commitment of line managers who can make or break a performance management scheme. Thought should be given at this stage on how this can be done as a key part of the development and implementation programme and thereafter. Approaches to doing this are described in Chapter 24.

Prepare a project plan

The project plan will define who will manage and be involved in the project, as a whole or different aspects of it, and set out the programme. Typical programme steps are described in the next section of this chapter. A decision would have to be made on whether outside help from management consultants is needed. They could bring experience and expertise to the assignment and act as 'an extra pair of hands'. However, there is much to be said for a home grown product as long as people are available who can do the work.

It is desirable to set up a project team to develop performance management composed of managers, staff, trade union representatives (if there are unions) and HR specialists. A project manager should be appointed who would be responsible for the detailed planning and implementation activities. The programme manager could report to a programme director who would chair a steering committee of senior managers which oversees progress and approves project team proposals. It is possible to deploy a number of experienced line managers to provide help, for example in running a pilot scheme and taking part in communications and training programmes. This approach was successfully adopted by AstraZeneca where the managers who were involved in development assisted with the implementation programme by coaching and mentoring less experienced managers.

Plan for involvement

The involvement of line managers and other employees in the development programme is essential for three reasons: (1) people support what they help to create, (2) good ideas about the system and how it can best work will be generated and (3) people have a right to be consulted on matters that affect them.

Involvement can be achieved to a degree by having line manager and staff representatives on a project team but this should be extended through focus groups and departmental meetings and by the use of employee surveys (example in Appendix A).

Plan communications

Considerable care needs to be taken to communicate to all concerned – managers, team leaders, staff and trade union representatives – the aims of performance management, how it will work and how people will be affected by it. The communication strategy should be a constant preoccupation of the developers of the scheme. They should consider how each feature of the process as it is being developed can be explained and presented to the people concerned.

Communication can be through documentation (an explanatory brochure), the intranet and face-to-face briefings (the more of the latter the better). The following is an example of a guide to performance management prepared by a not-for-profit organization.

A guide to performance management

Introduction

The purpose of performance management is to help and encourage everyone to raise their performance, develop their abilities, increase job satisfaction and achieve their full potential to the benefit of the individual and the organization.

What is performance management?

Performance management is a means of getting better results from the organization, teams and individuals by understanding and managing performance within an agreed framework of planned goals, and standards.

It is based on the simple proposition that when people know and understand what is expected of them, and have been able to take part in forming those expectations, they are most likely to meet them.

Why do we need performance management?

There are two main reasons for introducing performance management:

1   We want to focus everyone's attention on what they are expected to achieve in their jobs and how best to achieve it.

2   We would like to help everyone to identify and satisfy their development needs – to improve performance and realize their potential.

How does performance management work?

Performance management works like this:

- You and your manager will discuss and agree your objectives, action plans and development and training needs – this is called the performance agreement.

- During the review period (normally 12 months) you and your manager will keep under review your progress in meeting your objectives – as necessary you will agree revisions to those objectives and your priorities.

- Towards the end of the review period you and your manager will separately prepare for the performance and development review meeting – deciding in advance on any points you wish to raise and noting these down.

- A review meeting will then be held at which you can discuss with your manager how you got on during the review period and any other points you want to raise. You will then together draw up a new performance agreement.

- Your manager's manager will see the form and will add any comments he or she feels may be appropriate. You will also see these comments.

- You and your manager will then retain your own copies of the review form – no other copies will be held by anyone else.

Performance management will:

- focus on developing strengths as well as considering any performance issues;

- be based on open and constructive discussion;

- be an everyday and natural management process – not an annual form-filling exercise;

- be a positive process – looking to the future rather than dwelling on the past.

The part you will play

We hope that you will contribute to the success of this scheme in the following ways:

- by preparing carefully for the review – noting any points you want to raise with your manager;

- by entering into the spirit of the review meeting which is intended to provide an opportunity for you to have 'quality time' with your manager during which an open and friendly exchange of views will take place about your job and your prospects;

- by thinking carefully about how you are going to achieve the objectives and plans agreed at the meeting;

- by reviewing how you are getting on during the year and agreeing any actions required.

The part managers will play

All managers will be expected to play their part with you in preparing for the meeting, reviewing your performance and drawing up your performance agreement. They are being specially trained in how to do this. Managers are also expected to work with you in preparing and implementing your personal development plan.

Benefits to you

We hope performance management will benefit you by ensuring that:

- you know what is expected of you;

- you know how you stand;

- you know what you need to do to reach your objectives;

- you can discuss with your manager your present job, your development and training needs and your future.

Benefits to your manager

Managers will gain the opportunity to:

- clarify expectations with the individual members of their teams;

- have 'quality time' with their staff to discuss matters affecting work, performance and development away from the hurly-burly of everyday working life;

- provide better feedback to individuals about their performance and progress based on a mutual understanding of needs;

- identify areas of individual concern and provide guidance to enable individuals to make the best use of their abilities;

- build closer working relationships based on mutual trust and respect;

- identify individual training and development needs.

Benefits to the organization

The organization gains the opportunity to:

- integrate individual, team and corporate objectives;

- guide individual and team effort to meeting overall business needs;

- recognize individual contribution;

- plan individual careers;

- introduce relevant and effective learning and development programmes to meet identified needs.

An example of a communication issued to staff at the Royal College of Nursing (RCN) is shown in Table 22.1.

An example of communications from HRG is given in Appendix B.

Development programme

The development of performance management can be carried out in the seven stages shown in Figure 22.3 on page 286 and described below. At each stage arrangements should be made to consult and involve staff and, as appropriate, communicate to everyone what is happening, why it is happening and how it affects them.

TABLE 22.1   Communication on performance management issued at the Royal College of Nursing

What it is	What it is not	The benefits of doing it
• A formal meeting which is part of an ongoing discussion between the appraiser and the appraisee • A two-way discussion • A review of activity and performance over the past year • An exploration of any challenges that were faced during the year • An opportunity to explore ways of enhancing motivation and performance • A discussion of future work areas and joint agreement of objectives • An opportunity to discuss and agree development areas for the appraisee	• Simply a one-off, once a year exercise • Closed/secret • Disciplinary • Platform for bullying • One-sided • A surprise	If carried out correctly, the RCN appraisal process can benefit the appraisee, appraiser, counter-signer and the organization in a number of ways: • Support the organization in achieving its overall purpose • Link individual activities to departmental operational plans – support the department in better planning workload and deadlines • Create a joint understanding between the appraiser and the appraisee of areas of work • Appraisee can better understand what is required of them and how their areas of work contribute to the departmental operational plan and subsequently the overall purpose of the RCN • Appraiser has clear targets against which to measure performance of the appraisee • Can improve performance of the appraisee • Can improve morale/motivation of the appraisee • Give both the appraiser and the appraisee an understanding of the development needed and plan how best to support this

Stage 1 Agree objectives for performance management

The objectives of performance management should be discussed and agreed by the project team. These may refer to any objectives suggested in the preliminary stage but the team may amend them. Specific objectives could include:

- To improve organizational, team and individual performance.
- To provide for the closer alignment of organizational and individual goals.

FIGURE 22.3 Performance management development stages

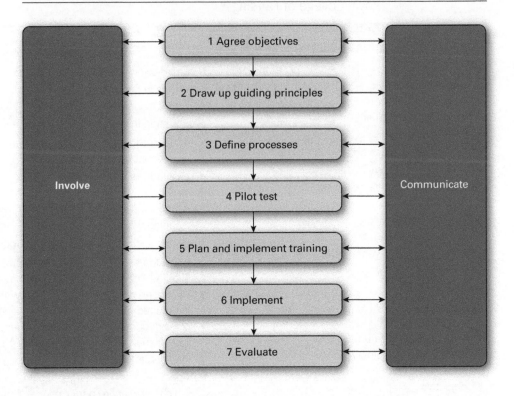

- To clarify expectations on what individuals have to achieve.
- To support the realization of the organization's core values.
- To develop the skills and abilities of employees.
- To foster a closer relationship between individuals and their managers based on the agreement of objectives, feedback and coaching.
- To provide for a more objective and fairer method of assessing performance.
- To empower individuals to manage their own performance and learning.
- To enhance levels of employee engagement.
- To support the talent management programme.
- To provide a means of rewarding employees as part of a total rewards system.

Stage 2 Draw up guiding principles on how performance management should work

The guiding principles should emphasize that performance management is regarded as a normal and continuous process of management which is owned by the managers and staff who are involved. It should be made clear that it operates as a partnership between managers and their staff who are equally involved in planning and reviewing performance and in implementing personal development and performance improvement plans.

The following is an example of guiding principles developed by a working party in a local authority:

- clearly stated work objectives/tasks subject to regular review and updating;
- clearly stated standards of performance;
- feedback on job behaviour;
- comments rather than performance ratings;
- identification of development needs;
- agreed training plan;
- reach agreement through a two-way process;
- incorporate appeal procedure;
- used as a day-to-day management tool;
- no link to pay;
- if no commitment from the head of department, don't do it.

Stage 3 Define performance management processes

Each stage of the performance management cycle needs to be defined. The first step is to describe the performance planning process – how role profiles are agreed and used as the basis for performance management, how goals are set, how performance measures are agreed, and how development plans are drawn up. Secondly, the basis upon which performance management should be a continuous process (performance management throughout the year) through informal reviews of progress and feedback should be explained. Finally, the approach to conducting performance reviews should be explained. Rating methods, if required, have to be decided and thought given to how to ensure that they are consistent and fair. Decisions are required on the use of rating scales and, if they are wanted, the scales drawn up. This could involve quite a lot of work if it is decided to use some form of graphic or behaviourally anchored rating scale (see Chapter 9). The link, if any, between performance management and merit or performance pay also needs to be determined.

Performance management processes include documentation. This is traditionally paper based and involves the design of performance management forms to be completed by managers and the individual concerned with guidelines on how they should be used. The points to be considered and an example is given in Chapter 19. The watch words are 'keep it simple'. Complex and lengthy forms are a major cause of performance management failure. It should be emphasized that the forms should simply act as an *aide memoire*. They should not be allowed to dominate the procedure.

Consideration can be given at this stage on the extent to which the process should be web-enabled as also described in Chapter 19. This will probably mean obtaining the software from a supplier but it will have to be customized and this will include designing the forms and displays to be used, and briefing and training managers and individuals in operating the system.

Stage 4 Pilot test

It is essential to pilot test performance management in two or three different types of departments. The procedures as set out on paper or as computerized must be exposed to real life conditions so that problems and issues in applying them can be identified. The tests will indicate what changes need to be made but they will also reveal what managers and staff have to learn about performance management. This will feed into the implementation programme during which steps are taken to ensure that everyone learns what they need to know. If the departments are selected carefully with a committed management team and staff who are likely to be cooperative, the pilot test can identify champions of performance management who can act as coaches and mentors and provide practical guidance.

The test should cover all the main performance management processes, ideally, over the whole twelve month cycle. If this is felt to be too long then at least three months and preferably six should be allowed. Superficial tests are worse than useless. Performance management takes time to establish. It should never be rushed.

Stage 5 Plan and conduct training

Training in performance management is necessary for both line managers and staff generally. It is particularly important that line managers have the skills required. These are demanding and the programme should provide for coaching, mentoring and ongoing guidance as well as formal training courses. A half or one day course which is the typical time the e-reward research established was devoted to training is not enough. Training arrangements are described in Chapter 25.

Stage 6 Implement

The implementation programme should cover communications, training and the provision of guidance and help.

Stage 7 Evaluate

It is important to carry out a thorough evaluation as described in Chapter 26 of how well performance management works after its first year of operation.

References

Coens, T and Jenkins, M (2002) *Abolishing Performance Appraisals: Why they backfire and what to do instead*, San Francisco CA, Berrett-Koehler

Deming, W E (1986) *Out of the Crisis*, Cambridge MA, Massachusetts Institute of Technology Centre for Advanced Engineering Studies

e-reward (2014) *Survey of Performance Management Practice*, Stockport, e-reward

Strebler, M T, Bevan, S and Robertson, D (2001) *Performance Review: Balancing objectives and content*, Brighton, Institute for Employment Studies

Managing performance management

23

Performance management is managing the business. It is what line managers do continuously, not an HR directed annual procedure. It is a natural process of management. But it is a natural process that can be enhanced if it is conducted systematically. That is why it is called a performance management system. The following questions will be answered in this chapter:

- Who should be covered by performance management?
- How should performance management be managed?
- What approach should be adopted?
- What documentation is required?
- To what extent can the processes involved be computerized by the use of web-enabled performance management?
- What is the role of HR?

Who should be covered by performance management?

Ideally performance management should cover everyone in the organization starting at the top. The approach might not be so elaborate for routine jobs in terms of the competency headings covered, for example, a leadership element may be inappropriate. But those in routine jobs are entitled to as much consideration as anyone else and this includes contributing to goal setting, properly conducted performance reviews with feedback, and opportunities for coaching and further development.

How should performance management be managed?

Performance management should be managed as a systematic process which is the concern of all of those to whom it applies. The aspects of performance management that need to be managed are:

- the communication of the aims of performance management – how it works and the responsibilities of those involved;

- the performance agreement process – providing guidance on the use of role profiles and goal setting;

- the performance review process – ensuring that reviews are carried out properly and documented (this is a major administrative area which may be computerized as is considered in detail later in this chapter);

- personal development planning – providing guidance and support in preparing and implementing personal development plans;

- skills development – providing coaching, mentoring and training in developing performance management skills such as goal setting, providing feedback, coaching and conducting performance reviews;

- monitoring and evaluation – monitoring the application of performance management, evaluating its effectiveness and taking action to improve it when necessary (this is a vital activity as described in Chapter 26).

The way in which performance management is managed will be affected by the context, which includes culture, the approach to management and management style. If the approach to managing is generally bureaucratic a more structured and controlled system with elaborate forms and procedures may be used. A more flexible approach to organization may mean that more scope is allowed for managers to carry out performance management within a policy framework. If the prevailing management style is autocratic, performance management may simply be a top-down method of controlling the workforce. A democratic management style would allow more scope for dialogue and agreement between managers and individuals. The organization structure will also affect the system (multinational, divisionalized, regionalized, centralized, devolved etc). As described in Chapter 18, in multinational organizations there may be a choice on the degree to which the approach should be convergent (ie the parent company's practices are replicated worldwide in order to achieve consistency in meeting universal standards) or divergent (ie HR policies and practices are tailored to meet local circumstances although adherence to certain guiding principles may be expected).

What approach should be adopted?

It has often been said in this book – but it bears repetition – that it is the processes of performance management as practised by line managers which are important, not the content of the system and how it is administered. The elegance with which forms and computerized systems are designed is relatively unimportant. Their purpose is no more than that of recording views and decisions; they are not ends in themselves.

Similarly, administrative procedures should not weigh down performance management. It is important to establish the principles of performance management and get everyone to buy into them, but administration and control should be carried out with a light touch. There should be scope for managers to decide on their own detailed approaches in conjunction with their staff as long as they abide by the guiding principles. However, performance management practice should be monitored through the evaluation approaches described in Chapter 26 which may reveal the need for general refresher training or the provision of coaching or guidance to individual managers.

Oppressive control will only prejudice managers against the process which they will think has been imposed upon them. This is against the whole thrust of performance management, which is to get managers and their staff to recognize that this is an effective process of management from which all can benefit.

Performance management is not a form-filling exercise, as many traditional merit rating or performance appraisal schemes appeared to be. Personnel managers who spent their time chasing up reluctant line managers to complete their appraisal forms and return them to the personnel department often unwittingly defeated the whole purpose of the exercise. Managers tended to be cynical about their rating and box-ticking activities and often produced bland and unrevealing reports which could be prepared without too much effort. They became even more cynical if they had any reason to believe that the completed forms were gathering dust in personal dossiers, unused and unheeded. And, this was often what happened.

A case could be made for having no forms at all for managers to complete. They could be encouraged to record their agreement and the conclusions of their reviews on blank sheets of paper or as a computer file to be used as working documents during the continuing process of managing performance throughout the year.

But there is much to be said for having a format which can help in the ordering and presentation of plans and comments and act as an *aide memoire* for reference during the year. And the mere existence of a form or a set of forms does demonstrate that this is a process which managers and their staff are expected to take seriously. Consideration is next given first to traditional methods of documentation and then to more recent developments in web-enabled performance management.

Performance management documentation

Performance management documentation can be on paper as described below, or, more commonly, it can be wholly or partly web-based. Before designing performance management forms it is necessary to be quite clear about their purpose. The following questions need to be answered:

1 What information does the HR department need about the outcome of performance reviews?
2 How is the quality of performance reviews to be guaranteed?
3 How can employees be reassured that they will not become the victims of prejudiced or biased reports?

Performance management forms as working documents

The main purpose of a performance management form is to serve as a working document. It should be in continual use by managers and individuals as a source of information on agreed objectives and plans when reviewing progress. It records agreements on performance achievements and actions to be taken to improve performance or develop competence and skills. It should be dog-eared from much use – it should not be condemned to moulder away in a file.

For this reason the forms should be owned by the manager and the individual (both parties should have a copy). Any information the HR department needs in ratings (for performance-related pay or career planning purposes) or requests for training should be incorporated in a separate form for their use.

The employee can still be protected against unfair assessments and ratings by providing for the manager's manager (the 'grandparent') to see and comment on the completed report. These comments could be shown to the individual who should have the right to appeal through a grievance procedure if he or she is still unhappy about the report.

There is, however, a good case for the HR department having sight of completed review forms for quality assurance purposes, especially in the earlier days of operating performance management.

Information for the HR department

The HR department may need to know:

- who the high flyers are – for talent management purposes;
- who are the people who are performing badly – to consider with the line manager what action needs to be taken;
- performance ratings for performance-related pay decisions;
- recommendations on training to assess any common training needs and to initiate training action;
- about the performance of any individual who might be considered for promotion, transfer or disciplinary action.

Another factor which helps to persuade many organizations to hold copies of the review forms centrally is that a decision in an unfair dismissal case may depend on the quality of record keeping as well as the honesty of the performance review process – performance review forms may be required for evidence. This can create a problem if a manager who has produced bland, superficial but generally favourable reports on an employee is later allowed to take disciplinary action for incapability. Employment tribunals do not look with favour on this type of inconsistency. It is always necessary for the HR department to compare review reports with the picture painted by managers when the latter request disciplinary action and to question any inconsistencies.

The approach adopted by most organizations is to require at least a copy of the review form and a performance agreement if this contains training and development recommendations to be held by HR. Managers and individuals would retain their own copies as working documents.

In the UK it is necessary to remember the provisions of the Data Protection Act 1998 which give employees the right to inspect any documents or records which contain personal data.

Form design

When designing performance management forms the aim should be to keep them as simple and brief as possible. Like all good forms, they should as far as possible be self-explanatory, but they can be supplemented by notes for guidance.

There are many varieties of performance management forms used by different organizations – some simple and some elaborate with, for example, a special 'performance planner' form. However, they typically include sections for:

- agreed goals;
- agreed performance and personal development plans;
- review of performance against objectives;
- review of achievements against the development plans.

If a competency framework exists, the form may include a section listing the competencies with space for comments.

Forms in organizations with performance-related pay (PRP) will often have an overall rating section. Those without PRP may still retain ratings as a means of summarizing performance.

There are three basic varieties of documentation:

1 A detailed performance management agreement and review form.

2 A simplified performance management agreement and review form.

3 A performance agreement form.

FIGURE 23.1 Performance management form (part 1)

PERFORMANCE AND DEVELOPMENT: AGREEMENT AND REVIEW SUMMARY	
Name:	Forename(s):
Job title:	Department:
Reviewer's name:	Job title:
PERFORMANCE AND DEVELOPMENT AGREEMENT	
Objectives	Performance measures
Competencies	Agreed actions

PERSONAL DEVELOPMENT PLAN			
Development need	How it is to be met	Action by	Target completion

Detailed performance management agreement and review form

A typical set of fairly complex forms which do not include an overall performance rating section is illustrated in Figures 23.1 and 23.2.

Simplified performance management agreement and review form

But even this fairly straightforward form may be too elaborate and it fails to be self-explanatory. A plea for simplicity has been made many times in this book. A performance management form is the visible part of a performance

FIGURE 23.2   Performance management form (part 2)

PERFORMANCE AND DEVELOPMENT REVIEW	
Objectives	Achievements
Competencies	Actions taken
Development needs	Actions taken
Comments by reviewer:	
Comments by reviewee:	
Signed: Date:	

management system and the simpler it is the better. An example of a basic but perfectly adequate form is reproduced in an abbreviated version in Figure 23.3. It could be used by both parties as a preparation form, which would include self-assessment by the job holder as well as a record of agreements made at planning or review meetings. It is reasonably self-explanatory although it would be essential to train people in its use.

Performance agreement form

A performance agreement form simply sums up what has been decided during the planning stage of the performance management cycle. It provides a framework for review during the year and is illustrated in Figure 23.4.

FIGURE 23.3   Simplified performance management form

Performance Management Form		
Job holder/job title	Manager	Period
Goals List below the key areas of the job (no more than six). A key area is something that has to be done by the job holder in order to achieve the overall purpose of the job. The areas should be defined very briefly (preferably in one sentence). For each area indicate what the job holder is expected to achieve and how the achievement can be measured or recognized.	**Achievements** Summarize what has been achieved in the period under review for each of the key areas. Note any factors that have contributed to or affected the achievement. The factors could be within the job holder's control (the way in which the work was carried out) or related to the job holder's experience and level of skill or ability. They may be external factors outside the job holder's control.	**Actions** Set down any agreed actions to be taken by the job holder or the manager to develop the job holder's skills and abilities or improve performance. The actions could include coaching, training or a personal development plan.
1		
2		
3		
4		
5		
6		
Signed Job holder..................................... Manager..................................... Date..................................	*Signed* Job holder..................................... Manager..................................... Date..................................	

FIGURE 23.4 Performance agreement form

Area of agreement	Agreement	Comments/review
Key result areas		
Goals		
Performance improvement plan		
Personal development plan		

Web-based performance management

The basic features of web-based or online performance management systems typically include the ability to capture performance ratings, interfaces for displaying performance standards and rating-process information. More advanced features comprise prompting managers and employees about performance management events, routing documents between employees, providing access to forms and providing automated reports. The forms used may be similar to those illustrated earlier.

Web-based performance management ensures widespread access and provides a standardized format for collecting and storing performance data. The software can make it easy for managers and employees to record role profiles and performance agreements including performance improvement and personal development plans and objectives, monitor progress against the plans, access performance documents online, and gather multi-source (360-degree appraisal) comments. All this data can be used to assist in performance reviews and record further agreements emerging from the reviews.

The aim is to reduce paperwork and simplify the process. A justification for 'e-appraisals' was provided by Barlow (2003):

> The time-consuming process of administering old-style performance reviews no longer needs to exist within any organization. E-appraisals are an automated process that dramatically cuts the amount of time and effort that is spent on the administrative procedure by HR staff. The time and effort required to write professional appraisals by line managers can be greatly reduced by the more sophisticated e-appraisal programmes. They enable employees to gain access via the internet to their record of performance as it develops throughout the year instead of having to rely on their memory of their successes, failures and learning needs.

Summers (2005) claimed that: 'In an internet-based performance management system, employees have "line-of-sight" visibility. They can set their goals to align with those of other managers, and they can see how these goals align all the way to the corporate goals'. The system provides 'the ability to pull information from multiple sources and aggregate it, to drive activity by interacting with users and to make information accessible and visible in truly meaningful ways'.

However, Pulakos *et al* (2008) commented that a problem with automated performance management systems is that in making evaluations easier to complete, they may result in a propensity for managers to get their performance management responsibilities done as quickly as possible – ticking the boxes – and perhaps not spend the extra time in performance-related interactions with employees. And as Fletcher (2001) pointed out, the more impersonal nature of entering and communicating assessments via a computer could lead to greater objectivity but less sensitivity and tact in handling the situation – apart from anything else, there is no chance to directly observe the recipients' reactions.

Web-based performance management systems were used by 36 per cent of the respondents to the e-reward 2014 performance management survey. Here are some reports from respondents on their web-based systems:

- 'We use a web-based system called one2onetracker. It is easy to use and access and managers can record their meeting minutes straight away to avoid duplication of writing up minutes, etc. HR also have administration rights where we can check up on those managers who have not conducted enough one-to-ones and we can do spot checks and talk to managers about any issues that are raised, etc.'

- 'We have an on-line performance management system. All forms etc are electronic. All written guidance is also on-line on our intranet. We have dedicated micro-sites for "performance and potential" and for "people managers". These contain guidance and e-learning tools.'

- 'Our on-line system is linked to our HR system to obtain information on completion rates, ratings etc.'

- 'The whole system is online and integrated with the rest of HRIS including payroll and talent management and L&D (there is section about training needs). This allows for up-to-date employee information, accurate reporting and production of intelligence at multiple levels in the organisation from top management to line supervisors and even employees. We also have tools for the HRBPs to track progress in their units so that they can intervene if needed (risk prevention and empowerment of HRBPs instead of post-event centred).'

- 'Recently introduced a web-based tool for recording the outcomes of PDR discussions which is accessible by both manager and staff member but is securely maintained outside of the County Council's systems.'

- 'Online appraisal for management population – easier to track completion and analyse results.'

- 'New performance management system (Oracle). Fits with ERP used for other HR processes so consistent from a data management point of view. Bought performance management module to get away from paper records.'

- 'It's a real time ongoing system that enables both manager and employee to complete progress and updates throughout the year.'

Other examples of web-based systems

Raytheon

The Raytheon web-enabled system incorporates a 'performance screen' and a 'performance and development summary' as well 360-degree assessment tools and details of how the Raytheon compensation system works. It enables goals to be cascaded down through the organization, although employees can initiate the goal setting process using the performance screen as a tool. Employees can then document their accomplishments against their goals on their performance screen.

Royal College of Nursing

FIGURE 23.5   Royal College of Nursing – diagram of online performance appraisal scheme

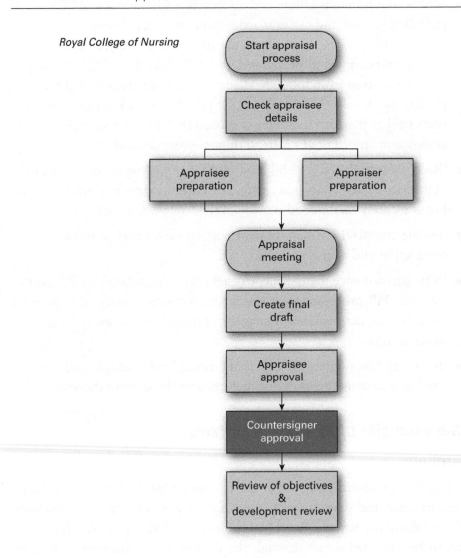

Royal College of Nursing

TRW Inc

As reported by Neary (2002) TRW Inc based their system on an 'Output Form' which included:

Page 1 Biographical Data

- identification information
- education
- experience summary

Pages 2–3 Performance Summary

- accomplishments against previous year goals
- TRW Behaviours
- TRW Initiatives
- legal and ethical conduct – diversity and cultural sensitivity
- previous year's professional development activities
- employee comments
- overall performance – manager's overall rating (four point scale) and comments

Page 4 Development Summary

- demonstrated strengths
- improvement opportunities
- performance goals for the upcoming year
- professional development activities for the upcoming year
- future potential/positions (employee perspective)
- future potential/positions (manager perspective)
- electronic sign off from both employee and manager

Once managers have reviewed the employees' input, they are required to sit down with their reports and have a face-to face dialogue about the employee's progress in the past year and plans for the coming year. To aid managers who may have many direct reports a 'manage employees' function is included so that managers can see an on-screen overview of the status of each of their direct reports.

Each year, data from the previous year's system is transferred to this year's system, eliminating the need for additional data input.

The Zambon Group

As described by Armstrong and Ward (2005) the Zambon Group (a multi-national chemical and pharmaceutical company based in Italy with 2,300 employees) developed a web-based performance management system as follows.

Consultants developed a blueprint for integrating the performance appraisal form with the procedures to ensure a greater level of objectivity and transparency. Crucial to the success was the selection of technology. The overall approach was to ensure that IT could maintain control of the services and databases in order to guarantee full compatibility with existing IT systems, both at a central and user level while HR could maintain the procedural software without the need for costly software development.

The two technologies chosen were *Microsoft InfoPath* and *Decision Flows*. *InfoPath* is an application that enables information workers to create dynamic forms that can help to share and manage data easily from different sources. *Decision Flows* lets business people create decision-making components without the need for software programmers. This combination helped with the rapid conversion of the existing performance appraisal forms and associated procedures into one integrated 'smart' form.

The developed process saves considerable time and costs. For example, ratings are derived from a simplified series of questions and answers.

The role of HR

At one time, the personnel department tended to be not only the sponsor but also the custodian of performance appraisal schemes. As a result line managers regarded them as the preserve of personnel and therefore not their concern. They filled up the forms, often because they had to, but unenthusiastically.

The emergence of the 'business partner' concept of HR has led to a change in direction. HR no longer runs the performance appraisal scheme, but the danger of simply giving it away had to be recognized. Their role becomes that of encouraging and facilitating the sort of performance management processes described in this book. And this is an important role. They work alongside line managers, helping them as necessary to develop their skills and encouraging their use. They assemble teams of committed and experienced managers who can act as coaches and mentors and stimulate the creation of communities of practice, ensuring that performance management is on the agenda. More specifically, they run training events and conduct surveys to evaluate the effectiveness of performance management. In essence, HR specialists exist to support performance management rather than drive it. A comment on the role of HR in performance management based on research carried out by the Work Foundation (Armstrong and Ward, 2005) is given below:

> HR's role in performance management is crucial. They tend to be the people that are in charge of designing and reviewing systems, convincing boards of a new approach, implementing new processes, running workshops for managers and staff, providing advice and support materials to staff and managers, and ensuring there is compliance with the system. However, they cannot be at every appraisal discussion; they can't ensure that managers and employees have 'quality' conversations; and they have a limited ability to improve the capability and engagement of managers in managing performance.

References

Armstrong, K and Ward, A (2005) *What Makes for Effective Performance Management?* London, The Work Foundation

Barlow, G (2003) Barriers to appraisals, *Competency & Emotional Intelligence*, 10 (6), pp 29–30

e-reward (2014) *Survey of Performance Management*, Stockport, e-reward

Fletcher, C (2001) Performance appraisal and management: the developing research agenda, *Journal of Occupational and Organizational Psychology*, 74 (4), pp 473–87

Neary, D B (2002) Creating a company-wide, on-line, performance management system: a case study at TRW INC, *Human Resource Management*, 41 (4), pp 491–98

Pulakos, E D, Mueller-Hanson, R A and O'Leary, R S (2008) Performance management in the US, in A Varma, P S Budhwar and A DeNisi (eds), *Performance Management Systems: A global perspective*, Abingdon, Routledge

Summers, L (2005) Integrated pay for performance: the high-tech marriage of compensation management and performance management, *Compensation & Benefits Review*, January/February, pp 18–25

The performance management role of line managers

24

Line managers play a crucial role in performance management. As Risher (2012) remarked: 'When the performance management system is "owned" by line managers, the level of effectiveness is significantly higher. There is a shared recognition that it is part of a manager's responsibilities.'

The 'black box' research conducted by John Purcell and his colleagues (2003) led to the conclusion that 'front line management or leadership played a pivotal role in terms of implementing and enacting HR policies and practices since it is the front line managers that bring policies to life'. Ellinger *et al* (2003) stated that short-term demands on line managers, time pressures, lack of rewards or recognition for assuming developmental roles, confusion about their roles, lack of an organizational climate conducive to employee development, and inadequate skills and competence may serve as barriers that impede performance management.

An important consideration in designing and operating performance management is how to gain the commitment of line managers and ensure that they have the skills required. The need is to fill the gap between rhetoric and reality; between what top management and HR want line managers to do and what line managers actually do. This chapter deals with the performance management role of line managers under the following headings:

- what the performance management role of line management is;
- issues with the performance management role of line managers;
- how the issues can be addressed.

The role of line managers

Performance management is what line managers do. They are there to achieve results through people and therefore have to manage the performance of their people. The aim of performance management systems is to help them to do this. They play a crucial role in each stage of the performance management cycle.

At the planning and performance agreement stage they agree with team members their roles, goals and performance improvement and personal development plans. They manage performance throughout the year by monitoring achievements against the plan, providing feedback and coaching as necessary. At the review stage they conduct formal review meetings and provide formal feedback as the basis for forward planning.

To do all this they need the following skills:

- preparing role profiles – defining key result areas and competency requirements;

- defining goals;

- identifying and using performance measures;

- giving and receiving feedback;

- taking part in review meetings – ensuring that there is a proper dialogue which enables the manager and the individual jointly, frankly and freely to discuss performance requirements and learning needs;

- assessing performance including rating, where appropriate;

- identifying learning needs and preparing and implementing personal development plans;

- diagnosing and solving performance problems (managing poor performance);

- coaching.

Issues with the performance management role of line managers

Performance management may be what line managers do but they don't always seem to do it very well. Respondents to the e-reward (2014) survey listed the following problems with line managers as the four biggest ones they had to face in their performance management systems:

- line managers did not have the skills required – 55 per cent;
- line managers did not discriminate sufficiently when assessing performance – 49 per cent;
- line managers were reluctant to conduct performance management reviews – 38 per cent;
- line managers were not committed to performance management – 24 per cent.

Following their research, Hutchinson and Purcell (2003) discussed 'performance appraisal' as an HR activity (they did not refer to performance management as a management activity). They noted that: 'Performance appraisal is an area in which front line managers have traditionally had direct involvement with their staff, and provides a good example of the key role these managers have to play in their delivery of HR policies'. They also found that:

> Looking at the sample of employees interviewed over the two years (n=608) we found that performance appraisal was rated as the least effective HR policy (in terms of levels of satisfaction) after pay, and in a fair number of organizations it was the least favourite HR activity. The reasons given were numerous, and included the views that the measurements and targets were felt to be unclear and/or not relevant, and that the system was too complicated and time consuming. Many of the problems could be directly linked to the behaviour of managers, as the interviews with employees revealed.

The research conducted by Armstrong and Ward (2005) identified the following problems with line managers and performance management:

> Our case study organizations were all finding it difficult to improve their managers' capacity to manage performance effectively. A particular issue for all of the organizations was the lack of consistency in capability. Some managers

were managing performance well, delivering fair and accurate feedback and setting goals that motivate. Others were doing much less well. A key skill gap was the ability to deliver feedback in a constructive way and having those 'difficult' conversations with underperformers.

Addressing the issues

These issues can be present in any up-to-date performance management systems which, even if they emphasize dialogue and agreement rather than control from above, still depend on the commitment and ability of line managers to carry out the process in a way which will meet the needs of all the stakeholders – the organization, the manager and, importantly, the individual. They are even more likely to arise in an old fashioned performance appraisal system which involves ratings and, often, a direct and formulaic link to performance-related pay.

It is relatively easy to design a performance management 'system'; it is much more difficult to make it work. There are no quick fixes. But it is important to ensure that all the stakeholders are involved in the development of the system (see Chapter 21) and that all concerned are given as much opportunity as possible to learn about performance management, through communications, formal training and, especially for line managers, less formal ways of helping people to learn the demanding skills involved such as coaching and mentoring. It is necessary to gain the commitment of line managers and also ensure that they are capable of carrying out their performance management responsibilities.

Gaining the commitment of line managers

Too often, line managers regard performance management in the shape of the formal review as a bureaucratic chore. They believe, rightly or wrongly, that they are doing it anyway so, they say 'Why should we conform to a system imposed on us by the HR department?' Even if they don't believe that formal reviews are a waste of time, some managers are reluctant to conduct them because they find it difficult to criticize people and imagine that they will be faced by unpleasant confrontations. Others are nervous about reviews because they feel that they lack the skills required to provide feedback, analyse performance and agree goals.

Gaining the commitment of line managers takes a lot of time, effort and persistence, but it has to be done. Here are some of the approaches that can be used.

Provide leadership from the top

Top management has a crucial role to play in implementing performance management. They have to communicate and act on the belief that performance management is an integral part of the fabric of the managerial practices of the organization. They should demonstrate their conviction that this is what good management is about and this is how managers are expected to play their part.

Communicate

Simply telling line managers that performance management is a good thing will not get you very far. But somehow the message has to reach them that managing performance is what they are expected to do. The message should come from the top and be cascaded down through the organization. It should not come from HR except as part of a training or induction programme. The message should be built into management development programmes, especially for potential managers. It should be understood by them from the outset that performance management is an important part of their responsibilities and that these are the skills they must acquire and use. The significance of performance management can also be conveyed by including the effectiveness with which managers carry out their performance management responsibilities as one of the criteria used when assessing their performance.

Involve

Involve line managers in the design and development of performance management processes as members of project teams or by taking part in pilot studies. This could be extended by the use of focus groups and general surveys of opinions and reactions. They can also be involved in reviewing the effectiveness of performance management. Commitment can be enhanced by getting line managers to act as coaches in developing performance management skills and as mentors to managers unfamiliar with the process. The more performance management is owned by line managers the better.

Encourage

Line managers can be encouraged to believe in performance management through communities of practice – gatherings of managers during which information is exchanged on good practice. They are more likely to take notice of their peers than someone from HR. But HR can still play a useful role in encouraging managers.

Keep it simple

Willing participation in performance management activities is more likely to be achieved if managers do not see it as a bureaucratic chore. If forms are used they should be as simple as possible, no more than two sides of one piece of paper. Web-enabled performance management eliminates paper work and can speed up the process but it must not be too complicated. It should be emphasized that performance management is not a form filling or data entry exercise and that the important thing is the dialogue between managers and individuals that continues throughout the year and is not just an annual event.

Reduce the pressure

Line managers can feel pressurized and exposed if they perceive that performance management is just about carrying out an annual appraisal meeting in which they have to tell employees where they have gone wrong, rate their performance and decide on the pay increase they should be given. This pressure can be reduced if the emphasis is on 'performance management throughout the year' as part of normal good management practice.

Pressure can also be reduced if managers do not have to make and defend ratings, although they still have to reach agreement on areas for development and improvement and what needs to be done about them. A further reduction of pressure can be achieved if pay reviews are 'de-coupled' from performance reviews, ie they take place several months later.

Developing skills

Systematic formal training in performance management skills as described in Chapter 21 is essential. This should take place when launching a new scheme but, importantly, also during management development programmes for potential managers and induction programmes for new managers. Coaching and guidance to individual managers should be provided to supplement formal training. This can be provided by HR specialists although, better still, experienced, committed and competent line managers can be used as coaches and mentors.

It is also necessary to monitor the performance of managers as performance managers. This is not just a matter of checking on completed performance management forms as practised in some organizations. HR specialists or line manager mentors can usefully follow up newly appointed or promoted managers to discuss how they are getting on and provide advice on dealing with any problems. 360-degree feedback or upward assessment can be used to review the performance management abilities of line managers when dealing with their staff and to indicate on an individual basis where improvements are required. Regular surveys can be conducted of the reactions of employees to performance management which can lead to the identification of any common weaknesses and the remedial action required.

An HR business partner had this to say about the situation faced by her organization and how it was dealt with:

> Performance management works very well with managers who are competent. Those who are less competent with the behavioural requirements of their role find it difficult, as this approach requires them to make some business judgements and discuss the rationale for them. Previously, they relied on the tick box approach where there was sometimes a perception that they did not need to discuss performance in detail. We have had to do quite a lot of coaching with managers to get them to feel comfortable with the new model as some feel the safety net of the tick box system has been removed. We have introduced role profiles which describe the 'how' and the 'what' and provide something against which managers and colleagues can be measured/assessed.

The Standard Chartered Bank model of their approach to developing performance management skills is shown in Figure 24.1.

FIGURE 24.1   Developing performance management skills at Standard Chartered Bank

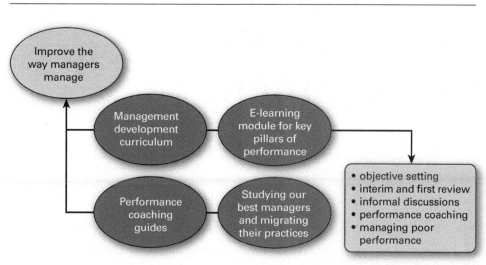

References

Armstrong, K and Ward, A (2005) *What Makes for Effective Performance Management?* London, The Work Foundation

Ellinger, A D, Ellinger, A E and Keller, S B (2003) Supervisory coaching behavior, employee satisfaction, and warehouse employee performance: a dyadic perspective in the distribution industry, *Human Resource Development Quarterly*, **14** (4), pp 435–58

e-reward (2014) *Survey of Performance Management Practice*, Stockport, e-reward

Hutchinson, S and Purcell, J (2003) *Bringing Policies to Life, The Vital Role of Front Line Managers in People Management*, London, CIPD

Purcell, J, Kinnie, K, Hutchinson, S, Rayton, B and Swart, J (2003) *People and Performance: How People Management Impacts on Organizational Performance*, London, CIPD

Risher, H (2012) Employers need to focus on improving performance management, *Compensation & Benefits Review*, **44** (4), pp 188–90

Learning about performance management

25

To introduce and maintain performance management successfully it is essential to ensure that all concerned – individuals as well as their managers – learn why it is important, how it functions, what they have to contribute and the skills they need. To do this a learning and development programme as described in this chapter is required. The programme should include arrangements for both formal and informal learning.

Incidence of training

The e-reward 2014 survey of performance management found that a considerable amount of training was carried out in the respondent's organizations. The most common type was ongoing guidance from HR, mentioned by 83 per cent of the sample. This was followed by the 67 per cent that carried out formal training for line managers and the 63 per cent that provided them with coaching. Training was given to staff by 42 per cent of respondents – a greater proportion than might be expected. Only 4 per cent said that they provided no formal training.

Where formal training was conducted it normally lasted half a day for staff (81 per cent of respondents). In contrast, formal training for managerial staff was more likely to take longer with 9 per cent of respondents saying it lasted more than two days, 4 per cent two days, 33 per cent one day and 52 per cent half a day.

Formal learning

Formal learning programmes can attempt to cover all aspects of performance management in two days or at least a day. Less than two days may only provide sufficient space to do no more than cover the basic features of performance management with little time left to practise skills – an essential element in training. Half a day is wholly inadequate. However, a training programme could start with a general introductory course and then provide modules in the shape of workshops concentrating on particular performance management processes or skills.

Respondents to the 2014 e-reward survey used the following methods:

- coaching from HR and the leadership team;
- online training (e-learning);
- practical case-study examples;
- road shows.

The most common subjects covered by the training were:

- evaluation and assessment skills;
- how to give feedback;
- how to deal with 'difficult' conversations;
- attaining consistency and avoiding bias;
- achieving quality rather than just quantity;
- regular updates of business objectives.

General courses

General introductory courses should be provided for managers and, also, for the people they manage. There is a case for including both parties on the same course on the grounds that performance management is a joint process and the skills required to set goals and review performance against those goals are essentially the same. While some skills such as giving feedback may be seen as primarily exercised by managers, those at the receiving end still need to know what is involved in providing and using feedback. Managers may need guidance on the techniques of conducting performance review meetings but the individuals involved are taking part in those meetings, the success of which will depend on their cooperation and responses as well as on how managers conduct them. Even if it is decided to run separate courses (the sheer number of employees to be covered may dictate this) the subject matter should be similar, although it may be presented either from the perspective of managers or those whom they manage.

A general course could include the following sessions:

- The purpose of performance management
- Setting goals
- Personal development planning
- Providing and using feedback
- Reviewing performance

Workshops

The following subjects could be covered singly or in combination by one or half-day workshops:

- setting goals;
- performance and development planning;
- providing feedback;
- conducting performance review meetings;
- assessing performance;
- using performance management to promote learning;
- coaching.

Road shows

The basic features of performance management can be presented in road shows – brief presentations which are moved round the firm or to different locations and are attended by all staff. Road shows are unlikely to cover any subject in depth and are probably better as a means of communication rather than training.

Training methods

Some of the material may be presented formally using PowerPoint slides with attached notes. But learning, especially skills development, should mainly be achieved by participative methods – guided discussions, role plays and other exercises – although it can be supplemented by e-learning covering the areas of knowledge needed.

Guided discussion

The aim of guided discussions would be to get participants to think through for themselves the learning points. For example, when covering review meetings the trainer asks questions such as:

- What do you think makes for a good review meeting? Can you provide any example from your previous experience?
- What do you think can go wrong with a meeting? Have you any instances?
- Why is it important to create the right environment?
- How do you set about doing so?
- What sort of things should be discussed in a review meeting?
- Why is it important for managers to let the individual do most of the talking?
- Why could self-assessment be useful?

Role plays

Role plays are usually based on a written brief which defines the same situation from each participant's point of view so that they can understand what it feels like to be in either position.

Course members are then asked to play out the roles and fellow members assess their performance (this in itself provides some practice in performance assessment). Each person playing the role will also describe his or her feelings about the review, and assess the other person's performance or behaviour.

Role plays are particularly useful as a means of developing performance review skills.

Exercises

Exercises can be used to enable participants to practise their skills. For example, practice in goal setting could take place by dividing the course members into pairs and getting then to agree in turn on each other's role profile, goals and key performance indicators.

The supplementary material provided with this book includes role plays and exercises.

Example of a performance management learning programme

A description of the performance management learning events conducted in a large pharmaceutical company is set out below.

Performance management workshop

Objectives

A two-day workshop providing the knowledge and skills necessary to operate the whole performance management process effectively. The workshop also offers an opportunity for refresher training where required.

By the end of the workshop participants will:

- be able to describe the four-stage performance management process and the key skills required;
- be able to apply a structured approach to help them establish team objectives, personal targets and development plans and conduct effective performance reviews;
- be able to explain the difference between performance review and career review;
- have practised the key skills required to operate each stage of the performance management process;
- be able, supported by coaching from their manager, to operate the performance management process back in the workplace.

Format

A two-day non-residential workshop.

Designed for

Those requiring an understanding of and a chance to practise the concepts and skills of performance management.

Coaching skills

Objectives

Coaching is the ability to take the opportunities presented by the job itself and use them in a conscious manner to improve the knowledge, skills, competencies, and therefore performance, of the learner. It is fundamental to performance management and generally to good management practice.

By the end of the workshop participants will:

- be able to describe and apply factors which help others to learn;
- be able to apply a systematic approach towards achieving learning through the conscious use of on-the-job opportunities;
- have practised skills/behaviours associated with effective coaching.

Format

A one-day workshop.

Designed for

People who have some existing experience of operating the performance management system.

Individual development workshop

The aim of this workshop is to enable participants to gain a clear understanding of what development planning is and how they can implement it effectively.

Objectives

By the end of the workshop participants will be able to:

- derive an agreed individual development plan;
- implement the skills associated with improving performance.

Format

A one-day workshop. In order to make the most practical use of the one-day event, participants will be invited to work on real issues and situations and tutors will demonstrate real examples. Case studies and role plays will not be used.

Designed for

Those who have some experience of performance management and who want to improve their understanding and skill in individual development planning.

Performance review workshop

Performance management is a continuous process aiming to increase business effectiveness by improving the performance of individuals. The planning, development and evaluation of performance throughout the year require frequent review between the people involved to monitor targets, discuss achievements, and progress development plans. This workshop will enable people to conduct effective discussions throughout the year and at the annual performance summary review session. It explores how reward in its widest sense can be used to reinforce performance.

Objectives

By the end of the workshop participants will be able to:

- describe good practice for reviewing performance;
- apply a structured approach to preparing for and conducting review meetings;
- create conditions that encourage good performance;
- apply a variety of methods to reward performance.

Format

A one-day workshop.

Designed for

People at all levels who have a good understanding of performance management and who want to enhance their ability to conduct effective performance review discussions and reinforce good performance.

Less formal learning

Formal training programmes are useful but not enough. Performance management skills are best developed through coaching and mentoring which can be supplemented by e-learning programmes. The HR department can play an important role in organizing these learning activities but it is best to use experienced line managers as coaches and mentors.

Reference

e-reward (2014) *Survey of Performance Management*, Stockport, e-reward

Evaluating performance management

26

It is hard to ensure that a performance management system functions effectively, however carefully it has been developed and introduced. As has often been emphasized in this book a performance management system is easy to conceive but hard to bring to life. Its operation must be monitored continuously and evaluated regularly by means of a performance management audit to provide information which will indicate how well it is working and identify any remedial actions required. This is evidence-based performance management.

The criteria, the contents of an audit, the methods used to conduct evaluation surveys and a typical approach are dealt with in this chapter which concludes with a summary of what can be done to improve performance management effectiveness in the form of an eight point plan. Further guidance on evaluation is provided in the toolkit in Appendix A.

Criteria

The criteria for evaluating performance management should have been defined when the system was introduced or amended. They will be based on how well its objectives have been achieved. If, for example, performance development is a major aim, how the impact of the system on performance can be measured should be described. The system design should specify how it is intended to operate and the evaluation will aim to determine the extent to which these operational requirements are being met.

Success criteria such as those set out below should be defined in advance and used as the basis for evaluation:

- Measures of improved performance by reference to key performance indicators in such terms as output, productivity, sales, quality, customer satisfaction, return on investment.

- Achievement of defined and agreed goals.

- Measures of employee engagement before and after the introduction of performance management and then at regular intervals.

- Assessments of reactions of managers and employees to performance management.

- Personal development plans agreed and implemented.

- Performance improvement plans agreed and implemented.

- Assessment of the extent to which managers and employees have reached agreement on goals and performance improvement plans.

There are two perspectives as identified by Lawler *et al* (1994) in evaluating a performance management system: (1) the effectiveness of the system as judged by management and (2) the effectiveness of the system as judged by employees. Performance management should meet both these needs. If it is to meet the needs of management it must help the organization to use the skills of employees and motivate and develop them to perform effectively. To meet the needs of employees it must help them to know what is expected of them, how well they are doing and how they can improve their performance to meet their own and the organization's goals.

Additionally, as pointed out by Lee (2005): 'All performance management systems should be judged by one standard – how well they create the climate necessary for performance conversations to occur so that the employee and supervisor can diagnose problems and work together to overcome them'.

Performance management audit

A performance audit should consist of the following steps (based on recommendations by Ed Lawler and colleagues quoted by Risher (2012)):

1 Surveys of managers and employees to obtain reactions to performance management processes.

2 Focus groups to discuss survey results.

3 Assessment of management training.

4 Analysis of ratings (by job level, occupation and organizational unit) – distribution, indications of any inflation, evidence of discrimination by gender or race.

5 Analysis of completion of reviews.

6 Analysis of any appeals.

7 Assessment of sample reviews by reference to the managers and individuals concerned to establish the extent to which:

- they were conducted properly in accordance with policy;
- goal and standards were agreed by the manager and the individual and complied with policy guidelines on the nature of an acceptable goal;
- assessments were made fairly by reference to information on performance and progress throughout the year;
- there was a constructive dialogue between the manager and the individual;
- the individual received useful feedback;
- action and personal development plans were agreed;
- both the manager and the individual were satisfied with the process.

Methodology

The best method of monitoring and evaluation is to ask those involved – managers and individuals – how it worked. As many as possible should be seen, individually and in groups by members of a project team and/or the HR function. Detailed checklists are provided in Appendix A but the main things to examine are set out in Table 26.1.

Individual interviews and focus group discussions can be supplemented by a special survey of reactions to performance management which could be completed anonymously by all managers and staff. The results should be fed back to all concerned and analysed to assess the need for any amendments to the process or further training requirements. Examples of a performance review evaluation form and typical attitude survey questions are given in the performance management toolkit in Appendix A.

TABLE 26.1 Performance management evaluation areas

For managers	For individuals
• How well the goal setting process worked.	• How well the goal setting process worked.
• How well the process of giving informal and formal feedback worked.	• The quality and helpfulness of any feedback received from their manager.
• How well the formal performance review worked.	• How well the formal performance review was conducted.
• Any evidence of performance improvement (individual and departmental) as a result of performance management.	• The extent to which the process provided justified indications or where improvement was necessary.
• The clarity of the process.	• Any examples of performance improvement as a result of performance management.
• The usefulness or otherwise of documentation or a web-based system.	• The extent to which the process provided guidance on learning and development needs.
• The quality of the guidance, training and support received.	• Any examples of useful coaching or training received as a result of the performance management system.
• The extent to which the whole process was worthwhile from their viewpoint as managers.	• The extent to which they were motivated by the process.

The ultimate test, of course, is analysing organizational performance to establish the extent to which improvements can be attributed to performance management. It may be impossible to establish a direct connection but more detailed assessments with managers and staff on the impact of the process may reveal specific areas in which performance has been improved which could be assumed to impact on overall performance.

A typical approach

When performance management was introduced in an NHS Trust it was decided that monitoring could be carried out by:

- recording and analysing performance assessments, this helps establish how managers are using performance management;
- one-to-one interviews with managers identifying how they are finding the experience of performance management and where they need more support;
- employee attitude surveys and focused discussion groups;
- reviewing improvements in the performance of the organization.

To maintain high standards it was deemed necessary to:

- maintain training in performance management for all new staff (including individuals who are promoted to management posts);
- top up training to keep the principles and practices fresh;
- use one-to-one coaching where necessary;
- conduct workshops for managers to share their experiences.

These guidelines are valid for any organization which wants to develop and maintain effective performance management processes. But concerted action is required to put the evidence they produce into good use as a means of improving the performance of performance management. An eight point plan to achieve this is set out below.

Improving the performance of performance management – an eight point plan

This eight point plan is designed to make use of the evidence from a performance management audit.

1 Analyse the results of the audit including any surveys and distribute a summary to all employees affected by performance management.

2 Consult senior management to obtain their views on any actions that need to be taken in the light of the outcomes of the audit.

3 Convene focus groups to analyse the audit results and consider what actions are required.

4 Summarize the results of the consultations in steps two and three and draw up an action plan. Depending on the findings of the audit the actions could include any of the following:

- Revisions to performance management procedures such as goal setting, performance assessment (rating) or documentation.

- Focused training for both managers and individuals in the form of modules dealing with issues such as performance planning (defining role profiles, goal setting and preparing and implementing performance improvement and personal development plans), providing and acting on feedback, conducting performance review meetings, assessing performance, and coaching.

- The provision of coaching and mentoring to overcome weaknesses displayed by any individual managers as revealed by the upward assessments contained in the survey.

5 Inform all concerned of the proposed actions.

6 Design the training modules, brief and train the trainers and brief and train anyone involved in coaching or mentoring.

7 Implement the action plan.

8 Monitor the implementation and evaluate the effectiveness of the action. This may take the form of a follow-up audit.

References

Lawler, E E (1994) Performance management: the next generation, *Compensation & Benefits Review*, **26** (3), pp 16–19

Lee, C D (2005) Rethinking the goals of your performance management system, *Employment Relations Today*, **32** (3), pp 53–60

Risher, H (2012) Employers need to focus on improving performance management, *Compensation & Benefits Review*, **44** (4), pp 188–90

APPENDIX A
Performance management toolkit

The toolkit is concerned with the design, implementation, operation and evaluation of new or substantially amended performance management systems on the basis of an analytical and diagnostic survey.

Contents

Introduction to the toolkit

Analysis and diagnosis toolkit

Design toolkit

Introduction to the toolkit

The purpose of the toolkit is to provide practical guidance to those who want to review existing performance management systems and processes or develop and implement new ones. The toolkit can be used by line managers as a guide to their performance management practices. It can also be the basis for developing understanding and skills through coaching, mentoring, formal training and e-learning.

Definition of a performance management system

A performance management system is defined as a set of inter-related activities and processes which are treated as an integrated and key component of an organization's approaches to managing performance through people and to developing the skills and capabilities of its human capital.

Structure of the toolkit

The toolkit is divided into the five sections described below and illustrated in Figure A1.

FIGURE A1   The performance management design, development, implementation and maintenance pathway

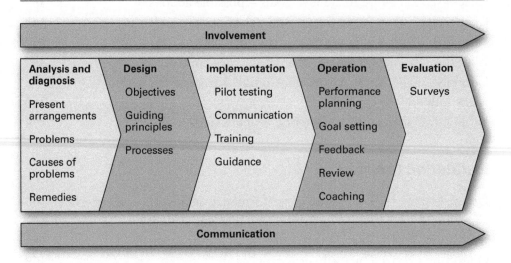

1 *The analytical and diagnostic toolkit* covers the analysis of present arrangements and the diagnosis of the causes of any problems. It provides the basis for the design or modification of a performance management system.

2 *The design toolkit* covers the development of the constituents of a performance management system – performance planning and agreements, goal setting, feedback, performance analysis and assessment, rating, coaching and the link to reward and personal development.

3 *The implementation toolkit* covers the processes of communicating, briefing, training and pilot testing which must be carried out to ensure the successful operation of performance management.

4 *The operational toolkit* covers the main performance management activities of completing performance agreements, goal setting, performance review, managing managerial performance and dealing with under-performers.

5 *The evaluation toolkit* covers methods of evaluating the effectiveness of performance management through checklists and surveys.

Analysis and diagnosis

It is necessary to analyse and understand the strengths and weaknesses of the present arrangements. As far as possible the analysis and diagnosis should involve line managers and employees through surveys, workshops and focus groups.

Initial discussions with stakeholders

The following questionnaires or a selection of them can be used to initiate discussions with stakeholders on performance management requirements:

- an overall analysis of performance management practices;
- performance management goals;
- evaluation of performance management practices;
- gap analysis of performance review practices;
- analysis of performance management practice.

QUESTIONNAIRE 1   Overall performance management analysis

Question	Significance of question
1. What is meant by performance?	'Performance' is often assumed to be simply about outputs or achievements. But it is also concerned with the manner in which the results were achieved, ie the 'how' as well as the 'what'. This distinction is significant because it affects how performance is measured or assessed. The assessment should not be confined to the extent to which objectives are reached but also to the behaviours or competencies that affected the results and that indicate what sort of improvements are required.
2. What is meant by 'a high-performance culture'?	A principal aim of performance management is to improve business performance by developing a high-performance culture. It is necessary to define what a high-performance culture is to understand how performance management can help to create one.
3. Can good or poor performance be identified?	This is at the heart of performance management. The processes used must establish how well people are doing in order to identify how they can build on their success. They must also indicate any aspects of less effective performance in order to plan improvements.
4. Can the causes of good or poor performance be established?	This follows question 3. Performance management processes need to ensure that performance is analysed in order to determine what has affected it and decide on any actions required.
5. How can people be encouraged to engage with their work?	Performance management is fundamentally about encouraging and helping people to be engaged with their jobs by becoming more aware of what they are expected to do, by receiving feedback on how well they have done it and by being given the opportunity to exercise and develop their skills.
6. What can be done about under-performers?	Performance management should always be positive and forward looking. But it is necessary to differentiate between people who are performing at different levels and agree on action to help the under-performers to improve.
7. Can all this be done fairly?	Performance management has to be seen to be fair by ensuring that it is based on a dialogue and agreed conclusions based on evidence rather than opinion. It is not 'appraisal' in the sense of a top-down judgement on people.

Performance management goals

Possible goals for performance management are set out below. A useful analytical exercise is to rate the importance of each of these goals and assess the effectiveness with which any relevant goals are reached. This can be done by individuals or in focus groups or workshops and the outcomes of the assessment analysed to indicate where changes or developments are required.

QUESTIONNAIRE 2　Performance management goals

Possible goals	Importance*	Effectiveness*
● Align individual and organizational objectives		
● Improve organizational performance		
● Develop a high-performance culture		
● Improve individual performance		
● Provide basis for personal development		
● Increase motivation and engagement		
● Inform contribution/performance pay decisions		
● Measure performance against quantified objectives		
● Encourage appropriate behaviours – 'living the values'		
● Clarify performance expectations in the role		
● Identify potential		
● Identify poor performers		

*Rate: 5 = high to 1 = low

Performance management gap analysis

The gap analysis shown below assesses the extent to which desirable characteristics of performance management exist in the organization. It provides the basis for the design and development of performance management systems and processes. Start gap analysis with senior management, line managers and staff by getting them to complete the grid individually or in groups by marking with an X the position in which they think the organization is at present and an O where it is believed the organization should be placed. A gap between X and O – between what *is* and what *should be* – reveals areas for development. The next step is to get those involved to discuss and agree priorities.

QUESTIONNAIRE 3   Gap analysis of performance management practices

Desirable characteristics	X = current O = desired	Undesirable characteristics
Performance management is perceived by top management as a key process for managing the business.	⌊___⌊___⌊___⌊⌋	Top management pays lip service to performance management.
Line managers are committed to performance management.	⌊___⌊___⌊___⌊⌋	Line managers see performance management as a chore.
Line managers have the skills to manage performance effectively	⌊___⌊___⌊___⌊⌋	There are serious deficiencies in the skill levels displayed by line managers.
Performance management is owned and driven by line managers.	⌊___⌊___⌊___⌊⌋	Performance management is seen as the preserve of HR.
Employees believe that performance management operates fairly.	⌊___⌊___⌊___⌊⌋	Employees do not trust line managers to review their performance fairly.
There is hard evidence that performance management improves business performance in our organization.	⌊___⌊___⌊___⌊⌋	There is no evidence that performance management improves business performance in our organization.

QUESTIONNAIRE 3 *continued*

Desirable characteristics	X = current O = desired	Undesirable characteristics
Performance management is based on agreed definitions of roles, key result areas and competency requirements.	└──┴──┴──┘	Performance management is not related to the reality of what people are expected to do and in terms of how they are expected to behave.
Clear objectives and performance standards are agreed at the performance planning stage.	└──┴──┴──┘	Objectives and standards, if agreed at all, are vague or undemanding.
Methods of measuring performance (key performance indicators) and assessing levels of competence are agreed at the performance planning stage.	└──┴──┴──┘	No attempt is made to agree performance or competency indicators.
Performance development plans are agreed at the planning stage.	└──┴──┴──┘	Performance development planning is generally neglected.
Performance management in the form of review and feedback is practised throughout the year.	└──┴──┴──┘	Performance appraisal takes place, if at all, as a dishonest annual ritual.
Line managers provide helpful feedback and support during formal reviews.	└──┴──┴──┘	The quality of feedback and support is generally inadequate.
Line managers recognize their responsibility for coaching people and act accordingly.	└──┴──┴──┘	Coaching by line management is sparse and often inadequate.

QUESTIONNAIRE 4   Analysis of performance management practices

Review practice	Fully in place	Partly in place	Not in place	Action
1. The content of the performance review is based on a role profile.				
2. Performance expectations are agreed with employees.				
3. Performance objectives are aligned with business goals.				
4. The review is based on evidence in the form of observable job behaviours.				
5. The review process is clearly defined for everyone involved.				
6. Employees participate fully in the review process.				
7. Reviewers are capable of making fair and consistent assessments.				
8. The review focuses on development and improvement needs.				
9. A higher authority checks and comments on reviews.				
10. Reviewers are trained in feedback and assessment techniques.				

Views on performance management

Besides the use of questionnaires as the basis for discussions with stakeholders, surveys covering all or large proportions of staff can be used to obtain views on present arrangements and a special survey can be made of the opinions of the line managers upon whom the success of performance management largely depends.

QUESTIONNAIRE 5 General survey of views on performance management

Rate the following statements on a scale of 1–5 where: 1 = fully agree, 2 = agree, 3 = not sure, 4 = disagree, 5 = strongly disagree	
Our performance management system:	
Translates corporate goals into divisional, departmental, team and individual goals	1 2 3 4 5
Helps to clarify corporate goals	1 2 3 4 5
Is a continuous and evolutionary process in which performance improves over time	1 2 3 4 5
Relies on consensus and cooperation rather than control and coercion	1 2 3 4 5
Creates a shared understanding of what is required to improve performance and how it will be achieved	1 2 3 4 5
Encourages self-management of individual performance	1 2 3 4 5
Encourages a management style that is open and honest and encourages two-way communication between managers and staff at all levels	1 2 3 4 5
Delivers continuous feedback on organizational, team and individual performance to all staff	1 2 3 4 5
Analyses and assesses performance against jointly agreed goals	1 2 3 4 5
Enables individual staff members to modify their objectives	1 2 3 4 5
Demonstrates respect for the individual	1 2 3 4 5
Has fair procedures	1 2 3 4 5

QUESTIONNAIRE 6   Questionnaire for line managers

Rate the following statements on a scale of 1–5 where: 1 = fully agree, 2 = agree, 3 = not sure, 4 = disagree, 5 = strongly disagree	
1. I believe that an effective system of performance management will help me to improve the performance of my team.	1 2 3 4 5
2. I am quite satisfied that I can manage performance well without the help of a formal performance management system.	1 2 3 4 5
3. I think that performance management could usefully ensure that the individual goals of my team members are aligned to departmental and organizational goals.	1 2 3 4 5
4. I recognize the need to be systematic about agreeing performance goals, providing feedback and reviewing performance.	1 2 3 4 5
5. I think my team members will benefit from a more deliberate planned approach to performance management.	1 2 3 4 5
6. I regularly provide good feedback to my team members, which in most cases they are prepared to accept.	1 2 3 4 5
7. I am quite confident that I will be able to define and agree goals with my team members.	1 2 3 4 5
8. I think I have the skills required to coach my team members.	1 2 3 4 5
9. I consider that it is possible to ensure that performance ratings are meaningful and fair.	1 2 3 4 5
10. I am confident that I can run a performance review meeting which has positive results and motivates my team members.	1 2 3 4 5

Diagnosis

Following the analysis any problems, their causes and possible remedies should be identified.

QUESTIONNAIRE 7   Diagnostic summary

List any significant problems identified by the analysis and indicate the likely causes of the problems and their likely remedies.		
Problem	Likely cause	Possible remedy

Design toolkit

The design should be based on the initial analysis and diagnosis and should involve stakeholders, ie senior management, line managers, employees and their representatives. It is advisable to build on existing practices in order to promote acceptance and assimilation.

There is always a choice in the design of the elements of a performance management system. The factors governing the choice will be the objectives of the system, the culture of the organization (including norms on the extent to which it is believed that a formal system is required and the amount of flexibility allowed in operating the system), the system of work, the structure of the organization and the views of management, line managers, employees and their representatives, and HR. The steps in the design programme are illustrated in Figure A2.

FIGURE A2   Steps in the design programme

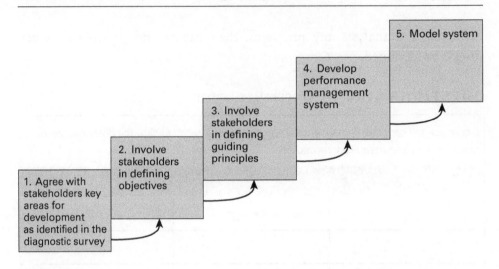

The instruments and guidelines set out below can be used to inform the design programme:

- areas for development;
- areas for choice;
- analysis of possible objectives and success criteria;
- checklist of possible success criteria;
- guiding principles questionnaire;
- analysis of the components of the performance management system;
- arguments for and against rating;
- arguments for and against forced distribution;
- model of a performance management system.

Areas for development

The areas for development will have been identified if a diagnostic survey has taken place. They can be summarized under the following headings.

QUESTIONNAIRE 8   Areas for development

Area	What needs to be done	How it can be done
Performance planning and agreement		
Goal setting		
Providing feedback		
Conducting performance reviews		
Assessment and rating		
Coaching		
Documentation		
Use of computers		
Increasing commitment of line managers to performance management		
Developing performance management skills of line managers		
Educating employees generally on the purpose of performance management, how it works, how it affects them and what part they play		

Areas for choice

There is plenty of room for choice in the design of a performance management system and much of the design programme will be taken up with an analysis of the pros and cons of the various alternatives as set out overleaf within the context of the organization and its people.

QUESTIONNAIRE 9   Areas for choice

Areas for choice	Examples of possible alternatives
Objectives of performance management	• To improve organizational performance • To improve individual performance • To provide the basis for employee development • To inform performance or contribution pay decisions • Others, including a combination of two or more of the above
Control and flexibility	• Processes based on guiding principles • Flexibility in operation in line with principles • Tightly controlled system • Common system throughout organization – no variations allowed
Role profiles	• Provide clear basis for planning and review, cover both key result areas (accountabilities) and competency requirements and are reviewed annually • Focus on required role outputs and inputs • Rely on existing job descriptions
Individual goals	• Aligned to organizational goals • Focus only on job requirements • Must be SMART • Include qualitative performance standards • Cascaded from above • Refer only to specific and time constrained tasks and projects • Refer to ongoing work goals as specified in the role profile
Personal development planning	• Regarded as a key part of the performance agreement • Treated as an incidental activity
Performance review	• Treated as a once-a-year event • Emphasis on continuous review and feedback • Top down • Dialogue • Ratings • No ratings (overall assessment or use of performance matrix)
Documentation	• Detailed forms to be completed by manager • Documentation minimized

QUESTIONNAIRE 9 *continued*

Areas for choice	Examples of possible alternatives
Relationship to performance or contribution pay	• Ratings inform position on pay matrix and therefore pay increase • Pay reviews take place at the same time as performance reviews • Pay reviews are 'decoupled' from performance reviews, ie take place some time later

Analysis of possible objectives and success criteria

It is essential that everyone involved is clear about the objectives of performance management and the criteria that will be used to evaluate the extent to which the objectives have been successfully achieved. Managers and employees should be involved in setting objectives and success criteria. They should consider not only what performance management will do for the organization but also what they hope it will do for them. It is advisable, however, not to try to attempt too much, especially when this is a new development. Some prioritization of objectives may therefore be required.

QUESTIONNAIRE 10   Analysis of possible objectives

Possible objectives	For the organization	For line managers	For employees	Possible success criteria (see checklist)
Rate the possible objective on a scale of 1–5 where: 1 = crucial, 2 = important, 3 = not sure, 4 = not very important, 5 = irrelevant				
Improve performance	1 2 3 4 5	1 2 3 4 5	1 2 3 4 5	
Develop a performance culture	1 2 3 4 5	1 2 3 4 5	1 2 3 4 5	
Identify people with high potential	1 2 3 4 5	1 2 3 4 5	1 2 3 4 5	

QUESTIONNAIRE 10 *continued*

Possible objectives	For the organization	For line managers	For employees	Possible success criteria (see checklist)
Identify under-performers	1 2 3 4 5	1 2 3 4 5	1 2 3 4 5	
Align individual and organizational goals	1 2 3 4 5	1 2 3 4 5	1 2 3 4 5	
Provide the basis for personal development	1 2 3 4 5	1 2 3 4 5	1 2 3 4 5	
Enable people to know where they stand	1 2 3 4 5	1 2 3 4 5	1 2 3 4 5	
Provide the basis for performance pay decisions	1 2 3 4 5	1 2 3 4 5	1 2 3 4 5	
Other	1 2 3 4 5	1 2 3 4 5	1 2 3 4 5	

CHECKLIST 1   Checklist of possible success criteria

- Measures of improved performance by reference to key performance indicators in such terms as output, productivity, sales, quality, customer satisfaction, return on investment.
- Achievement of defined and agreed objectives.
- Measures of employee engagement before and after the introduction of performance management and then at regular intervals.
- Assessments of reactions of managers and employees to performance management.
- Assessment of the extent to which managers and employees have reached agreement on goals and performance improvement plans.
- Personal development plans agreed and implemented.
- Performance improvement plans agreed and implemented.

Definition of guiding principles

It is important to involve stakeholders in agreeing a set of guiding principles which can be used as a basis for performance management design, operation and evaluation and can be communicated to employees. A questionnaire is shown below.

QUESTIONNAIRE 11   Guiding principles

Possible guiding principle	Assessment of importance/ relevance 1 Vital 2 Very important 3 Fairly important 4 Not very relevant
Clearly stated work goals/tasks subject to regular review and updating	1 2 3 4
Clearly stated standards of performance	1 2 3 4
Feedback on job behaviour	1 2 3 4
Comments rather than performance ratings	1 2 3 4
Identification of development needs	1 2 3 4
Agreed development plan	1 2 3 4
Reach agreement through a two-way process	1 2 3 4
Incorporate appeal procedure	1 2 3 4
Used as a day-to-day management tool	1 2 3 4
No direct link to pay	1 2 3 4
Requires commitment from all concerned	1 2 3 4
Other	1 2 3 4

Development of performance management system

The development of a performance management system involves first selecting and describing the components of the system (Table A1), then considering the pros and cons of rating and forced distribution (Tables A2 and A3) and finally modelling the system (Figure A3).

TABLE A1   Analysis of the components of the performance management system

Component	Contents	Considerations
Performance planning and agreement	• Agreeing role profiles • Agreeing objectives (see also goal setting) • Agreeing performance measures • Agreeing development needs (see also personal development planning) • Agreeing areas for performance improvement • Recording decisions in an agreement	• Format of role profiles • Methods of preparing and updating role profiles • Choice of measures • Format of agreement
Goal setting	• Identifying key result areas • Identifying key performance indicators • Agreeing targets and standards of performance	• Methods of goal setting • Ensuring 'SMART' goals are agreed • Selecting appropriate measures
Personal development planning	• Deciding areas for development • Planning methods of development	• Format of development plan • Approaches to development • Emphasis on self-directed development
Feedback	• Provision during year • Provision during formal review	• Developing feedback skills • Use of informal and formal feedback

TABLE A1 *continued*

Component	Contents	Considerations
Performance reviews	• Purpose • Content • Timing	• Use of informal reviews throughout year • Preparation for formal reviews • Conduct of formal reviews
Performance analysis	• Methodology • Use of metrics	• Performance analysis skills • Data collection and analysis
Performance assessment and rating	• Use of overall assessment • Use of rating • Use of forced distribution rating	• Provision of guidelines for overall assessments • Arguments for and against rating (see Table A2 below) • Decisions on type of rating to be used, if at all • Developing assessment/rating skills • Providing rating guidelines, if appropriate • Arguments for and against forced distribution (see Table A3 below)
Link to performance pay	• How assessment/ratings will inform performance pay decisions • The timing of pay reviews and performance reviews	• Arguments for and against performance pay
Coaching	• Methods • Responsibility of line managers for	• Developing coaching skills
Administration	• Documentation • Use of computers	• Design of documentation • Design of computer system • Decision on extent to which a standard approach to performance management should be used

TABLE A2   Arguments for and against rating

Arguments for rating	Arguments against rating
• Ratings let people know where they stand • It is necessary to sum up judgements about people. • Ratings give people something to strive for. • They provide a basis for assessing potential • They are needed to inform performance pay decisions.	• Ratings are likely to be subjective and inconsistent. • To sum the overall performance of a person with a single rating is a gross oversimplification of what may be a complex set of factors affecting that person's performance. • It is hard to rate qualitative aspects of performance. • To label people as 'average' or 'below average', or whatever equivalent terms are used, is both demeaning and demotivating. • Line managers tend not to differentiate between ratings. • The use of ratings to inform decisions on performance pay or inclusion in a talent management programme will dominate performance reviews and prejudice the real purpose of such reviews, which is to provide the basis for developing skills and improving performance.

TABLE A3   Arguments for and against forced distribution

Arguments for forced distribution	Arguments against forced distribution
• Identifies 'best' and 'worst' performance so that action can be taken. • Achieves a more appropriate (ie 'normal') distribution of ratings. • Overcomes the 'centralizing' tendency of raters, ie a preference for rating in the middle 'boxes' and avoiding extremes. • Helps to achieve consistency in rating between different raters.	• Based on some form of rating or ranking system which suffers from all the disadvantages inherent in any rating approach (see Table A2). • No evidence that ability is distributed normally. • Assumes that the same distribution of ability/performance occurs in all departments, which is unlikely to be the case. • Managers do not like to be forced into a straight-jacket. • Employees resent the fact that their future is determined by some form of artificial quota or ranking system or that their ratings may be 'moderated' downwards to fit a forced distribution. • A 'rank and yank' system can produce a climate of fear in an organization and will at least inhibit and at worst destroy any possibility that performance management is perceived and used as a developmental process.

Modelling the performance management system

A model of a performance management system is a useful way of summing up how it operates. It can be used in communication and training programmes to provide an easily absorbed picture of what performance management is about. Typical models illustrate the cyclical nature of a performance management system as shown in Figure A3.

FIGURE A3   Model of a performance management system

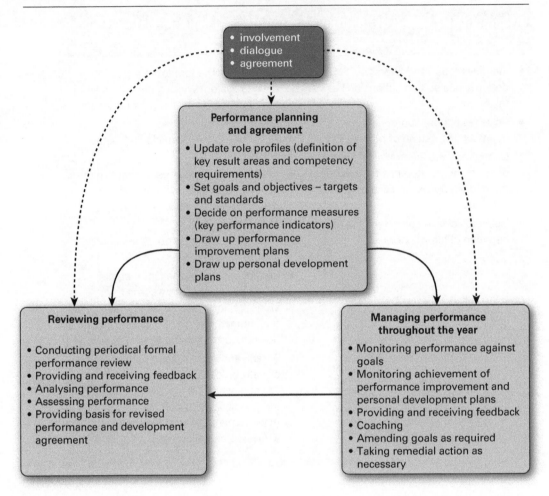

Implementation toolkit

The implementation programme as illustrated in Figure A4 should start with a pilot test of performance management process and approaches to communication and training which can inform full communication and training programmes and, subject to any modifications required, the launch of the system.

FIGURE A4   Implementation programme

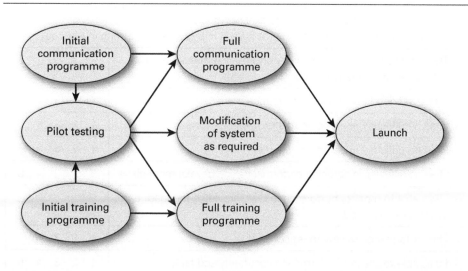

Pilot testing

Before embarking on full implementation it is essential to pilot test the process. This should be done in two or three departments where the managers are sympathetic to performance management and will therefore give it their backing. The test should be preceded by a briefing and training for participants in the processes and skills they should use. Ideally, it should extend over the whole of the performance management cycle, ie twelve months. But a period of between six and twelve months will provide an adequate test. The purpose of the test, which should be explained to those taking part, is to ensure that an appropriate and acceptable form of performance management is introduced. Another way of testing is to do it top down – get senior managers to try it out first so that they know all the wrinkles before cascading it throughout the organization.

The following questionnaires can be used to evaluate the test.

QUESTIONNAIRE 12   Pilot test questionnaire for managers

Rate the following statements on a scale of 1–5 where: 1 = fully agree, 2 = agree, 3 = not sure, 4 = disagree, 5 = strongly disagree	
1. The objectives and processes of performance management were described clearly to me.	1 2 3 4 5
2. I received good training in performance management skills.	1 2 3 4 5
3. I had no difficulty in agreeing role profiles.	1 2 3 4 5
4. I had no difficulty in agreeing objectives.	1 2 3 4 5
5. I had no difficulty in agreeing performance and development plans.	1 2 3 4 5
6. I was able to monitor performance well, providing feedback and coaching as required.	1 2 3 4 5
7. The performance review meeting went very well.	1 2 3 4 5
8. I was able to assess performance accurately and fairly.	1 2 3 4 5
9. I believe that performance management will enable me to do my job as a manager better.	1 2 3 4 5
10. I believe that performance management is a waste of time.	1 2 3 4 5

QUESTIONNAIRE 13   Pilot test questionnaire for employees

Rate the following statements on a scale of 1–5 where: 1 = fully agree, 2 = agree, 3 = not sure, 4 = disagree, 5 = strongly disagree	
1. The objectives and processes of performance management were described clearly to me.	1 2 3 4 5
2. I received good training in performance management skills.	1 2 3 4 5
3. I had no difficulty in agreeing my role profile.	1 2 3 4 5
4. I had no difficulty in agreeing my objectives.	1 2 3 4 5
5. I had no difficulty in agreeing my performance and development plans.	1 2 3 4 5
6. I was able to monitor my own performance well and was provided with feedback and with coaching as required.	1 2 3 4 5
7. The performance review meeting went very well.	1 2 3 4 5
8. I was able to assess performance accurately and fairly.	1 2 3 4 5
9. I believe that performance management will enable me to do my job better.	1 2 3 4 5
10. I believe that performance management is a waste of time.	1 2 3 4 5

Communications

It is vital to have a communications strategy which keeps all concerned from the very beginning of the exercise informed of what is being planned, what it will look like and how it will affect them. A checklist is set out below.

CHECKLIST 2   Communications checklist

1. Has the best use been made of different methods of communication, eg team briefing, DVDs and brochures?
2. Have the objectives of performance management been explained?
3. Have the various processes involved been explained?
4. Have the benefits of performance management to the organization, line managers and individual employees been explained?
5. Have the links, if any, to performance management been explained?
6. Has every attempt been made to convince employees that performance management will be operated fairly?

Training

Training for both managers and employees in performance management skills is essential. A checklist is set out below.

CHECKLIST 3   Performance management training checklist

1. Have all managers received training in the operation of performance management generally and in basic performance management skills, ie defining role profiles, goal setting, drawing up performance and development agreements, providing feedback, analysing and assessing performance, conducting performance reviews and coaching?
2. Have employees received training in their role in agreeing and implementing performance and development plans, goal setting, monitoring their own performance, generating their own feedback and preparing for and participating in performance reviews?
3. Have arrangements been made to provide coaching and mentoring for line managers in performance management skills?

Performance management operations toolkit

The operations toolkit is concerned with the major performance management process of agreeing performance and development plans, goal setting, providing feedback, preparing for and conducting performance reviews, coaching and dealing with under-performers. Checklists for each of the above activities together with a checklist on assessing managerial performance are set out below.

CHECKLIST 4   Performance and development agreement checklist

1. Is there an up-to-date role profile that sets out key result areas and competency requirements?
2. Have 'SMART' objectives been set for each of the key result areas?
3. Have individuals been encouraged to formulate for themselves performance and personal development plans?
4. Has a realistic performance development plan to enhance strengths and overcome any weaknesses been agreed?
5. Has an attainable personal development plan been agreed?
6. Are plans based on an analysis of past performance and an assessment of future demands (new skills to be acquired, new tasks for the role holder, changes in the role or scope of the function)?
7. Do the plans indicate success criteria – how the individual and the manager will know that the desired results have been achieved?
8. Has the agreement been reached through constructive dialogue, with the full involvement of the individual and without any sort of coercion from the manager?
9. Have individuals been empowered to implement the plans?
10. Has provision been made for monitoring and reviewing progress without being oppressive?

CHECKLIST 5   Goal setting checklist

1. Has the goal setting process been based on an agreed and up-to-date role profile that sets out key result areas?
2. Are goals clearly related to key result areas in the role profile?
3. Are individual goals integrated with corporate goals?
4. If goals have been cascaded downwards, is there some scope for individuals to discuss and modify their own goals?
5. Has goal setting been carried out jointly by the manager and the individual?
6. Do goals clearly and specifically support the achievement of team and department goals?
7. Are goals specific and time related?
8. Are goals challenging?
9. Are goals realistic and attainable?
10. Have success criteria for each goal been determined?

CHECKLIST 6   Feedback checklist

1. Is feedback provided on actual events or observed behaviour?
2. Is feedback presented as a description of what has happened and not expressed as a judgement?
3. Is feedback related to specific items of behaviour rather than transmitting general feelings or impressions?
4. Is feedback based on questions rather than statements?
5. Has feedback been restricted to key issues?
6. Does the feedback focus on aspects of performance the individual can improve?
7. Is feedback positive?
8. Is feedback constructive?
9. Has feedback been built into the job so that it can be generated by individuals?
10. Does feedback provide a sound basis for action?

CHECKLIST 7   Review meeting preparation – manager's checklist

1. How well do you think the individual has done in achieving his/her goals during the review period?

2. To what extent have the actions and behaviour of the individual been in line with competency requirements?

3. How well have any improvement, development or training plans as agreed at the last review meeting been put into effect?

4. What goals relating to the individual's key tasks would you like to agree with him/her for the next review period?

5. Has the individual had any problems in carrying out his/her work? If so, what sort of problems and what can be done about them?

6. Are you satisfied that you have given the individual sufficient guidance or help on what he/she is expected to do? If not, what extra help/guidance could you provide?

7. Is the best use being made of the individual's skills and abilities? If not, what should be done?

8. Is the individual ready to take on additional responsibilities in his/her present job? If so, what?

9. Do you think the individual and the organization would benefit if he/she were provided with further experience in other areas of work?

10. What direction do you think the individual's career could take within the organization?

11. What development or training does the individual need to help in his/her work and/or to further his/her career with the organization?

12. Are there any special projects the individual could take part in which would help with his/her development?

CHECKLIST 8   Review meeting preparation – individual's checklist

1. How well do you think you have done in achieving your objectives during the review period?

2. How well have any improvement, development or training plans as agreed at your last review meeting been put into effect?

3. What goals relating to the key tasks in your present job would you like to agree with your manager for the next review period?

4. Have you met any problems in carrying out your work? If so, what sort of problems and what can be done about them?

5. Do you think your manager could provide you with more guidance or help in what he or she expects you to do? If so, what guidance or help do you need?

6. Do you think the best use is being made of your skills and abilities? If not, what needs to be done about it?

7. Do you feel you are ready to take on additional responsibilities in your present job? If so, what would you like to do?

8. Would you like to gain further experience in other related areas of work? If so, what?

9. What direction would you like your future career to take with the organization?

10. What development or training would you like to help you in your job and/or further your career with the organization?

CHECKLIST 9   Performance review meeting contents checklist

1. Have achievements been discussed in relation to goals and performance/personal development plans?

2. Has self-assessment by the individual been encouraged, including any comments about the manager's support, resource availability or objectives?

3. Has the level of competency achieved against the headings and descriptors in the individual's role definition been discussed?

4. Has there been a discussion on the extent to which the individual's behaviour is in accord with the organization's core values?

5. Have any problems in achieving agreed goals or standards of performance been identified?

6. Have the reasons for such problems been agreed, including any factors beyond the individual's control as well as those that can be attributed to the individual's behaviour?

7. Have any other problems relating to work and the individual's relationships with his/her manager, colleagues and, if appropriate, subordinates been discussed?

8. Have any actions required to overcome problems been agreed?

9. Have any necessary changes to the role profile in terms of key result areas or competency requirements been agreed?

10. Have performance measures been reviewed and revised if necessary?

CHECKLIST 10   Approach to performance review meeting checklist

1. Has the manager prepared for the meeting by reference to a list of agreed objectives and notes on performance throughout the year?

2. Has the meeting been conducted in accordance with a clear structure covering all the points identified during preparation?

3. Has an informal environment in which a full, frank but friendly exchange of views can take place been maintained?

4. Has good feedback been provided?

5. To what extent has the meeting taken the form of a dialogue between two interested and involved parties, both of whom are seeking a positive conclusion?

6. Has praise been used effectively?

7. Have individuals been encouraged to do most of the talking?

8. Has self-assessment been encouraged?

9. Has the focus been on performance not personality?

10. Has the analysis of performance been encouraged?

11. Have unexpected criticisms been avoided?

12. Has the review meeting ended on a positive note with an agreed action plan?

Managing underperformers

The following checklists set out the questions which can usefully be answered when dealing with different aspects of substandard performance. However, it is important to remember that poor performance may be caused by faults in the system more than in the people who work within it.

CHECKLIST 11   Failure to achieve goals – possible reasons

1. Did the individual fully understand what he/she was expected to achieve?
2. Were these expectations reasonable in the light of the individual's experience and qualifications to do the job?
3. Did the individual get sufficient leadership, guidance and support from his/her manager or team leader?
4. Did the individual get sufficient support from his/her colleagues?
5. Did the individual have the resources required?
6. Were there any other factors outside the individual's control such as an inadequate system of work or unforeseeable external events and pressures that affected his or her performance?
7. Was the problem caused by inadequate knowledge or lack of skill in any respect?
8. To what extent, if any, was the failure to achieve targets or meet performance standards simply due to a lack of effort or interest on the part of the individual?

CHECKLIST 12   Failure to achieve goals – possible actions

1. Clarify goals and as necessary reformulate them to make them attainable (but not too easily).

2. Re-design the job (adjusting tasks and responsibilities) to provide a sounder basis for obtaining better results.

3. Improve the system of work.

4. Improve leadership, guidance and support from the manager or team leader.

5. Re-examine the composition of the team and its methods of working, followed if necessary by a team-building programme.

6. Improve the feedback on results to the individual, and monitor performance following the feedback to ensure that action is taken as necessary.

7. Encourage individuals to develop the additional knowledge or skills themselves while providing guidance and coaching as required. If a self-development approach is inappropriate or insufficient, arrange for specific training or coaching in areas where deficiencies in knowledge or skill have been identified.

8. Help individuals to learn from their mistakes so they know how to minimize the risk of repeating them.

9. Encourage individuals to recognize that certain aspects of their behaviour have contributed to the sub-standard results and get them to agree to the achievement of specified modifications in behaviour.

10. Agree an overall performance improvement plan.

CHECKLIST 13   Handling attitude and behavioural problems

1. Why do you believe that there is a problem over the employee's attitude or behaviour?

2. What evidence do you have that the attitude/behaviour is creating a performance problem? (Quote actual examples.)

3. Have you discussed with the individual at the time any instance of poor performance that you believe could be attributed to negative attitudes or behaviour?

4. How did the individual react when asked to comment on any such instances?

5. What steps have you taken to enable the employee to recognize his/her own problem or situation and discuss it with you?

6. Have you taken into account the fact that in general it is easier to change behaviour than deep-seated attitudes?

7. Have you been successful in obtaining agreement on the cause of the problem and what should be done about it?

8. If so, have you agreed how the problem should be managed by the individual with whatever help you and, possibly, other people could provide?

9. Will additional coaching or mentoring help?

10. Is this a problem that you would refer to another counselling source (eg a member of the human resource department) for resolution?

CHECKLIST 14   Unwillingness to accept objectives

1. How certain am I that this is an attainable goal or standard?

2. Have I any 'benchmarking' evidence that targets or standards of this nature have been achieved by other people in similar circumstances?

3. Is it reasonable for me to ask this particular individual to achieve this goal or standard in the light of his/her experience or qualifications or the circumstances in which the job is carried out?

4. Does the individual have any reasonable grounds for rejecting the goal or standard?

5. If not, why is he/she adopting this attitude?

6. Do I insist on this goal or standard in spite of the individual's objections? If not, to what extent am I prepared to modify the goal?

CHECKLIST 15   Factors outside the individual's control

1. Unforeseeable changes in the circumstances in which the job is carried out – either internal or imposed by external events.
2. Poorly defined responsibilities.
3. Inappropriate or unachievable goals or targets.
4. Insufficient guidance or support from the manager or other individuals at higher levels in the organization.
5. Inadequate cooperation or support from colleagues.
6. A faulty system of work.
7. Inadequate resources – money, staff, equipment or time.
8. Insufficient training.
9. The job demands levels of skill or knowledge that the individual does not have – and could not reasonably be expected to possess.
10. Insufficient support or guidance.

CHECKLIST 16   Performance or behavioural characteristics within the individual's control

1. Poor leadership.
2. Insufficient attention to people responsibilities.
3. Poor judgement.
4. Indecisiveness.
5. Uncooperativeness.
6. Poor team member.
7. Lack of planning and organizing skills.
8. Unwillingness to learn from experience.
9. Unwillingness to learn from training or coaching programmes.
10. Laziness.

A competency framework for managers is shown in Table A4, overleaf.

TABLE A4   Competency framework for managers

Leadership
- Develops cohesive groups and teamwork.
- Guides others to the accomplishment of objectives.
- Resolves conflicts.
- Provides direction under uncertain conditions.

Managing skills
- Delegates work responsibility among employees for maximum efficiency.
- Monitors employees' performance to achieve organizational goals and maintain control.
- Sets clear, understandable objectives and priorities for department, self and with each employee.
- Schedules and develops contingency plans.
- Motivates people toward effective, cooperative group and individual efforts.

Learning and development
- Conducts performance reviews according to established guidelines.
- Provides good feedback to employees at the time of the event and in performance review meetings.
- Praises and recognizes positive performance of employees; builds confidence in employees by supporting their appropriate decisions and actions.
- Provides support to employees in preparing and implementing personal development plans.
- Takes prompt corrective measures when employees' performance needs improvement.
- Encourages and assists individuals through coaching, training and other methods to acquire knowledge, skills and expertise necessary for effective job performance and promotion.

Decision making and problem solving
- Identifies and anticipates potential problems.
- Recognizes critical situations and takes appropriate action.
- Investigates and analyses problems and situations adequately and appropriately for the circumstances
- Solicits and encourages ideas and input from others, involving them in the decision making process.
- Considers the whole organization when making decisions.
- Looks for, evaluates and considers alternatives and options in solving problems prior to making decisions and recommendations.
- Willing to accept responsibility for decisions whatever the outcome.

TABLE A4 *continued*

Innovation/creativity
- Recommends new methods and ideas.
- Accepts ideas and builds on them; adds value to given efforts.
- Questions constructively why things are done in a particular way.

Flexibility/adaptability
- Willing to accept new assignments and complete them according to set standards.
- Can handle a wide variety of assignments.
- Willing to consider new ideas and methods.
- Open to constructive criticism and suggestions.

Teamwork
- Collaborates effectively with colleagues and other internal customers.
- Obtains co-operation from others.

Responsiveness
- Understands and responds to needs and requests quickly and willingly.
- Makes his/her expertise available to others.
- Represents the department's services in a precise and acceptable manner.

Communication
- Communicates all matters of importance up and down the organization in an accurate, timely manner.
- Provides complete and reliable information.
- Participates easily and influentially in meetings.
- Listens carefully to others.
- Writes and speaks clearly, concisely, accurately and persuasively.

Technical/professional expertise
- Has the knowledge required in specified areas to achieve objectives.
- Has the skills required in specified areas to achieve objectives.

Evaluation toolkit

It is essential to evaluate the effectiveness of performance management in meeting the objectives and in each of the main processes involved. Evaluation can take place against success criteria (Questionnaire 14) and by means of the overall checklist (Checklist 17). It can also be conducted through an assessment of reactions to performance management (Questionnaire 15) and an engagement survey (Questionnaire 16).

Evaluation against success criteria

Reference needs to be made to the performance of performance management with regard to established success criteria. Unless such evaluation takes place regularly and leads to any remedial action required the system is likely to decline.

QUESTIONNAIRE 14   Evaluation of performance against success criteria

Evaluate effectiveness as follows: 1 = high level of achievement, 2 = acceptable level of achievement, 3 = poor level of achievement	
Measures of improved performance by reference to key performance indicators in such terms as output, productivity, sales, quality, customer satisfaction, return on investment.	1 2 3
Achievement of defined and agreed objectives for performance management.	1 2 3
Measures of employee engagement before and after the introduction of performance management and then at regular intervals.	1 2 3
Assessments of reactions of managers and employees to performance management.	1 2 3
Assessment of the extent to which managers and employees have reached agreement on goals and performance development plans.	1 2 3
Performance development plans agreed and implemented.	1 2 3
Personal development plans agreed and implemented.	1 2 3

Overall checklist

CHECKLIST 17   Overall performance management evaluation

1. Are performance agreements being completed properly?
2. Do they generally spell out realistic goals, attribute and competence requirements, work plans and performance improvement and development plans?
3. Are goals being agreed properly?
4. Are they related clearly to key result areas?
5. Do they generally meet agreed criteria for good objectives, ie are they demanding but attainable, relevant, measurable, agreed and time based?
6. Are they integrated with organizational and departmental goals?
7. Are individuals and teams given scope to contribute to the formulation of higher-level goals?
8. Are appropriate performance measures being agreed?
9. Are managers providing good feedback throughout the year as well as during formal review meetings?
10. Are both managers and individuals preparing properly for performance review meetings?
11. How well are managers conducting such meetings?
12. How effective has performance management been in motivating employees?
13. Is performance management providing a good basis for recognizing high performance and valuing those who achieve it?
14. How effective has performance management been in developing skills and capabilities?
15. How well have managers and team leaders carried out their roles as coaches or mentors?
16. Have ratings been fair and consistently applied?
17. How well is poor performance recognized and dealt with?
18. How well have the performance management forms been completed?
19. How effective have the briefing and training programmes been?
20. What impact has performance management had on individual, team and organizational performance?

Reactions to performance management

QUESTIONNAIRE 15   Reactions to performance management

Rate the following statements on a scale of 1–5 where: 1 = fully agree, 2 = agree, 3 = not sure, 4 = disagree, 5 = strongly disagree	
1. I am quite satisfied that the objectives I agreed were fair.	1 2 3 4 5
2. I felt that the meeting to agree objectives and standards of performance helped me to focus on what I should be aiming to achieve.	1 2 3 4 5
3. I received good feedback from my manager on how I was doing.	1 2 3 4 5
4. My manager was always prepared to provide guidance when I ran into problems at work.	1 2 3 4 5
5. The performance review meeting was conducted by my manager in a friendly and helpful manner.	1 2 3 4 5
6. My manager fully recognized my achievements during the year.	1 2 3 4 5
7. If any criticisms were made during the review meeting, they were acceptable because they were based on fact, not opinion.	1 2 3 4 5
8. I was given plenty of opportunity by my manager to discuss the reasons for any of my work problems.	1 2 3 4 5
9. I felt generally that the comments made by my manager at the meeting were fair.	1 2 3 4 5
10. The meeting ended with a clear plan of action for the future with which I agreed.	1 2 3 4 5
11. I felt motivated after the meeting.	1 2 3 4 5
12. I felt that the time spent in the meeting was well worth while.	1 2 3 4 5

Engagement survey

Data on levels of engagement obtained from an employee opinion survey as set out below provide one of the most important means of measuring the effectiveness of performance management in terms of its impact on people. Such surveys should be conducted before the introduction of performance management and thereafter every year or other year to establish trends.

QUESTIONNAIRE 16   Engagement survey

Rate the following statements on a scale of 1–5 where: 1 = fully agree, 2 = agree, 3 = not sure, 4 = disagree, 5 = strongly disagree	
1. I am very satisfied with the work I do.	1 2 3 4 5
2. My job is interesting.	1 2 3 4 5
3. I know exactly what I am expected to do.	1 2 3 4 5
4. I am prepared to put myself out to do my work.	1 2 3 4 5
5. My job is challenging.	1 2 3 4 5
6. I am given plenty of freedom to decide how to do my work.	1 2 3 4 5
7. I get plenty of opportunities to learn in this job.	1 2 3 4 5
8. The facilities/equipment/tools provided are excellent.	1 2 3 4 5
9. I get excellent support from my boss.	1 2 3 4 5
10. My contribution is fully recognized.	1 2 3 4 5
11. The experience I am getting now will be a great help in advancing my future career.	1 2 3 4 5
12. I find it easy to keep up with the demands of my job.	1 2 3 4 5
13. I have no problems in achieving a balance between my work and my private life.	1 2 3 4 5
14. I like working for my boss.	1 2 3 4 5
15. I get on well with my work colleagues.	1 2 3 4 5
16. I think this organization is a great place in which to work.	1 2 3 4 5
17. I believe I have a good future in this organization.	1 2 3 4 5
18. I intend to go on working for this organization.	1 2 3 4 5
19. I am happy about the values of this organization – how it conducts its business.	1 2 3 4 5
20. I believe that the products/services provided by this organization are excellent.	1 2 3 4 5

APPENDIX B
Performance management case studies

This appendix contains case studies for AXPO, CEMEX UK, DHL, Hitachi Europe and IHS.

AXPO

Axpo is in the business of the generation, utilization, purchase, sale, exchange and trading of electrical and other energy and the provision of services of all kinds in the fields of energy and the environment. The head office is in Switzerland, and there are regional bases in 17 European countries, including the UK. There are 2,500 employees.

The performance management system

Axpo operates a single, standardized performance management system for all its staff in Switzerland and the European subsidiaries. The main aim is to improve individual performance, ensuring that the objectives are aligned with those of the organization.

Objective setting

The kind of objectives set for employees covered by the performance management system vary from division to division; for example, 90 per cent of objectives are safety related in the nuclear plants. The objectives for middle and senior managers are more closely linked to business results than those in the system for the bulk of staff. For some mid-office roles such as HR, objectives are primarily project-based. People doing back office administration roles will usually have task-based objectives, for example, completing a certain set of reports without making more than a fixed number of errors. The objective-setting process is currently under review – all departments have been asked to identify cost savings which must be incorporated into their targets.

HR business partners scan through the objectives set for individuals each year, paying particular attention to those employees whose managers have a 'track record of playing fast and loose with the system'. Nicholas Long, Axpo's International Compensation and Benefits Manager says: 'We are looking for objectives where there is no notion of how they will be measured or evidenced. In these cases, we go back to the line manager concerned and ask how a particular objective will be appraised. Employees rarely raise questions about their own objectives.'

When will HR intervene? HR partners will step in if they notice that an individual has agreed the same set of objectives for, say, the third year in a row, or if an objective appears arbitrary or lacking in a baseline from which to measure progress (for example, 'to improve the quality of X reporting'). According to Long, some of the non-financial objectives set are too qualitative, without a specific hurdle, the crossing of which would signify the objective is met. HR also jumps in if an objective does not have a concrete deadline for measuring progress.

Performance review

HR owns the performance management process. Line managers take the lead in review meetings, explaining how the employee has met objectives or not and giving a verbal rating. After the meeting, the employee has the opportunity to tick a box agreeing to the rating, or not, in which case matters are escalated to HR. This happens in around one in 30 cases, usually because the original objectives were not clear.

Employees also make a self-assessment, which is not passed on to the line manager during the performance review, but is useful for them in preparing for appraisal meetings.

Performance rating

Rating is carried out through a five-point scale – 1 is 'unacceptable', while 5 is 'really good'. Axpo works on the basis that it does not want the performance management system to produce an average rating of more than 'x' on the scale (with 'x' defined by Executive Management).

Some managers are prone to handing out ratings of 4 or 5 to all members of their team because the system is seen as the mechanism for determining bonuses and incentives rather than as a performance management tool. If a manager awards too many top ratings for their teams to fit with the required distribution, HR will pass them back for review. Rating inflation has the potential to affect the actual amount of bonus people receive as an overall pot is set and initially divided on the basis of the total number of rating points awarded across the business in any one year. The more rating points awarded, the less each of these bonus points is worth in cash. HR also massages the rating allocation in the background if required; for example, if all members of a particular team are given a 5, these may be taken down to 4s for the purposes of bonus payment.

Line managers and performance management

Long argues that the commitment, capacity and confidence of line managers in operating a performance management system are critical to its success: 'Some managers are really excellent and work with the tools at their disposal, using them to maximum impact, for example, to produce personal development plans for employees'. This group represents around 30 per cent of managers in the organization, concentrated in the company's Eastern European operations.

A second group of managers see performance management as primarily HR's job and argues that they do not need to 'waste their time' on it: 'It is very difficult to change this mind set, which affects around 50 per cent of our managers'.

The final group, representing around 20 per cent of managers, will 'do nothing on performance management unless HR hits them with a stick'. These are typically managers in Axpo's smaller operations who have a great deal of autonomy and who tend to to be furthest away from the head office in Switzerland.

Line manager training

Line manager training is at the heart of engaging some managers. These people and the company hold an annual one-hour presentation for managers on the potential pitfalls arising from poor operation of the performance management system, for example, ineffective objective setting. The HR team will also coach individual managers around behavioural issues in teams; for example, how to handle a situation where an individual meets their targets but does so in a way that is detrimental to the team, or relationships in the team.

The HR team also travels to the company's different countries of operation once a year to talk to line managers about different performance management scenarios, stressing that the line of least resistance – avoiding confronting poor performance – is likely to cause greater problems in the future.

CEMEX UK

CEMEX UK is a supplier of cement, ready-mixed concrete and aggregates with 4,000 employees. It is a subsidiary of the Mexican company CEMEX.

Aims of performance management

The aims of the Performance and Potential Assessment (P&PA), scheme at CEMEX UK are to:

- promote strategic alignment and respond to business needs;
- facilitate clear communication and understanding of standards;
- ensure objective grading and differentiation of potential levels;
- promote continuous feedback and development;
- reinforce high performance attitudes.

The annual cycle

CEMEX's performance management scheme runs over the calendar year as follows:

- The company's overall budget is set in January and from this the most senior managers' objectives are established which are then cascaded down the organization.

- Around July, there is a mid-year review of initial objectives set and discussions on how the individual is progressing over the first part of the year.

- Finally, between November and January an ultimate meeting takes place where line managers and individuals meet and staff are rated between one and five by their line managers.

Objective setting

CEMEX states that the purpose of objectives is to communicate clearly the kind of work to be performed. The company says that there are three types of objectives that can be set:

- Operative/functional: activities designed to strengthen the quality of service and to make the existing processes or procedures more efficient by innovation.

- Continuous improvement: responsibilities that are inherent to the position and functional area of the employee.

- Development and training: activities that will help the employee improve their performance.

Setting objectives is a two-way process and all objectives must align with the common acronym 'SMART'. Two more conditions are laid down – first, that objectives should be relevant and second, that they should be limited in number (no more than ten on the grounds that research has shown that any more than this amount limits impact and causes dilution).

Objectives are cascaded down through the organization which promotes their alignment of objectives with the corporate strategy and ensures the level of challenge among the overall team is calibrated. In practice, direct supervisors can cascade objectives down by up to two levels, while indirect supervisors can do so by one level.

In addition, the various objectives are weighted and each has a specific unit of measure. For example, a sales person might have a specific amount of a product to sell which means that there is no ambiguity and it is easy to determine whether this sort of target has been achieved or not. By using clear evaluation criteria with a description of what it means to accomplish them, CEMEX believes that there can be no disagreement when it comes to determining a score for the year.

Mid-year and final review

CEMEX recognizes that the individual's and company's situation can change over the course of the year so a further mid-year review is held in July. This ensures that managers can amend objectives as a consequence of any work or other changes that have taken place. The end of year meeting takes place between November and January when there is a one-to-one discussion between the employee and their immediate supervisor. At the meeting, a final rating is agreed which helps determine the bonus to be received the following March.

360-degree appraisal

CEMEX's performance management scheme also incorporates a 360-degree appraisal process whereby managers, staff and clients provide additional feedback. Although the results of this are considered when determining bonus levels, this process is designed mainly to gauge the future potential of the individual with the main rating more important in the bonus decision.

The 360-degree appraisal does consider outcomes, but perhaps more important is an emphasis on 'how' people accomplish their objectives, drawing on the company's nine key competencies:

- *Team work:* genuine willingness to work with others in a cooperative, assertive and transparent manner to achieve a common goal, placing group interests above those of the individual.

- *Creativity:* generation and development of ideas, considering both internal and external context to create and take advantage of business opportunities in CEMEX.

- *Focus on stakeholders:* adaptation of personal behaviour to the values, priorities and objectives of CEMEX, looking for the benefit of the different stakeholders.

- *Entrepreneurial spirit:* development of opportunities to improve the business, within and outside one's own working environment, undertaking risks and overcoming obstacles.

- *Strategic thinking:* understanding the circumstances that prevail in the external environment and those within the company, to make decisions that lead to the achievement of CEMEX's strategies.

- *Customer service orientation:* willingness to serve and anticipate the needs of the client, both internal and external, and to take the necessary actions to satisfy them.

- *Development of others:* continuous commitment to stimulate learning and development of others, in order to further their professional success.

- *Information management:* ability to search, generate, manage, and share relevant information for decision-making in the organization.

- *Development of alliances:* identify and maintain long-term relationships with individuals, groups and institutions, both within and outside the organization, which contribute to the achievement of CEMEX's strategies.

The 360-degree process allows up to six people to appraise each staff member. These include any individuals that have observed their behaviours in relationship to the competencies and should include at least one internal client, at least one internal supplier and at least one peer. Once the individual has selected their evaluators, the immediate manager either approves or rejects those chosen. This may even involve the rejection of the entire proposal, in which case the employee will need to come up with a new set of evaluators. When examining a proposal, line managers are advised to avoid approving the same evaluators over a number of years in order to promote greater diversity.

Guidance on feedback

The following guidance is provided to both those giving and receiving feedback.

Managers

- Criticisms or praise should be communicated continually throughout the year and should be followed up at the end-of-year meeting.

- The purpose of feedback should be explained, pointing out that reviews can make the employee a more valuable member of staff and provide greater opportunities for job satisfaction, usefulness and promotion.

- Start with positive performance and do not overload – choose one or two critical issues or behaviours to concentrate on.
- Focus on the specific behaviours that the person can change.
- Offer suggestions, support and include clear action plans with follow-up dates.

Staff

- Approach feedback as a partnership process not a debate.
- Take notes if possible.
- Select a convenient time so you are not rushed.
- Ask for clarification if what is being said is not clear.
- Seek a balance between positive and negative feedback, if you only get one, ask for the other.

Online tool

CEMEX's online tool, known as CEMEX Plaza, enables managers and staff to enter and store all of the information and results produced from the 360-degree appraisals.

Bonus scheme

Bonuses are determined by an individual's rating in their end-of-year appraisal meeting as long as threshold financial performance has been achieved by their own unit, the UK. In some cases, for more senior staff, the performance of CEMEX Worldwide can also be a factor. Objectives are graded on a five-point scale, with a corresponding numerical value:

Significantly above target = 5

Above target = 4

On target = 3

Below target = 2

Unsatisfactory = 1

The final rating is the weighted average of the different objectives.

Non-performers

Anyone that receives a score of '2' or below at their end-of-year meeting is considered to be performing below the level that CEMEX expects and in such cases action is taken. The initial step in the process is to set up a specific programme to help the employee improve. If this is not successful a 'safety track' is put in place with 'mini objectives' that are shorter term than the annual ones. Where necessary the line manager, along with the HR department, engages in training and development and coaching to help the employee improve their performance.

DHL

DHL is a global market leader in the international express and logistics industry with 45,000 staff in Europe.

The performance management process

DHL's annual performance management process begins in August when the bonus framework and core elements of the scheme are designed at the top level. Following this, in mid-November, based on the aims decided upon in August, targets are set for the year by a panel of senior staff. Once devised, these targets are cascaded down the organization into individual personal objectives following discussions between line managers and HR.

The cascading process is designed to ensure that targets are refined and altered to align with each individual's actual job. Further discussions then take place to decide what each target means for employees in practice and their implications for competencies. Around the same time, attainment levels and scoring based on the previous year's performance take place to determine bonus levels and salary rises. Following this, with targets already set, around the middle of January, an outline for recording performance targets for personal and financial performance for the coming year is designed and in mid-February, the company's financial results become known. This makes it possible to determine the pot available for bonus payments and salary increases relating to the previous year. Bonuses are paid in either March or April while salary reviews take place in April.

Setting the tone for the year

The initial stage of establishing overall objectives and the target-setting framework sets the tone for the year. From year to year, conditions change, with the priorities of senior management reflecting the current state of affairs. As a result, each year there are a number of overarching themes such as serving customers, for example, or health and safety. These core individual key objectives (IKOs) are strictly adhered to, although local managers can determine themselves how to manage their attainment. In contrast, more flexibility exists for other objectives with managers at lower levels able to alter them to align with their particular needs. There is further flexibility in the system with regard to its timing.

Performance management tools

To ensure the smooth running of the system, managers and staff alike are provided with a number of tools to help them during the performance management process. These include:

- *A performance evaluation template:* This template enables the appropriate competency model to be reviewed and evaluated.
- *An objective agreement template:* This template is located within the performance evaluation template and is used to capture both performance and personal objectives.
- *Competency models:* are available as support tools for personal development planning.
- *Technical competencies:* These represent a support framework for identifying core technical competencies for key operational roles.
- *Development guides:* Guidelines for use in the support of developing a personal development plan.
- *Personal development plan (PDP):* A template for assessing an individual against management competencies and developing actions for them to progress their career.
- *Career ladder:* A guide to support the development of a personal development plan.

- *Passport of success:* A small booklet retained by the individual (non-management) that identifies completed training.
- *Site succession plan:* A plan developed utilizing information from the performance review and PDP process.

The annual face-to-face meeting

A key element of the performance management cycle is the face-to-face meeting between line managers and each member of their teams. For operational employees (non-management) the company recommends, as a minimum, this should be a discussion of around 30 minutes, while for managers, a one-hour meeting is suggested. During the meeting, the managers and their direct reports examine performance over the last 12 months with reference to the previous year's objectives. Discussions cover what was achieved, whether support provided was sufficient and, if relevant, what could have been done differently for a more effective result.

Following this they agree performance objectives for the coming year, along with any support in the form of training and development that can be offered. Objectives are documented in a 'target agreement form', information on levels of attainment captured on the 'performance evaluation tool', while training and support needs are recorded in the 'performance development plan'. In addition, as mentioned, further support tools used include competency models, development guides, technical competencies and career ladders. Where tools, guides or advice are provided, the company states that any suggestions are minimum standards and if managers wish to invest more time and effort in any procedures they can. For example, while there are guidelines for the number of meetings to discuss progress throughout the year, the company informs managers that they can arrange more, if they feel it is appropriate.

Nevertheless, the company adds the proviso that where managers diverge from policy to a significant degree they must gain agreement and support from their own management and HR. DHL says that the key aim of the meeting is to discuss and agree objectives for the forthcoming year, adding that 'setting and agreeing objectives focuses an individual on their performance areas and defines clear outcomes and results'. In total, no more than five individual objectives are established: up to three relating to individual performance and two, personal development. The company also says that both types of objective need to adhere to the SMART acronym.

Development objectives

Unlike performance objectives, development objectives are primarily the individual's responsibility to identify, with support provided by managers via the supply of appropriate resources and by contributing objectivity in discussions on staff potential. In some circumstances, DHL guidance says that it may be appropriate to develop a full performance development action plan, while in others this may not be necessary. In either case though, the tools mentioned above are available to assist. DHL says it is committed to personal development planning because it supports the growth of individuals across the organization, stating that 'growing its people develops talent to meet the organization's future management and leadership requirements'. Further, it is a 'motivator for the individual and allows development priorities to be clearly identified creating opportunities to fully achieve their potential'.

Competencies

Closely linked to objectives, competencies play an important part through-out DHL's performance management process. In addition to the management of performance, they are used for recruitment, selection, induction, job sizing and feed into decisions on pay increases. There are different competencies for different roles.

Progress meetings

In addition to the main performance management meetings, managers are advised to arrange progress meetings throughout the year. The number will depend on the individual in question, but the company suggests that there should be at least one every 12 months. In this meeting, discussions cover how attainment against objectives and competencies is progressing, whether training and development support aligns with expectations and whether additional support can be provided. Moreover, in some cases, certain senior employees are consulted on their own aspirations, and questions, such as whether they want to move upwards or into a different role or perhaps to change location, are asked.

Performance measurement/scoring

At the end of the year in the subsequent annual meeting the process begins again while, at the same time, ratings for the last 12 months are given based on performance against objectives and the individual's competencies. To aid in the evaluation process, the 'performance evaluation tool' is used which includes a competency and development needs assessment. Using this, progress against last year's performance evaluation is discussed, particularly drawing on successes during the year. Individual achievement is based on a combination of two ratings. First, there is a measure of achievement against personal objectives – also known as personal targets or individual key objectives (IKOs). This concentrates on *what* is achieved, as distinct from a second rating which examines *how* things are achieved, drawing on competencies. While there is no particular formula, both ratings are taken into account when making decisions on pay, bonuses and career progression. Under the first measure, target achievement level is linked to IKOs and scores are on a scale of zero to 133.33 per cent. On-target performance gives a score of 100 per cent. Competency ratings are on a scale of one to five where five is exceptional and one, unsatisfactory as follows:

- *Far exceeds:* Consistently demonstrating the competency behaviours effectively, role model.
- *Exceeds:* Demonstrates the competency behaviours beyond what is expected.
- *Fully meets:* Behaviours fully correspond with what is expected in the current role.
- *Partially meets:* Demonstrates minor deficiencies (coachable) in the behaviour.
- *Does not meet:* Does not demonstrate behaviours expected in the current role.

When it comes to decisions on salary increases, ratings are moderated by employees' positions in their pay bands, local budget constraints and the market. Ratings are used to determine bonus levels and they also tie in to decisions on promotion and succession planning.

Succession planning

Following the evaluation and rating stage, the line manager's immediate superior reviews the results and, in the light of them, considers, among other things, succession and career planning. By using the overall results, senior managers can determine where there are skills gaps or other deficiencies. In addition, it enables them to take a closer look at individual employees to consider whether they might be more suited to be employed elsewhere in the organization. Similarly, managers can examine strengths and weaknesses, which might flag up a shortage of certain abilities, such as commercial acumen, for example. Such issues can therefore be addressed and recruitment can be directed appropriately. Moreover, it also helps when employees leave the organization, making it simple to determine the corresponding skills and behaviours that leave the organization with that individual. To aid with this task, managers are also able to draw on an additional rating for certain senior staff, termed 'potential for job'. This gauges potential for the future and helps by feeding into future decisions on promotion and succession planning.

Hitachi Europe

Hitachi Europe has a well-established performance management system that has been in place for a number of years. It is designed primarily to enhance staff development in order to add value to the organization and all of the company's 450 staff are covered by the system.

The process is created to be an open, two-way discussion between employees and their managers with meetings taking place at least twice a year. During meetings, staff and managers focus on current and past performance and future development and although there is no direct link to pay, the system does help inform pay decisions. In contrast, appraisal results for two-thirds of staff are directly linked to one of the company's five bonus plans with performance ratings determining payout levels.

The process is as much about building relationships with employees in order to agree what is reasonably attainable in the year as it is about setting objectives. It is effective because it focuses people's intentions and produces new thinking on the way they work rather than simply continuing to perform at the same level day-in-day-out.

The performance management cycle

Hitachi Europe's year begins in April and prior to this, managers and staff are advised to consider performance over the previous year and expectations for the coming 12 months. Around March, managers meet with employees to devise a performance development plan which, in practice, involves two discussions:

- performance planning discussion;
- development planning discussion.

The performance planning discussion is focused primarily on whether past objectives have been achieved and what future targets should be. In contrast, the development planning discussion helps the manager and employee consider the individual's development needs and ties-in with training and other requirements necessary to help them achieve future objectives.

Hitachi Europe's performance management guidance says that the purpose of these meetings is:

> To ensure that an open, two-way discussion takes place between an employee and their manager. The discussion should review both past performance and development and identify whether past objectives have been met and to agree future objectives. The objectives set should align to both group and team objectives.

Performance planning

During the performance planning meeting, managers are encouraged to use examples to illustrate to employees where they have performed adequately, exceptionally and below expectations. In addition, they also refer to information acquired via consultation with other managers and colleagues of the employee.

This rounded approach ensures they have a good understanding of how the employee is performing and while the focus of the discussion is on the employee's performance, managers must also be prepared to discuss the role they themselves played in helping or hindering the employee in achieving their objectives. Throughout the meeting, Hitachi Europe says that there should be mutual understanding and agreement especially regarding decisions on past objectives and key actions for the future.

Objectives

Objectives emerging from discussions should be SMART – specific, measurable, achievable, realistic and time bound. From a time perspective, while the process is an annual event some objectives are likely to have differing time scales. In some cases, these may cover periods of less than six months, so managers and staff are given the option to meet more frequently than the usual two times a year if they wish.

While the company's guidance says that objectives need to be business-related, in practice, this is not always strictly the case for all staff. Those in more senior roles, for example, have objectives linked to overall business objectives such as market share and profit targets, while lower down the hierarchy, aims are often more closely aligned to specific jobs and sales-specific targets. In practice, the company says that objectives are really intended to encourage the individual to perform beyond the level normally associated with their job role.

In addition to setting objectives, performance planning meetings provide time for managers to outline key dates and deadlines and while the documentation associated with the process is paper-based, all forms and related information are also available on the firm's intranet.

Development planning discussion

Unlike the performance planning meeting the development planning discussion is employee-led. This is because Hitachi believes it is the employee's responsibility to consider their own development requirements for the coming year. To help them do this, there are a number of development tools available, while managers also guide and coach where necessary. The range of development tools available is explained in a dedicated section available in the company's guidance and includes information on a learning log, a development record and a career plan.

In addition, in the past the company used a competency framework as part of a previous incarnation of its performance management system and while this is no longer formally in use, employees can refer to its 'success factors', as the company says they are a useful reference point when exploring and diagnosing development needs.

Using these tools, and prior to the development planning discussion, employees are encouraged to consider their development needs, looking back over the past 12 months and looking forward over the coming year. Moreover, they need to review their previous development objectives thinking about what they wish to achieve in the future. To aid in the process employees are advised to collate evidence in order to clarify their strengths and areas for improvement. Using this information, they can prepare a plan of recommended solutions to aid in their development for discussion with their manager.

While these meetings are employee-led, in some cases, Hitachi employees may be unclear or need guidance on their development needs so managers can help them reach a decision. Similarly, and where appropriate, managers can challenge the proposed development options, but in both cases, only after the employee has voiced their own opinions.

Hitachi is aware of the dangers of the manager leading the process and provides clear guidance outlining certain boundaries to which they should adhere. While the guidance says that is acceptable for managers to question employees' proposed development strategies, for example, it adds that they should avoid trying to make career choices for the employee. Similarly, they are told not to try to push someone to develop if they are not ready to, letting the employee make up their own mind.

Training not always the best option

The company finds that in many cases employees conclude that they require a training course as this is an obvious option. Despite this, Hitachi advises employees to avoid jumping to this conclusion as there are a number of other less-obvious but more appropriate options that are often also available. The company guidance, for example, highlights on-the-job training and learning because it believes that these are the most effective ways of developing and acquiring new skills, knowledge and experience. This is not to say that training is discouraged, however, as the company states that training courses are a very good way of supporting development needs, providing a foundation for future skills and knowledge.

Interim reviews

In the autumn, six months on from the initial meetings, managers and employees meet again to have an interim review. The point of the discussion is to make sure that the personal development plan remains on track and objectives are still relevant. The meeting is a formal stage of the process but there is no rating at this point. Nevertheless, the outcomes of discussions are used to help inform pay rises that take place a few months later, effective from January.

Six months after the interim review, the year ends and managers and staff again meet to review objectives and discuss performance over the previous 12 months. If objectives are not attained, the conversation examines why this was the case, with managers considering their own as well as the individual's role when determining why targets were not achieved. Employees also have the opportunity to explain why they believed targets were not met, outlining any mitigating circumstances. Based on this interaction, outcomes of discussions lead to a performance rating being awarded and any failed targets usually feed into the following year's objectives. Unlike some other organizations, ratings do not align with a forced distribution and the four potential levels are:

'O':   Failed to meet objectives

'S':   After assessing performance against objectives has met some of the objectives

'M':   Meets expectations and has completed all objectives

'M*': Achieved significantly more than the agreed objectives so performance was exceptional.

Consistency

A common concern with most, if not all, performance management schemes, is maintaining consistency across the whole organization. To ensure this is achieved, Hitachi Europe's HR staff review objectives at the start of the year to check that they are both 'SMART' and realistic. Further, once the process is completed, results are evaluated to determine whether particular departments or divisions have especially high or low outcomes. In addition, even when there are no discernible differences in departmental rankings as a whole, HR staff still examine any individual outliers to determine whether an unfair rating has occurred.

Where inconsistencies are found, HR staff meet with the line managers concerned and revisit each part of the process to ensure they are taking a consistent and impartial approach. In some cases, rating inconsistency is a symptom of another underlying problem or issue. Some managers, for example, might feel that their staff's salaries are too low, while others may have difficulties managing the expectations of their team against objectives and the individual's competencies.

IHS

IHS provides critical information, analytics and expertise to a range of business sectors and governments in more than 31 countries. It is the parent company of Jane's defence publications and the Construction Information Service in the UK. It has 7,700 employees in the Americas, Asia-Pacific and EMEA (Europe, Middle East and Africa). The head office is in Englewood, Colorado, USA, with centres of excellence around the world.

The performance management system

A single, standard performance management system for all its employees was introduced in 2013. The overarching objective for performance management at IHS is to drive organizational performance. Goals tend to be top down, reflecting the company's organizational objectives. IHS is very committed to having a line of sight between individuals' objectives and those of the organization.

Discussions on performance take place between line managers and colleagues twice a year, with the initial discussion at mid-year focusing on progress against objectives. Performance reviews are managed through an online platform branded as MySuccessFactors, and this platform also addresses other aspects of an employee's career development life cycle. These include support on objective settings as well as setting development plans which link in with the learning and development module for training courses.

Rating

Objectives: These account for 75 per cent of a colleague's overall rating in the performance cycle. Colleagues are encouraged to have a minimum of three objectives and to weight them according to importance (the total must add to 100 per cent). For example, a team of accountants may have a primary goal to complete a certain set of reports by a fixed point at the end of each month; this objective can be cascaded to individuals in their detailed objectives.

Competencies: These account for 25 per cent of an overall rating. During the self-assessment part of the review process, colleagues are asked to rate how they demonstrate each of the role's competencies, providing specific examples of how they have demonstrated these during the course of the year. As with objectives, individuals weight the competency components in their self-assessment. There are five core competencies: customer focus; decision-making and problem-solving; effective communication; results orientation; and people and team leadership (for those with direct reports) or teamwork and collaboration (for those in individual contributor roles). The competencies are based on the organizational level within IHS.

Individual Development Plan: Colleagues are expected to enter at least one individual development objective that, if met over the year, will enhance their skills, behaviours and performance in the role.

Ratings for the objectives and competencies part of the review are based on a five-point scale, with numerical values attached to descriptions as follows:

- Significantly exceeds: 4.5 to 5.0
- Exceeds: 3.9 to 4.4
- Meets: 3.0 to 3.8
- Partially meets: 2.5 to 2.9
- Does not meet: Less than 2.5

Rating calibration

The compensation team reviews how managers in each sector evaluate their teams. Although this moderation takes place, the organization does not have quotas or a forced distribution of individual performance management ratings, as each business operates independently.

Paying for performance

IHS operates pay-for-performance and there is a 'link between the performance management process and merit pay', but both are designed to be independent of each other, so that discussions around pay are kept separate from the conversations managers have with people around ratings. As noted by

Alissa Shelton Twiss, Global Compensation Partner: 'Some managers find it difficult enough to have personal conversations – many are technical professionals who find the "softer" elements of management tricky. We always put the focus on the performance conversation, without the complication of adding in pay.'

Line managers use an online compensation tool, including guidelines on the payment of merit pay, to allocate a fixed merit pay budget between people in their team who have received at least a 'meets' performance rating. The annual merit pay budget is typically decided based on a combination of market surveys and business performance.

AUTHOR INDEX

SUBJECT INDEX